Praise for True North...

"*True North* is the best new regional guidebook to come out in a long while. Written with wit and authority, it takes readers beyond the tourist clichés in Duluth and along [Lake] Superior's North and South shores. The authors' love of the region and its quirks comes through, making for a very useful guide that's also fun to read."

– Chris Welsch, Travel Editor, *Minneapolis Star-Tribune*

"Even people who think they know the Twin Ports will be delighted by *True North.* It includes all my favorites, plus lots of places I want to check out."

– Beth Gauper, Travel Editor, *St. Paul Pioneer Press*

"Reading *True North* is like having a relative in Duluth. The authors reveal the Twin Ports and North and South Shore secrets that those of us who live here share with those who come to visit."

– Sam Cook, columnist & outdoors writer, *Duluth News-Tribune*

"I love it! Everyone in Duluth and up and down the shore should have a copy of *T.......*

– Dave Walter, Duluth's WEBC-AM ......

"*True North* is a storehouse of quirky information...that .... right direction but might enlighten som.....

– Kyle Eller, *Duluth Budgeteer N.....*

"[An] excellent little travel boo.....

– Mike Nardine, Duluth's *Northland Read.....*

"BEST REGIONAL GUIDE BOOK" 2002 Sawyer Awards, Duluth's *Ripsaw News*

True North

Alternative and Off-Beat Destinations In and Around Duluth, Superior, and the Shores of Lake Superior

Tony Dierckins & Kerry Elliott

Xcommunication

X-communication
1002 North Thirteenth Avenue East
Duluth, Minnesota 55805
(218) 724-2095
www.x-communication.org

True North: alternative and off-beat destinations in and around Duluth, Superior, and the shores of Lake Superior

Text by Tony Dierckins & Kerry Elliott
Layout & Design by Tony Dierckins
Copy editing by Scott Pearson
Proofreading and additional copy editing by Chris Godsey

Please see page 268 for complete photo and illustration credits.

Updated Edition, 2003

Library of Congress Control Number: 2002100704

ISBN: 1-887317-20-1

03 04 05 06   10 9 8 7 6 5 4 3 2

The authors would like to thank:

Kent Aldrich, Dan Amell, David "Drew" Anderson, Sally Anderson, Ted Anderson, Tim Anderson, Tim Bates, Barbara Cadigan, Isabel Carlson, Guy Evans, Chris Godsey, Simon Gray, Adam Guggemos, Susan Gustafson, Chris Hazelton, Jim "Senator" Held, George Kessler, C. Patrick Labadie, Grady Larimper, Mark Lindquist, Suzi Ludwig, Paul Lundgren, Scott Lunt, Tim & Toni McEvoy, Jack & Hank McEvoy, Lynette Maki, Julie & Joe Maiolo, Brad Nelson, Maryanne Norton, Bob Olson & Julie Zimmerman, Jerry Paulson, Scott Pearson, "Dr." Dan Proctor, Tami Tanski Sherman, Carlene Sippola, Jean Sramek, Bob Swanfeld, Jon Swanson, Joe Taatjes, Sean Taylor, Judi Turner, Mark "Sporty" Voigt, and Tom Wigstrom & Lisa Spencer...

...the Thursday Night Brewhouse/Starfire Lounge Brain Trust (er...Brain Rust?)...

...Pat Maus of the Northeast Minnesota Historical Center...

...The great staff of the Duluth Public Library...

...Bob Berg and the Duluth Preservation Alliance...

...Gerri & Gordon Slabaugh and the wonderful folks at Adventure Publications...

...and everyone else whose assistance and suggestions helped shape this book.

Contents

Help Us Out!

Because this book had to go to the printer long before it could be placed in stores—and because this isn't one of those "pay-us-and-we'll-put-you-in" guide books (we actually visited each business and checked them out in cognito)—we realize that some of the information may have changed—some shops and restaurants may have moved, changed their business hours, or even closed. We also realize we may have overlooked some places worthy of mention. If you find that something has changed or that we've left out one of your favorite places, let us know and we'll work it into the next edition.

We'd also like to add to our "Outdoor Adventures," "Annual Events," and "Local Lore" sections (or any other part of the book, for that matter), so if you know of anything that might be appropriate, please tell us about it.

Just e-mail us at truenorth@x-communication.org.

Introduction

Outside the Superior Street entrance to Duluth's Greysolon Plaza (the former Hotel Duluth), you'll find a compass embedded in the sidewalk. The direction arrow pointing north is set at a 45-degree angle to the right, not straight-up-and-down as one would expect. You see, Duluth's streets and avenues don't follow the traditional east-west/north-south grid common to most towns. Instead, the streets of Duluth follow the Lake Superior shoreline. The compass appears to be off center, yet it points true north. And so in these parts you won't find true north simply by following the main streets, just as you can't get a true appreciation of this region simply by sticking to the beaten paths that lead to the more typical, "touristy" stops.

Not that those destinations aren't popular for good reason. There are many wonderful places that visitors and local residents regularly visit: Superior's Fairlawn Mansion (Pattison estate) and Barker's Island, Duluth's Canal Park, the Aerial Lift Bridge, the Lakewalk, the beach on Park Point, Great Lakes Aquarium and Freshwater Discovery Center, Glensheen Mansion (Congdon estate), Betty's Pies, Gooseberry Falls, Split Rock Light House, Bayfield's quaint shops, etc. We could fill a book describing all the great "touristy" things to see and do in the Twin Ports and along Lake Superior's shores. But of course, many others already have.

We're proud that we're not like other places. We like being a little off center. We like the idea that Duluth's Eighth Street Video is located on Ninth Street, that part of the city's Skyway system runs undergound, that the Chester Park Laundry doubles as a tropical bird aviary, that Duluth's annual "Christmas City of the North" parade is held before Thanksgiving. Duluth may be a little bit off center, but it is always true north.

But this region isn't all about Duluth any more than Gooseberry Falls defines the North Shore, and we'd like to introduce you to places you may not know about. We think you'll find that most of the places featured in our book prove to be much more interesting than some of the, shall we say, homogenized establishments that cater to their expectations of your taste.

This project started out to be just about Duluth, but as we shared our idea with others, they told us of more places we simply had to include, many of which are found along Lake Superior's North and South Shores. And so while the book remains centered on Duluth, it has reached along both shores along Minnesota Highway 61 and Wisconsin Highway 13.

We've done our best to omit chains, franchises, and businesses that are not locally owned. In Duluth we decided to concentrate on places found below Skyline Parkway (with one or two very special exceptions), not to imply that there is little worth seeing up in the 'Heights, only that there is little to distinguish the Central Entrance strip and the Miller Hill Mall shopping corridor from any suburban shopping center.

In our first edition, we also left out all of Canal Park because it is Duluth's most wellworn tourist area. This time around we've added a new chapter—"The Beaten Path"—that guides readers to *locally owned, non-chain* establishments in Canal Park and the Fitger's Brewery Complex. Since you're inevitably going to spend some time among the madding tourist crowd, you can also choose to spend your money at shops and restaurants that keep proceeds in the community.

In this edition we've also updated and expanded the rest of the book. We've added more outdoor adventures and interesting old buildings, squeezed in a few more events, increased the number of shops and museums, found new places to eat, and removed establishments that have closed. We've even added a map of Downtown Duluth (including the Skywalk system) and expanded the information in the "Places to Stay" section.

Not all the entries in the book would normally qualify as "alternative" or "off-beat"—a few are probably well known to visitors. We've included them here because of some unique feature they offer, such as their history, location, or product. Essentially, everything we've included illustrates the fact that there's more to this region than most visitors—and many local residents—ever experience.

We hope you find the book useful and that it helps you find your own version of true north—but keep in mind that around here, true north isn't always where you'd expect it to be.

– The Authors.

Tips for Travelers
(maps, getting around, unusual laws,
radio stations, etc.)

Tips for Travelers

One of our goals for this book is to show visitors that there's more to Duluth than Canal Park, more to Superior than Barker's Island, more to the South Shore than Bayfield, and more to the North Shore than Gooseberry Falls—all wonderful places, but not a complete representation of all that the area has to offer.

And so we created this section to help you find your way around once you leave paths worn smooth by visitors. We've included maps—one showing the North and South Shores as well as individual maps of Duluth and Superior—featuring major thoroughfares to help you get to the places we've highlighted in other chapters. There's even a map of Duluth's Skywalk system and downtown. We've also included a page filled with tips on driving in Duluth, from negotiating hills in the winter to figuring out which side of the street to park on. And since you'll be in the car, we've listed all the stations your radio will pick up so you can find your favorite format. (By the way, Twin Cities residents, Twin Ports radio stations start coming in just north of Hinckley.)

This section also gave us an opportunity to have some fun, as you'll discover when you read our reasons to go to Superior and our list of some rather obscure and outdated Minnesota and Wisconsin laws. We've even added a page that attempts to explain the area's weather and—to make every last moment of your visit more interesting—we've included some ideas to make even the ride home something different, at least for those who live south of the Twin Ports in Minnesota (and who make up the vast majority of visitors to this area).

And just to make locals easier to understand, here's a mini glossary:

"Bridged" = Stuck in the car, waiting for a ship to pass through the Canal when the Lift Bridge is up.

"Northland" = Advertising and media term for Northwestern Wisconsin and the Minnesota Arrowhead region.

"Old Downtown" = The area between Lake Avenue and 5th Avenue East along Superior and First streets.

"Rats with Wings" = Seagulls. (*Please* don't feed the gulls!)

Lake Superior

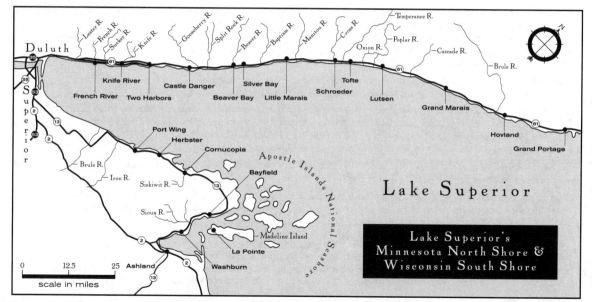

Lake Superior's
Minnesota North Shore &
Wisconsin South Shore

Driving Duluth

- For the most part, streets (Superior Street, 1st Street, etc.) run relatively east and west (or "across"); avenues run relatively north and south (or "up and down"). Lake Avenue and Superior Street is the "zero" intersection: numbered avenues start from Lake Avenue (1st Avenue East is the first avenue east of Lake Avenue, and 1st Avenue West is the first avenue west of Lake Avenue) and numbered streets start from Superior Street (1st Street is the first street above Superior Street).

- Because of the numerous creek ravines that run through the city, many of Duluth's streets and avenues come to sudden dead ends where it would be impractical to build bridges.

- Several streets in and around downtown are one-ways from Mesaba Avenue to 24th Avenue East, including Michigan Street (heading east, it ends at 4th Avenue East), 1st Street (heading west), 2nd Street (heading east), and 3rd Street (heading west, beginning one way at 22nd Avenue East). Also, 14th Avenue East is a one-way heading up the hill, and 12th Avenue East heads one way down the hill.

- When driving east on 2nd Street between Mesaba Avenue and 6th Avenue East, drive at a steady 30 mph and you should find the traffic lights lit green the whole stretch.

- Due to its narrow streets, Duluth enforces alternate-side parking year round throughout most of the city. The "parking side" switches each Sunday, and residents must move their cars between 4 P.M. and 8 P.M.

- The steepest hill in Duluth is 5th Avenue West above 5th Street—a 26-percent grade.

- Winter driving on slippery hillside roads can be tricky, particularly if you don't have a four- or front-wheel drive vehicle. Fortunately, the plow crews move quickly in Duluth. If you do find yourself driving Duluth when the streets are thick with snow or ice, try this: stick to main thoroughfares, especially when you have to go uphill, and approach your destination from above (it's easier to go down a hill in poor conditions than to go up).

Getting from Canal Park to Downtown[*]

Too many Duluth visitors miss out on the wonderful downtown shops and restaurants because they don't want to drive from their hotels in Canal Park or they are uncomfortable crossing I-35 on Lake Avenue on foot.

You can get to "Old" Downtown (between Lake Avenue and 5th Avenue East) using the Lakewalk. Find the stairs near the bathroom facilities just past Endion Station and follow them up. You'll find a small park that covers the highway, complete with benches and statuary, and intersected with sidewalks. The sidewalks lead to boardwalks near Michigan Street. These boardwalks will lead you to three different intersections in "Old" Downtown: Second Avenue East and Superior Street, First Avenue East and Superior Street, and Lake Avenue and Superior Street.

Another way to get downtown is through the Skywalk. Cross the blue drawbridge at the stern of the William A. Irvin to the Duluth Entertainment & Convention Center (DECC). The DECC connects to the Skywalk system and leads directly to the Wells Fargo Building at Third Avenue West and Superior Street.

What you'll find in "Old" Downtown (and in this book): Electric Fetus, Lizzard's Gallery, Chinese Dragon, Last Place on Earth, Lester River Fly Shop, First Oriental Grocery, Great Northern Music, Hacienda Del Sol, Romano Grocery, Chinese Garden, NorShor Theatre, Green Mercantile, Browser's N'eTc., Original Coney Island, Greysolon Plaza, and the Old City Hall and Jail.

What you'll find Downtown (and in this book): Fragments of History, Tony's Trading Post, Global Village, Jitters, Explorations, My Buddy's Place, India Palace, Coco's to Geaux, Duluth Tobacco & Gift, Duluth Athletic Club, Cantonese House, Sammy's Pizza, Coney Island Deluxe, Thai Krathong, Dirtygirlz Cooperative, Chef Yee's, Exchange Deli, Angela's Bella Flora, Duluth Civic Center, Duluth Union Depot, Board of Trade Building, Alworth Building, Wirth Building, and much more.

[*]Without driving.

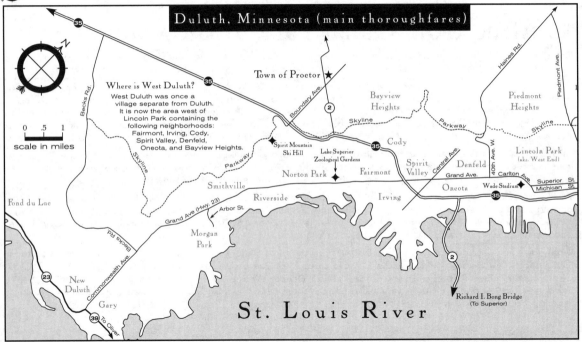

Duluth, Minnesota (main thoroughfares)

Town of Proctor ★

Where is West Duluth?
West Duluth was once a village separate from Duluth. It is now the area west of Lincoln Park containing the following neighborhoods: Fairmont, Irving, Cody, Spirit Valley, Denfeld, Oneota, and Bayview Heights.

scale in miles
0   .5   1

Spirit Mountain Ski Hill

Lake Superior Zoological Gardens

Bayview Heights

Piedmont Heights

Cody

Skyline

Parkway

Spirit Valley

Denfeld

Lincoln Park (aka. West End)

Fairmont

Norton Park

Smithville

Riverside

Irving

Oneota

Grand Ave.

Wade Stadium

Superior St.

Michigan St.

Fond du Lac

Grand Ave (Hwy. 23)

Arbor St.

Morgan Park

New Duluth

Gary

To Oliver

Richard I. Bong Bridge (To Superior)

St. Louis River

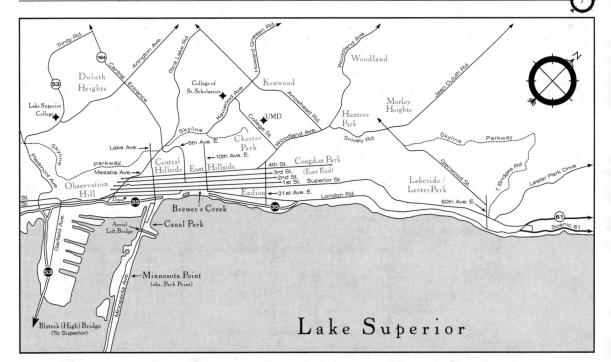

Downtown Duluth & the Skywalk System

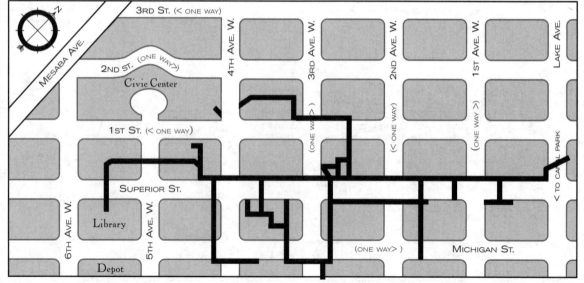

"Old" Downtown

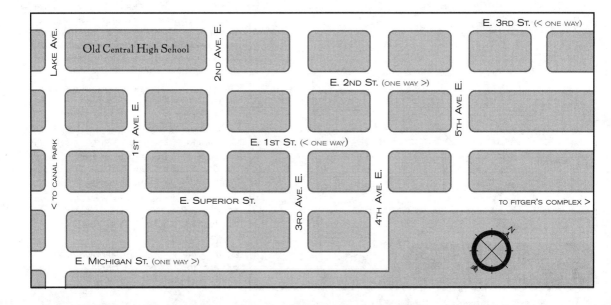

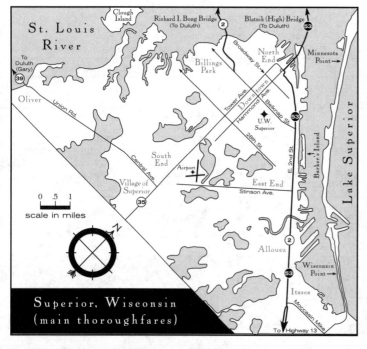

Superior, Wisconsin
(main thoroughfares)

Visit Superior

Too few visitors to Duluth ever cross the river to Superior, and that's a shame. Superior is home to museums, historic sites, and many taverns and restaurants. Many before you have found it a great place to visit or make their home:

Gangster Al Capone once suggested to a friend that she'd find Superior a hospitable place to live (see next page).

Movie star Arnold Schwarzenegger lived in Superior while attending his alma mater, UW-Superior (rumor has it that's his cabin atop Silver Cliff on Minnesota Highway 61 past Two Harbors).

And Superior is home to Raymond "Bud" Somerville, the first inductee into the United States Curling Association's Hall of Fame.

By the way, in Superior, Highways 2 and 53 are the same as East 2nd Street when they pass through town.

Ten Reasons to Go to Superior

Why do so few visitors to Duluth ever make the short drive to Superior? Maybe it's because of the whole Minnesota vs. Wisconsin issue, the Packers vs. Vikings rivalry, or the slew of bad driver jokes tossed in both directions. But whatever the reason, if you don't head "O.T.B." (over the bridge), as local residents like to say, you're not getting a true north experience. If you can't find your own reason to go or aren't satisfied with those mentioned on page 10, we've listed a few more for you below. The list contains ten reasons, but not necessarily the top ten.

- Twenty-six bars operate along one ten-block strip of Tower Avenue, plus nine more a block or less off Tower.

- Bars stay open until 2:30 A.M. on weekends (they close earlier in Minnesota).

- Superior has more places to eat at 2 A.M. than does Duluth.

- Liquor stores are open on Sundays (liquor stores are closed in Minnesota on Sundays).

- You can smoke in restaurants (Duluth has banned smoking in its restaurants).

- Lower cigarette taxes = cheaper cigarettes. (Please, for your own good, don't smoke!)

- As Al Capone once told a friend, Superior "is full of speakeasies and brothels...the law won't give you any trouble there" (of course, that was during Prohibition).

- Two bridges cross between Duluth and Superior: The Richard I. Bong Bridge and the Blatnik Bridge, also known as the High Bridge. So, technically, you can go to Superior on a bong and come back on a high (we have no idea what this means).

- Closet Green Bay Packer fans from Minnesota can cheer the Pack in relative safety.

- You can't get to the South Shore from Duluth without driving through Superior!

Obscure Minnesota Laws

Not many of these laws are still on the books, but we want you to be prepared. Remember, ignorance of the law is no excuse.

In Minnesota...

- A person may not cross state lines with a duck atop his or her head. (Also, citizens may not enter Wisconsin with chickens on their heads.)
- It is illegal to sleep naked.
- All men driving motorcycles must wear shirts. (The law does not mention whether women must wear shirts.)
- It is unlawful to tease or torment skunks or polecats.

In Duluth...

- All bathtubs must have feet.
- Dogs may not nap in barber shops or beauty salons. The law also makes it illegal to let a dog, horse, or any other animal sleep in a bakery.

Further up the map...

- If you visit Hibbing, keep close tabs on your cat, for "If any cat is found running at large, or is found in any street, alley, or public place, it shall be the duty of any policeman or other officer of the city to kill such cat."
- If you travel to International Falls, keep in mind that cats are not allowed to chase dogs up telephone poles.
- And if you stop by Virginia, remember that you're not allowed to park your elephant on Main Street.

Obscure Wisconsin Laws

When visiting the Dairy State, keep a close watch on your activities surrounding dairy and faux-dairy products, for in Wisconsin...

- At one time, margarine was illegal.
- Butter substitutes are not allowed to be served in state prisons.
- All yellow butter substitutes were banned after people began smuggling them in from Illinois.
- It was once illegal to serve apple pie in public restaurants without cheese.
- While all cheese making requires a cheese maker's license, making Limburger cheese requires a *master* cheese maker's license.

Furthermore...

- You must manually flush all urinals in a building.
- Citizens may not murder their enemies.
- It was once illegal to kiss on a train.
- It was once illegal to cut a woman's hair.

And to clear things up...

- "...Whenever two trains meet at an intersection of said tracks, neither shall proceed until the other has."

Radio Stations

Commercial-Free & Public Radio

KUMD • 103.3 FM • Duluth • "Duluth Public Radio"
A member-supported, independent public radio station broadcasting from the UMD campus. Eclectic mix with an emphasis on the singer/songwriter and modern blues. "World Café" weekday afternoons from 2-5 P.M.

WTIP • 90.7 FM • Grand Marais • "Public Radio for the North Shore"
An eclectic mix of folk, bluegrass, singer/songwriter, acoustic, classical, American Indian, Celtic—you name it— along with some programming from KUMD.

WSCN-FM • 100.5 FM • Duluth • Minnesota Public Radio & NPR / Talk *(WLSN 89.7 on the North Shore)*
NPR, news, information, and entertainment: "Talk of the Nation," "All Things Considered," "Fresh Air," "This American Life," "A Prairie Home Companion." "The Jazz Image" with Leigh Kammam late into Saturday night.

WSCD-FM • 92.9 FM • Duluth • MPR & NPR / Classical music *(WMLS 88.7 on the North Shore)*
Classical music along with some WSCN programming (e.g., "A Prairie Home Companion").

KUWS • 91.3 FM • Superior • Wisconsin Public Radio & NPR
NPR, news, and a great mix of music broadcasting from the campus of the University of Wisconsin, Superior.

WOJB • 88.9 FM • Superior • Woodland Public Radio / Lac Courte Orielles tribe
Great mix, including live pow-wows. Hard to get in Duluth, but halfway into Superior it comes in loud and clear.

Radio Stations, continued

KBMX 107.7 "Mix 108"
107.7 FM • Duluth
Hot Adult Contemporary

KDAL-AM
610 AM • Duluth
Talk with News, Weather, & Sports

KDAL-FM "Magic 95.7"
95.7 FM • Duluth
Adult Contemporary

KDNW
97.3 FM • Duluth
Christian

KKCB "B-105"
105 FM • Duluth
Country

KLDJ "KOOL 101.7"
101.7 FM • Duluth
Oldies

KQDS
94.9 FM • Duluth
Classic and New Rock

KQDS AM
1490 AM • Duluth
CNN Headline News

KRBR "The Bear"
102.5 FM • Duluth
New Rock

KTCO
98.9 FM • Duluth
New Country

KUSZ "USA Radio"
99.9 FM • Duluth
Country

KXTP "Radio X"
970 AM • Duluth
Talk Radio

106X
104.3 and 106.3 FM • Duluth
Modern Rock

WEBC Radio
560 AM • Duluth
Talk

WDSM
710 AM • Duluth
Sports

WNCB
89.3 FM • Duluth
Christian Hits

WNXR
107.3 FM • Superior
Oldies & Brewers' Baseball

WWAX "Kiss 92"
92.1 FM • Duluth
Top 40

WWJC Radio
850 AM • Duluth
Christian Information

WXXZ
95.3 FM • Grand Marais
Classic and New Rock

Informative Web Sites

If you're looking for more information about Duluth, Superior, or places to go or things to do up and down the Lake Superior shores, try these Web sites:

Alternative Press / Weekly Entertainment Schedule:
www.ripsawnews.com (the *Ripsaw*, a regional arts and entertainment weekly)

Unique Duluth Information and Image Sites:
www.duluthshippingnews.com (daily reports and schedules of arrivals and departures from the Duluth Harbor)
www.duluthpreservation.org/index.html (home of the Duluth Preservation Alliance)
www.duluth-mn-usa.com/ (a great collection of postcards, photos, and other images of Duluth past and present)
www.inredllc.com/duluth/architecture/architec.htm (images of and information about Duluth's old buildings and homes)

General / Visitor Info:
www.visitduluth.com (Duluth Convention and Visitors Bureau)
www.northshorevisitor.com (commercial visitor's guide to the North Shore)
www.dnr.state.mn.us/parks_and_recreation/state_parks (Minnesota state parks)
www.exploreminnesota.com (a state-sponsored visitor's guide to Minnesota)
www.visitsuperior.com (a guide to Superior and Douglas County)
www.travelwisconsin.com (a state-sponsored visitor's guide to Wisconsin)

Mainstream Press:
www.duluthsuperior.com (*Duluth News-Tribune*, Duluth's daily paper, a member of the Knight-Ridder chain)
www.duluth.com (*Duluth Budgeteer News / Duluth.com Newpaper*, weekly Murphy-McGinnis newspapers)
www.superior-wi.com (*Superior Evening Telegram*, a daily Murphy-McGinnis newspaper)
www.lakesuperior.com (*Lake Superior Magazine*, a monthly magazine dedicated to the Lake Superior region)

Colder by the Lake?

Most out-of-towners have a pretty bad impression about the weather "up north," especially in Duluth. "How can you live up there?" they ask. "With all that snow and it gets so ding-dang cold?" Well, they may not say "ding-dang," but they do think it's rather cold in these parts. And they're right. Kinda.

The oft-repeated refrain from TV weathercasters is "colder by the lake." This refers to the frequent and wide difference in temperature from the harbor to "over the hill" in the 'Heights and further up at the airport, where the official temperature is measured. In the summer, "colder by the lake" is generally the rule, as the frigid waters of Lake Superior act as an air conditioner, keeping the average summer temperature at 62 degrees (Duluth is the coldest major urban center in the contiguous United States). Meteorologists have reported as much as a 40-degree difference between the airport and harbor on a summer's day. In the winter, however, it is often warmer by the lake, as residents below the hill are protected from icy northwest winds.

But don't take anything for granted—even the forecast. The Lake Superior region is one of those places that lays claim to the adage "If you don't like the weather, wait five minutes." The lake makes weather predicting rather unpredictable and keeps the jobs of area meteorologists very interesting.

The Twin Ports don't get as much snowfall as one might expect, but the North Shore does get more snow than any other place in Minnesota. The real dumping ground is the South Shore, also known as the snow belt, which receives more than its fair share of lake-effect snow. Common from November to February, lake-effect snow is any snow—from flurries to squalls—that the presence of the Great Lakes causes or helps to develop.

Lake Superior is also susceptible to great blasts of wind many have mistakenly called Nor'Easters (a similar phenomenon found along the eastern seaboard) that make sailing treacherous. Some call these winds "the gales of November" after the reference in Gordon Lightfoot's famous ballad, "The Wreck of the Edmund Fitzgerald."

Take the Long Way Home

If you're from the Twin Cities and have visited before, you know what a pain traffic along I-35 can be on a Sunday evening when it seems that everyone is trying to get back from mowing the lawn at the cabin with enough time to mow the lawn in the suburbs. Next time, leave early so you can relax and enjoy the trip. Try these ideas:

Take the Scenic Route
Instead of I-35, follow Grand Avenue south until it becomes Commonwealth Avenue and, eventually, Scenic Highway 23, and enjoy a leisurely drive until the highway connects with I-35 near Askov.

Take Skyline out of Town
Heading west on Skyline Parkway will eventually bring you to the on-ramp of I-35 at Boundary Avenue. If you stay on Skyline to the end, you'll find yourself at Becks Road. A right will take you to I-35, a left to Scenic 23.

Go through Wisconsin
Wisconsin's Highway 35 out of Superior will take you all the way to Stillwater, Minnesota, or Hudson, Wisconsin, so if you're from the eastern suburbs, this is a fun way to go. You'll have to jump on Highway 8 at St. Croix Falls and head west to stay on 35.

Treat Your Tank & Tummy
Stop in Cloquet and fill your tummy at Gordy's Hi-Hat, a classic drive-in restaurant open during the summer offering old-fashioned burgers and fries and thick malts to wash them down. When you're full, top off the tank with a taste of architectural history at the Phillips 66 service station at the corner of Route 45 and Route 33—it was designed by Frank Lloyd Wright.

Outdoor Adventures

(day trips & some stunning views)

Outdoor Adventures

Obviously you can't have a chapter titled "Outdoor Adventures" in a book that covers the North and South Shores without mentioning Lake Superior itself. We thought you'd like to know a little something about that big body of water that dominates—and has shaped—the landscape that surrounds it. Lake Superior was formed about 10,000 years ago, near the end of the most recent ice age. As the giant glaciers melted, they formed lakes, including Glacial Lake Duluth, Superior's predecessor (Skyline Parkway runs along what was once its beach). With its surface 602 feet above sea level, Superior has the highest elevation of all the Great Lakes. It is also largest in area with 31,280 square miles (an area equal to Connecticut, New Hampshire, Massachusetts, Rhode Island, and Vermont combined), and the cleanest and coldest as well (average temperature, 40 degrees Fahrenheit). It contains three quadrillion gallons of water, or about ten percent of the world's fresh water. From east to west Lake Superior extends 383 miles; it stretches 160 miles across at its widest and reaches depths of 1,279 feet.

There's a lot to do along Superior's shores (2,700 miles of shoreline surround the lake), but far too many visitors limit their adventures to a drive along the highway and a stop at Gooseberry Falls or the Split Rock Lighthouse. We want you to see more of it. At the same time, we realize that not everyone is an outdoor enthusiast who packs plenty of gear and is ready to kayak or rock climb at a moment's notice. Most of us don't even remember to pack a decent pair of athletic shoes.

If you did, you're in luck. The following 38 pages are filled with adventures you can experience without gear—we did them all with nothing more than a beat-up pair of hiking boots, and most often even those weren't required. Almost all of the adventures are found less than a mile from shore (most even closer than that) and many are found inside the Duluth city limits (only Eagle Mountain on page 45 takes you more than three miles from the shore). You can get to all of them in a car, and none of them require even as much as a state park pass.

Bring a camera.

Amity Creek: Seven Bridges & The Deeps

Amity Creek is a western feeding branch of the Lester River that converges with the larger waterway just above Superior Street within the boundaries of Lester Park. On its way downstream toward the Lester and Lake Superior, Amity winds through gorges of rhyolite and over basalt ledges, forming many waterfalls along the way.

One of the more popular spots along the Amity is The Deeps, a large pool formed by erosion at the base of a waterfall just upstream from the Lester near Occidental Boulevard (which becomes Seven Bridges Road). A footbridge above the waterfall connects to hiking trails. What do folks do at The Deeps? They jump in.

While most of the Amity is quite shallow, some areas in The Deeps reach forty feet down. Local adrenaline junkies like to leap from nearby cliffs, and have been doing so for years. Launching spots such as "Stumpy," "The Tower," and "The Pine" offer jumpers a challenge. (Cliff jumping is extremely dangerous; jumpers do so at their own risk.)

The seven arched stone bridges of Seven Bridges Road cross the Amity. Former mayor Sam Snivel (who served Duluth from 1921 to 1937) donated 60 acres of land for the road and convinced other land owners to give property and funds for the project (see pages 36 and 37 for more details).

"The Deeps" of Amity Creek, a popular cliff jumping site.

Bagley Nature Center

Located on the UMD campus, Bagley Nature Center is 55 acres of old hardwood forest that includes a variety of habitats as well as Rock Pond, the western branch of Tischer Creek, and its centerpiece, Rock Hill, which rises 1,271 feet above sea level (659 ft. above Lake Superior) An observation deck sits atop the hill.

The Nature Center is used by UMD for environmental studies and recreation, but is open to everyone. During summer months, Bagley offers 2.7 kilometers of hiking trails, none too difficult, unless you're hiking uphill. In the winter the trails are groomed for classic cross-country skiing. (No dogs or hikers in winter; no mountain bikes year round). The hill also makes for great sliding in the winter (UMD once operated a ski hill on the site; only concrete ruins of the tow-rope system remain). There are two locations for campfires, but you must bring your own wood.

Bagley Nature Center's Rock Pond, just below a tree-covered Rock Hill.

The original 16-acre site, including Rock Hill, was donated by Dr. William Bagley and his daughter, Dr. Elizabeth Bagley, one of the first women to practice medicine in Duluth and the personal physician and close friend of Elisabeth Congdon (see pages 242 and 245). University purchases expanded the park to 55 acres.

The center is located northwest of UMD, off Buffalo Street (which connects St. Marie Street, north of campus, with Junction Avenue, west of campus). Park free in the lot during summer; a limited number of parking meters are available in the same lot during the school year.

Chester Park

Chester Park is one of Duluth's original three parks (along with Lincoln and Zenith) and includes a trail system popular among UMD and St. Scholastica students and East Hillside residents—especially dog lovers (if you don't like dogs, be aware that you're bound to encounter a pup or two along the trail). The park takes its name not from Chester Congdon, as many believe, but from Charles Chester, who homesteaded a property along the creek near what is now 5th Street, just east of 13th Avenue East, on May 31, 1856 (ruins of his home remain).

The park's 108 acres include 2.5 miles of hiking trail along Lower Chester (the area below Skyline Parkway), which is home to a pair of footbridges, several waterfalls, and a cauldron known as Devil's Hole. Four miles of cross-country ski/hiking trails can be found in Upper Chester (also known as Chester Bowl). Upper Chester also contains soccer fields (flooded in the winter for ice skating), a small ski hill, and some ski jumps. The Chester Bowl ski jumps were the training grounds for several national champions and members of the U.S. Olympic Ski Jumping Team. Many of the park's stone walls and stairways were constructed by the WPA in the 1930s. Mountain bikers, please take note: the trails are very fragile; bikes are *not* allowed.

You'll find ample parking in the lot at Skyline Boulevard and Chester Parkway, which runs along the east side of the creek starting at the 8th Avenue East Bridge. You can also park along the bridge at 4th Street between 13th and 14th avenues east.

One of Chester Creek's waterfalls near Skyline Boulevard.

Congdon Park & Tischer Creek

The 38 acres along Tischer Creek that make up Congdon Park were donated to the city in 1908 by Chester A. Congdon, who along with his wife, Clara, built a family mansion, Glensheen, at the site where the creek empties into Lake Superior. In 1925 Mayor Sam Snively saw to it that the park was developed, establishing gravel-covered trails, stone stairways, and wooden bridges—even a bridle path once graced the park. The park fell into disrepair over the years, but in 1972 the Duluth Junior League, along with the Department of Parks and Recreation, restored the park as a nature trail with the help of local Boy Scouts and UMD students.

Steep red rock cliffs line portions of Congdon Park's Tischer Creek.

The park rests between Superior Street and Vermilion Road and winds along the creek near 32nd Avenue East. A stairway leads down to trails within the deep walls that form the park's boundaries. High cliffs of red rock, produced by lava roughly one billion years ago, show how much the creek has eroded the stone over the eons. White cedars appear to grow straight out of the cliffs (a trick of erosion), and Norway pines and a variety of hardwoods line the creek. Several waterfalls grace Tischer Creek; one forms a large swimmin' hole. The park is a popular spot for Duluth East students to visit to "avoid" class.

You can enter Congdon Park at 32nd Avenue East and Superior Street. Look for stairs leading down into the creek gorge near the park's sign, on the uphill side of Superior Street just west of the bridge. You can park along 32nd Avenue East near Congdon School.

Enger Park & Twin Ponds

Most people know Enger Park for its six-story, bluestone tower, but there's a lot more to the greenspace than a great view. The park contains a gazebo, a pavilion, gardens, and the Peace Bell, making it a popular site for outdoor weddings.

The Peace Bell is a replica of a cherished temple bell in Ohara, Japan. The Japanese government took the original bell from Ohara in 1940 to be melted down as part of the war effort, but for some reason the bell never met the furnace. After the war, American sailors aboard the *U.S.S. Duluth* took the bell as a spoil of war and sent it to their ship's namesake city. The bell was returned to Ohara in the 1950s. Years later, the town of Ohara had a replica of the bell made for its sister city, Duluth, and the new bell was dedicated at Enger Park in 1994. It was then dubbed the Peace Bell.

In keeping with the Japanese theme, beautiful gardens with a trickling fountain/stream and winding footpaths make up most of Enger Park. The groomed areas are surrounded by rock outcroppings that lead to thick stands of trees. A gazebo to the east provides a view without climbing the tower's six stories of stairways, and a stone pavilion complete with a fireplace, picnic tables, and restrooms provides visitors with a comfortable spot for a meal.

Just east of the park along Skyline Parkway you'll find Twin Ponds. As Lake Superior is often too cold to take a dip, many Duluthians use the ponds for swimming.

Enger Park's Peace Bell..

Hartley Park (a.k.a. Hartley Nature Center)

Hartley Park (sometimes called "Hartley Nature Center") is made up of 660 acres of diverse natural habitat, including streams, ponds, forests, and wetlands, on the site that was once a farm owned by Guilford and Caroline E. Hartley, who left many landmarks throughout Duluth (see pages 258 and 264).

The park contains about five miles of trails—three of which are maintained for cross-country skiing—that are popular among runners, hikers, and dog owners. It's also home to a 50-acre wetland, streams, and an abundance of wildlife such as bears, white-tailed deer, mink, fox, owls, and a variety of other birds.

The view of Duluth and Lake Superior from Hartley Park's Rock Knob.

Perhaps the most obvious natural landmark in Hartley Park is Rock Knob, a 100-foot stone hill that many park visitors use as a vantage point to view the park and its surroundings. On a clear day, you can see Lake Superior while Duluth's houses and buildings remain hidden by trees.

Ruins of some of the outbuildings—including a large food-storage cellar—and other remnants of the Hartley family farm can be found throughout the park.

Hartley Park is open until dark during winter and until 10 P.M. in the summer. To get there, take Woodland Avenue north past Minneapolis Street and look for the sign on your left. For more information on the park, call (218) 724-6735.

Kitchi Gammi Park (a.k.a. Brighton Beach)

Most people who haven't been there in a while still call Kitchi Gammi Park "Brighton Beach." In fact, Brighton Beach is just part of the park (and the road that goes through it is named for the beach). Found along the Lake Superior shore just a quarter mile east of Lester River where London Road converges with Scenic Highway 61, Kitchi Gammi Park provides visitors with various picnicking and outdoor-cooking spots, restrooms in the summer, and a quaint gazebo overlooking the lake. It even has some swingsets and a sandbox for the kids. Visitors can thank Chester and Clara Congdon for the park, which is part of the land they donated to ensure the Lake Superior shoreline in Duluth past the Lester River remains undeveloped.

But Brighton Beach remains Kitchi Gammi's central attraction. This stretch of shore isn't what most people think of when they consider going to the beach. It's sort of a compromise between the craggy rocks of Stoney Point and the sandy shores of Minnesota Point. In other words, it's covered in rocks—big ones for climbing over and sunning upon and small ones perfect for skipping upon the water. You can swim here, but no lifeguards patrol the area.

Some of these rocks are often gathered into circles for driftwood fires on cool fall and summer nights, as the park provides a view of the city lights of both Duluth and Superior. If you're an early riser, take a drive out to the park and watch the sunrise over the unbroken horizon.

The rocky "beach" at Kitchi Gammi Park, with Wisconsin in the distance.

Leif Erickson Park (Along the Lakewalk)

Perhaps the best-known park in all of Duluth, Leif Erickson Park offers folks using the Lakewalk an opportunity to stop and smell the roses—literally. Next to the park's entrance—marked by a statue of Leif Erickson that credits the Viking with discovering America 1,000 years ago—is Duluth's Rose Garden, a lovely spot featuring stone benches, a gazebo (a popular wedding setting), and an incredible variety of roses and shrubs. The Rose Garden actually sits upon I-35 as the highway passes through tunnels beneath.

Across the footbridge and down next to the Lakewalk visitors will find a vast greenspace of groomed lawn that forms a natural ampitheatre and, at its base, a wonderfully whimsical stone stage framed by castle-like "towers." This setting makes the park a natural for such events as the annual Duluth International Folk Fest and the Lake Superior Shakespeare Festival. Behind the stage the park meets the lake shore. The beach is lined with stones, some boulders large enough to explore and others small and ideal for skipping.

Leif Erickson Park's "castle" stage, with Lake Superior in the background.

The park also features a replica Viking ship that was built in Bergen, Norway, in 1926 and sailed to Duluth. It is currently wrapped in blue shrink wrap to protect it. The Leif Erikson Restoration Project (LERP) is raising funds to create a roof to cover the ship.

You can access the park from the Lakewalk or park your car along London Road between 10th and 14th avenues east or in the lot across from the Armory.

Lester Park

Lester Park is located a few blocks upstream from the mouth of Lester River at the edge of Duluth's Lakeside neighborhood. Its eastern border runs along Lester River Road, and it's bordered on the west by Amity Creek and Seven Bridges Road (see page 21). The park includes miles of hiking and cross-country ski trails and a central park area near the parking lot that has picnic tables, grills, fields, shelters, playground equipment, and portable toilets in the summer.

The hiking and ski trails lead along both Lester River and Amity Creek. Portions of the river run through a fairly deep gorge in parts of the park, and hikers can either stroll on the smoother trails above the river or along rougher trails next to the water. For the view, get close to the river, where you'll find steep cliff walls, waterfalls, and swimming holes below the cascades.

Just downstream from the point where the Lester and Amity merge, cliff jumpers will find another spot to test their nerves. Old bridge footings and natural cliff walls form platforms for jumps as high as 60 feet, but most range from 20 to 30 feet. (Cliff jumping is extremely dangerous; jumpers do so at their own risk.)

To get to Lester Park, take Superior Street past 60th Avenue East to Lester River Road and turn left. You'll find a parking lot on your left less than a quarter mile up the road.

In September, Lester River runs shallow as it approaches Lake Superior.

Lincoln Park

Just about every town in America has a Lincoln Park, and Duluth is no exception. Duluth's Lincoln Park is the centerpiece of the West End—or Lincoln Park—neighborhood. The small park (just 1.5 miles of hiking trails) surrounds Miller Creek below Skyline Parkway down to West 3rd Street.

The park's central grounds consist of an expansive groomed lawn surrounded by a wonderful stone pavillion to the south and, to the north, Elephant Rock, an outcropping so large it looks out of place. The pavillion can be used for public gatherings and was recently renovated. North of Elephant Rock trails line either side of Miller Creek and are connected by several small footbridges. The creek itself is lined with rocks as it runs through the park and features several waterfalls and cauldrons large enough to serve as swimming holes. It is a popular spot for dog walkers.

Lincoln Park's Elephant Rock.

Behind the pavillion, the creek cascades gently down large, flat rocks; when the creek is low in late summer or fall, many local kids can be found hydroplaning down the rocks on the creek's naturally formed "slip-n-slide." A road also runs through the park and along the creek, allowing hiking access at different points.

There is no local historic significance behind the park's name—it comes from an adjacent elementary school named for President Abraham Lincoln. Access the park off West 3rd Street at 25th Avenue West.

Minnesota Point (a.k.a. Park Point)

Minnesota Point, a.k.a. Park Point, is the northern half of the largest freshwater sandbar in the world (Wisconsin Point, of course, is the southern half). Most of Minnesota Point is a residential area, but the entire stretch of shore on the lake side—all of it sandy beach—is open to the public. Most visitors stop where the road ends, at the recreation center just shy of Sky Harbor Airport. But for others, this is where the adventure begins.

Behind the airport you'll find the entrance to the Minnesota Point Hiking Trail. An old-growth forest of naturally regenerating red and white pines (some about 200 years old) begins shortly thereafter and continues almost to the end of the point at the Superior Entry. The sandy soil is often a challenge to hike, and bicyclists would be ill-advised to try these trails (besides, they'll also damage a delicate ecosystem). Stay on the trail: much of the ground cover is thick with poison ivy.

Along the trail, hikers will encounter the ruins of the oldest standing lighthouse on Lake Superior. Built in 1858, the Minnesota Point Lighthouse operated for 20 years. The ruin of the U.S. Lighthouse Station Depot rests nearby (see page 88).

To get to the hiking trail, simply cross the Aerial Lift Bridge and drive along Minnesota Avenue until you run out of road at the Sky Harbor Airport. Pass through the fence and follow the trail behind the buildings.

Wildflowers grace the beach near the Minnesota Point Hiking Trail.

Mission Creek Trail

Mission Creek Trail is perhaps the most historically significant trail in Duluth. It is named for the Ely Mission, which was founded on the current site of the Fond du Lac Community Church in 1834. Fond du Lac was home to the first mail route in the area; established in 1857, carriers used dogsleds to take mail as far away as Canada, and the route started on what is now the Mission Creek Trail. A brownstone quarry run by C.A. Krause operated on the creek in the 1880s, and much of the rock (Fond du Lac sandstone) was used in such historic Duluth buildings as Old Central High School (see page 77). A portion of the trail was once a road, built by the WPA, that connected with Skyline Parkway. Mission Creek was also a popular recreation area and included Ojibway Lodge, an ice skating rink, a ski hill, and even ski jumps.

The 3.25-mile trail follows a path created by American Indians long before the area was settled by Europeans. Half of the trail criss-crosses the creek over several footbridges while the other half takes hikers through a heavily wooded area filled with birches, maples, and a variety of other trees. It starts next to a holding dam near the site of the old quarry and at one point connects with the Willard Munger Trail.

To get to the trail, go south on Grand Avenue (Highway 23) to 131st Avenue West, turn right at Fond du Lac Park and follow the road until it ends at a gate. If the gate is open, follow the dirt road until you reach the trailhead (if the gate is locked, you will have to walk in—about a half mile).

Mission Creek Trail: thick with hardwoods that explode in fall colors.

Oneota Cemetery

Most people don't think of cemeteries as spots for outdoor adventures, but if you've ever taken the time to look around while you remember your lost loved ones, you've probably noticed what beautiful places they can be. If you don't find cemeteries morbid, you'll find a natural and architectural (not to mention historical) treat in Duluth's cemeteries.

Take Oneota Cemetery, for instance. Established in 1895 in what was then Oneota Township (just above Spirit Valley in West Duluth), the cemetery includes some wonderful old markers, a variety of hardwood trees, and—because of its location next to Skyline Parkway—a great view of St. Louis Bay.

Among the notables buried in Oneota are George Stuntz (and his dog Kayuga), the surveyor who mapped out most of Duluth and Superior, and environmental politician Willard Munger (for whom the Munger Trail is named).

To get to Oneota Cemetery, take Central Avenue north from I-35 to Highland Street and turn left—Highland runs right past the cemetery before connecting with Skyline Parkway.

An eroding marker set in 1890.

The tree stump marker of H.A. Michelson.

Forest Hill & Park Hill Cemeteries

One of Forest Hill's striking markers.

Forest Hill Cemetery, which can be accessed through the gate at Woodland and Carlisle Avenues, is the final resting place for many Duluthians. It is also a sprawling park filled with trees, ponds, nesting geese during the summer, and some very interesting grave markers.

The names on the markers in the older portion of the cemetery read like a who's who of Duluth and Northeastern Minnesota history. You'll find markers and mausoleums for Congdons, Alworths, Denfelds, Hibbings, Chisolms, and enough Hartleys to fill the Kitchi Gammi Club (and even some with last names such as Munger-Hartley and Hartley-Congdon, reflecting the past social circles of Duluth's elite). The resting place of Captain Charles S. Barker, for whom Superior's Barker's Island is named, is marked by a large stone cube graced with a round, bronze relief of the Captain's profile.

Some of the markers even reflect the region itself, such as the Walbank mausoleum, laid in 1890 and made of Lake Superior Brownstone. A stone obelisk dedicated to those of Scottish descent who have passed stands near a cannon memorializing Duluthians who died in the Civil War.

Park Hill Cemetery, located behind Forest Hill on Vermilion Road, also contains some historic grave sites, though the folks buried here didn't enjoy the financial success of those in Forest Hill. Most notably among Park Hill's interred are lynching victims Isaac McGhie, Elmer Jackson, and Elias Clayton (see page 240), who were once buried in unmarked graves. A few rows away lies Olli Kinkkonen, a Finnish immigrant lynched for his political views (see page 241).

Western Waterfront Trail

The 2.5-mile Western Waterfront Trail winds along the St. Louis River valley and was designed to allow users to get as close as possible to the water and wetlands that surround it.

One leg of the crushed limestone trail follows a path along the river that takes hikers around two of its bays, ending up at a parking lot at 63rd Avenue West. Another crosses Kingsbury Creek and traverses the perimeter of Indian Point Campground before stretching along the St. Louis until it reaches the Riverside neighborhood. The scenery on the Western Waterfront Trail is very different from that of most other Duluth parks. It includes expansive wetlands that are home to a variety of waterfowl, wildflowers, and other plant life. Rather than looking down toward the lake, hikers can gaze up toward Spirit Mountain, making the trail a great spot from which to enjoy the hardwood forest's fall colors.

The trail has two access points: a parking lot at Grand Avenue and 71st Avenue West (next to the Tappa Keg Inn and across from the Lake Superior Zoo) and another at Grand Avenue and Pulaski Street (take a left just past the Willard Munger Inn). Both access points also provide a gateway to the Willard Munger Trail, a paved bicycle/inline skating trail that rolls all the way to Hinkley, Minnesota. If you're from out of town and wish to give the Munger Trail a try, you can rent bicycles and other gear at the Willard Munger Inn.

Wetlands of the St. Louis River valley along the Western Waterfront Trail.

Skyline Parkway: a car or bike tour

The 28-mile roadway known as Skyline Parkway sits almost 500 feet above Lake Superior and stretches along a ridge which was—millions of years ago—the beach of Glacial Lake Duluth. The road once reached from Occidental Boulevard (Seven Bridges Road) along Amity Creek near the Lester River all the way into Jay Cooke State Park. It can still be accessed at Occidental and East Superior Street, but now ends where it intersects with Becks Road near Gary-New Duluth.

The parkway was first imagined by William K. Rogers, president of Duluth's first park board, and was presented to the Duluth City Council in 1888. By 1900 it was only five miles long. During the 1920s, Mayor Sam Snively—dedicated to making Duluth "the most beautiful city in the Northwest"—saw to it that the roadway was extended. The mayor had already built Seven Bridges Road with private funds. By 1927 the parkway ran to Jay Cooke State Park and in 1927 was named

Duluth's Skyline Parkway

Skyline Parkway, continued

Skyline Parkway. (Before that, the road had been named Carriage Drive, Rogers Boulevard, and Terrace Parkway.) In 1935 Snively began work to connect Skyline to Seven Bridges Road, a task that would not be completed until 1939, two years after he left office.

Today, much of the parkway is interrupted by larger thoroughfares that took priority over a leisure route. Starting at Spirit Mountain and heading west, the road remains unpaved. One of its original stone bridges can

be seen along this stretch, which features a stunning view from Bardon's Peak.

Today, Seven Bridges Road consists of eight bridges (there were originally nine; two were abandoned when Skyline Parkway was completed; a newer bridge near Superior Street is not considered part of Seven Bridges Road). To learn more about Skyline Parkway and Seven Bridges Road, see Mark Ryan's Web site at www.geocities.com/SoHo/Lofts/4839/SevenBridges/.

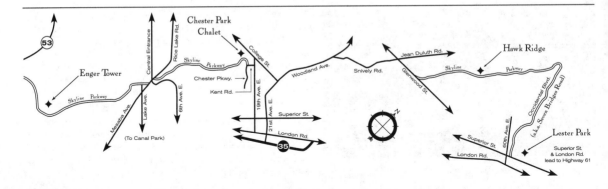

Billings Park

Superior's Billings Park is just about the best place for a family picnic in all of the Twin Ports. Its man-made facilities include pavilions, grills, picnic tables, restrooms (including a facility for disabled people) as well as horseshoe pits, swings, a small backstop for softball, and plenty of lawn for volleyball, bocce ball, or croquet.

The park sits next to the St. Louis River (it includes boat access), and trails provide hiking access (along a gentle, gravel-lined trail) to the shore—and to the great view of Spirit Mountain across the river (perfect for fall colors). The trail and park are home to a variety of plant life, including lily pads, rushes, cattails, raspberries, and black-eyed susans. Near the picinic facilities, the park is neatly groomed and blooms with a variety of trees, shrubs, and flowers.

Billings Park once included a swimming beach and boat house and the waters surrounding it were once the site of various water sports, including sailboat races. You can still sit on the remnants of granite bleachers once used by crowds to watch the various competitions on the river. Unfortunately, while the St. Louis River has become cleaner over the last few years, the river is currently too polluted for the city to allow swimming at the park.

The park is located at New York Avenue and 18th Street. Take Belknap Street west until the road veers left, then follow the signs to the park. South from the park you can drive through the Superior Municipal Forest to Pokegema Park.

A footbridge leads to a tiny island in Billings Park.

Wisconsin Point

While Wisconsin Point and Minnesota Point make up the world's largest sandbar, the points differ greatly from one another. Minnesota Point is highly developed with homes, community buildings, businesses, and even an airport. Wisconsin Point has been left almost completely natural. This may well be because it is considerably more narrow than its Minnesota counterpart.

All the better for its recreational users. Most of the Point is covered by pine forest and a vast stretch of beach. The beach is a popular spot for late-night summer parties, when the shoreline is likely to be dotted with bonfires and revelers. Hikers and bikers will enjoy the Osaugie Recreation Trail, a 5.5-mile trek running between the Nemadji River to Moccasin Mike Road and on to the end of the Point, where a lighthouse stands at the end of a long stone pier.

The Point is also home to the site of a traditional Fond du Lac Chippewa burial ground that dates from the 17th century. The graves were moved to Superior's St. Francis Cemetery in 1918, but the site is well marked and many visitors still leave offerings of respect, such as tobacco, dream catchers, and other less traditional gifts. Please respect the site as you would any other burial ground.

To get to Wisconsin Point, take Highway 53 southeast to the outskirts of Superior and turn left onto Moccasin Mike Road—the road will take you all the way to the end of the point (see the map on page 10).

The lighthouse at the end of Wisconsin Point.

Snow Sliding on Duluth's Hills

Any city like Duluth—built on a hillside and socked with winter from October to May—has to have a serious sliding history. In the 1880s, the Duluth Snowshoe and Toboggan Association was all the rage, and members included former mayor H.B. Moore and financier W.H. Alworth. Members often marched en masse from their unofficial headquarters at the St. Louis Hotel to a sledding hill somewhere near downtown off Superior Street (newspapers accounts are vague about the exact location). In other days gone by, local residents braved traffic by sliding down Duluth's steep streets.

Jack and Hank McEvoy sliding behind Holy Rosary School.

The DSTA is long gone, and street sliding has become extremely dangerous, but that doesn't keep local residents from sliding. One popular hill can be found off Seven Bridges Road near the Lester Park Junior Hockey Association's rink. Another is located behind the parking lot next to Holy Rosary school at 2802 East 4th Street (you have to climb over the fence). UMD students and neighbors enjoy sliding down Rock Hill in the Bagley Nature Area near UMD's Oakland Apartments (see page 22), and brave souls use the ski hills at Chester Park (see page 23). The city's golf courses also provide some great runs for toboggans, sleds, and saucers.

Snow sliding hasn't always been just for fun. The Finnish called it *luskiainin*, and sliding was an important part of their agrarian culture. It was thought that sliding helped the flax grow: the further you went down the hill (and often out onto the lake), the higher the flax would grow. Falling off was considered bad luck.

Stoney Point & the Buchanan Wayside

North Shore · Lakeside at Mileposts 15 & 16 on Scenic 61

Stoney Point is a stretch of rocky shoreline along a loop of road off Scenic Highway 61. The western point of Stoney Point Road connects to Highway 61 at Milepost 15, just across the road from Tom's Logging Camp (an interactive, family-friendly museum). The waves can be particularly dramatic at Stoney Point, forcing spray high into the air when they meet the rocks. Kayakers and even surfers take advantages of the waves along this stretch of 61 to play in the lake.

Since the 1990s Stoney Point has become increasingly popular among shorecasters and picnickers. In fact, many local residents asked us to not mention it, but it's way too late to put that genie back in its bottle. Visitors should be aware that many people live nearby, so be careful to respect their property and privacy. And of course, respect Stoney Point and pick up after yourselves when you leave.

Less than a half mile from Stoney Point, the Buchanan Wayside marks the spot of an abandoned town named for President James Buchanan. The town, laid out in 1856, was the seat of the land office for Northeastern Minnesota. After the office relocated, the settlement disappeared. The wayside is made of stone walls that enclose a small picnic area and historic marker. It also provides access to a stretch of shoreline very much like that of Stoney Point, making it a great alternative if Stoney's crowded.

The rocky shore adjacent to the Buchanan Wayside along Scenic 61.

Split Rock River Loop

North Shore • Inland at Milepost 43 on Highway 61

Split Rock's split rock?

The Lake Superior Hiking Trail runs up and down the North Shore inland from Highway 61, providing hikers with days and days of adventure and camping spots, but gearless day trippers can enjoy it as well. One of the most spectacular legs of the trail is Split Rock River Loop, a five-mile hike that gently rises along Split Rock River.

From the wayside parking area, take the trail up the west side of the river, but pay attention to the map at the trail's entrance, or you could find yourself on the path to Gooseberry Falls State Park instead of Split Rock. A few waterfalls and sheer red rock walls make up just some of the river's beauty. About 1.5 miles up the path you'll find a large rock column that has been split in two—many consider this the source of the river's name. About another mile up, a bridge crosses to the river's east bank. The trail follows the river from above and eventually leads hikers to a high peak that overlooks the river valley—a great spot to see fall colors. However, after following the trail down to the highway, you will find yourself almost half a mile from your car and must walk along the highway to reach it.

Split Rock's name may have come from its landmark rock formation or from early fishermen who saw the optical illusion of two large cliffs a mile east of the river's mouth "split apart" as they approached in boats from the lake. The Ojibwe called the river Gin-On-Wab-Iko-Zibi or "Eagle Iron River." Park at the wayside at Milepost 43 on the inland side of the road.

Palisade Head

North Shore • Lakeside at Milepost 57 on Highway 61

About four miles up the shore from Silver Bay, you'll find Palisade Head, a cliff that climbs 320 feet above Lake Superior near the mouth of Palisade Creek. A winding road brings you to the summit of Palisade, and trails among rock outcroppings provide opportunities for exploration and picnicking. Keep the kids and dogs close: it's a long way down.

The reason most folks come to Palisade Head is the view. The Apostle Islands, 30 miles away off Wisconsin's South Shore, can be seen on clear days, as can the Sawtooth Mountains (actually lava deposits) up along the North Shore, and Shovel Point (sometimes called "Little Palisades") in Tettegouche State Park.

In recent years, Palisade Head and Shovel Point have become a magnet for rock climbers looking for a challenge. The sheer face of Palisade—igneous rhyolite overlaying soft basalt that has been undercut by Lake Superior's waves—provides just what they're looking for. Kayakers can also be found playing among the waves below.

Don't bother stopping by in the winter—the county does not plow the road.

Palisade Head from the lake, a view few landlubbers get to see.

Baptism River's Waterfalls

North Shore · Lakeside at Milepost 58 on Highway 61

The Baptism River's 70-foot High Falls.

The North Shore's Baptism River is home to several waterfalls, but the most spectacular is High Falls, a 70-foot drop a mile or so up easily hiked trails. Only at the 130-foot waterfall on the Pigeon River at the Canadian border will you find a higher falls in Minnesota. The river also contains Two-Step Falls downstream from High Falls. Though not as tall, Two-Step spills over some spectacular rock formations and is well worth the hike down a steep stairway.

Day trippers can park in the lot adjacent to the Tettegouche State Park headquarters (the Baptism is actually part of the park). Well-groomed trails lead hikers to both falls and, further inland, climb to the Lake Superior overlook, which provides a view of the river valley leading into Lake Superior.

Tettegouche is also home to Palisade Head and Shovel Point. A trail near the park headquarters leads to an overlook at Shovel Point, providing another great view of the lake.

The park, by the way, takes its name from an old logging camp established near Mic Mak Lake by eastern Canadians (Mic Mak is the name of a New Brunswick Indian tribe). You can park free at the wayside next to Tettegouche State Park if you're staying for fewer than six hours.

Crystal Beach Sea Cave

North Shore • Lakeside at Milepost 60 on Highway 61

Without a kayak, the Crystal Beach sea cave is a pretty tricky place to get to, but it's well worth the time and trouble. The cave—more of an arch, really—is one of the largest on Lake Superior, carved from the rock by the lake's relentless waves. You can't get in the cave from the beach without a kayak or canoe, but you can see it fairly close up. It lies to the east of a horseshoe-shaped beach surrounded by cliffs where Crystal Creek empties into Lake Superior. Ruins of abandoned structures indicate that this area was once used for some kind of commercial enterprise.

Gaining access to the beach is the tricky part. First, there's no place to park (Superior Outlook Bar & Grill is across the highway where 61 meets with Highway 1; ask if you can park in its lot and make sure to patronize it if you do—the owner is a friendly gent and knows how to get to the trail). On foot, cross to the lake side of the highway and over Crystal Creek—be very careful. You'll find a rocky trail leading down just past the guardrails and the "Crystal Creek" sign. Follow the trail down and you'll find yourself at the beach. By the way, some folks from the Silver Bay area call this spot "Peterson's Beach," and it was once a popular spot to enjoy a fire and a few beers.

The Crystal Beach sea cave as seen from Crystal Beach.

Caribou River Falls

North Shore · Inland at Milepost 70 on Highway 61

You won't find caribou anywhere near the Caribou River—they've been gone for more than 100 years—but you will find one of the best waterfalls along the North Shore, especially if you go during the spring thaw or after a good hard rain when the swollen river practically leaps off the cliffs on its way to the big lake.

The Caribou River Falls, just a half-mile hike from the highway.

The river and its falls are part of Caribou Falls State Park, which is little more than a parking lot, some outdoor toilets, and a hiking trail that leads to the falls and, eventually, to the Manitou River and Crosby Manitou State Park (about six miles away). The trail starts at the parking lot, and you need only hike half a mile up before you get to the falls. When you reach the falls, the trail gets a bit tricky as it descends to the base of the falls on a path of loose rock. But it's well worth the maneuvering, as the trail brings you very close to the falls for an incredible look at the descending plume. Amazingly, trees grow from the sides of the sheer cliffs that surround the cascade's cauldron (probably more a trick of erosion than a statement of heartiness).

The trail continues to the top of the falls, where a small bridge traverses the Manitou and hooks up with the Lake Superior Hiking Trail.

Father Baraga's Landing at Cross River

North Shore • Lakeside at Milepost 79 on Highway 61

Missionary Frederic R. Baraga, born in Yugoslavia in 1797, came to America in 1830 to devote his life to the American Indians of the Upper Great Lakes and was named bishop of Upper Michigan in 1853. But before that, he had a little trouble in a canoe. Crossing 30 miles of open Lake Superior waters from La Pointe on Madeline Island ten years before he became bishop, he and some native guides encountered a storm that almost took their lives. But they eventually found harbor at the mouth of a gently flowing river, and Baraga nailed a wooden cross to a stump and wrote upon it: "In commemoration of the goodness of almighty God in granting to the Reverend F.R. Baraga safe passage from La Pointe to this place, August, 1843." The river became Cross River, and the wooden cross has since been replaced by one made of concrete.

You can visit the cross and enjoy the scenic beauty surrounding the mouth of the Cross River without hardly walking a step. A short road off Highway 61 leads to a small parking lot (and boat landing) practically next to the cross itself (a short path leads to the cross). Outcroppings of igneous rock provide great spots for picnicking or just playing around on the rocks. The area also has picnic tables, but no camping is allowed.

People live nearby, so drive carefully, clean up after yourself, and respect all private property.

Father Baraga's Cross.

Temperance River's Hidden Falls

North Shore · Inland at Milepost 80 on Highway 61

A mile up the road from Cross River is Temperance River State Park, home to the dangerous beauty of Hidden Falls (the name Temperance comes from the lack of a "bar" at the river's mouth). You can park along the highway waysides on either side of the Highway 61 bridge that crosses the river, then follow the maps to the more than six miles of trails that traverse the park. But watch your step and hang on to the kids and dogs— you get dangerously close to steep drops. (Sadly, missteps have led to a few tragedies over the years.)

The Temperence River's Hidden Falls cut deeply into rock.

Within the park, a series of cascades brings the river down 162 feet through a rocky gorge within the space of only half a mile. The last cascade is found only 100 feet from the river's mouth. Along this span, the river's erosive power has carved deep cauldrons into the native rock.

The park's six miles of foot trails (and eight miles of cross-country ski trails) allow visitors to take long or short hikes at their discretion. It's just a 10-minute round trip to the lower footbridge and 30 minutes to the upper footbridge and back. A series of seven scenic overlooks can be found in less than an hour's round-trip hike from the parking areas.

Heartbreak Ridge (a great drive for fall colors)

North Shore • Inland at Milepost 82 on Highway 61

No tragic story of lost love inspired the name Heartbreak Ridge. It comes from a time when draft horses were used in the timber industry to pull logs out of the forest. The steepness of the ridge was too much for the sturdy horses in the winter, when it was sleek with ice and snow. Consequently, loggers could not move logs up and down the rise, and bypassing the ridge caused them extra work, thereby breaking their hearts.

Call it Breathtaking Ridge if you want, because this spot is home to thousands of sugar maples, which explode into reds, oranges, and yellows in autumn. A drive along the ridge is often the first stop for fall color enthusiasts on their annual autumn pilgrimage along the North Shore.

Leaf watchers say there are two seasons for watching the trees burst. The inland trees start changing about September 10, and peak color occurs between September 20 and October 10. The second season—when ash, birch and poplar turn yellow against flaming sumac along Highway 61—runs from about October 5 until the 20th. Since Heartbreak Ridge is inland, get out there before mid-October.

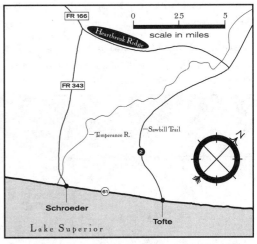

To get to Heartbreak Ridge, take the Temperance River Road (Forest Road 343) to Forest Road 166. Go east on FR 166 until you reach the Sawbill Trail (County Road 2). Heading south on the Sawbill takes you back to Highway 61.

Onion River's Cauldron

North Shore • Inland at Milepost 86 on Highway 61

You'll find the Onion River by stopping at the Roy Berglund State Scenic Wayside just north of Milepost 86. More of a creek than a river, the Onion trickles into Lake Superior, but about a quarter mile or so upstream you'll find a gently cascading waterfall. At the base of the waterfall is a pool local residents have dubbed "The Cauldron."

The Onion River's cauldron hardly roils with the force of water fed to it from above, making it an ideal swimming hole. There are plenty of flat rock surfaces for kicking back to dry off after a dip or to spread out a picnic lunch.

The Onion River's waterfall, which forms its refreshing cauldron.

To get to The Cauldron, take the rough trail located about 15 feet to the right of the Ray Berglund signpost (between the parking lot's 6th and 7th posts). The trail leads you up the east edge of the Onion and at times runs close to the edge of a drop leading down to the river, so keep the kids in hand. Look for a path leading down after a quarter mile or so of hiking (if you reach the area where trees have been cleared for power lines, you've gone about 30 yards too far). The trail continues beyond the falls for those who want a longer hike. Don't forget to clean up after yourself—in recent years inconsiderate visitors have left the place a mess.

Ray Berglund, by the way, was a St. Paul man who worked as a lumberman and loved the natural beauty of the North Shore. He lived from 1895 to 1948.

Eagle Mountain: Lowest to Highest

North Shore • Inland at Mileposts 92/109 on Highway 61

Well, it's a bit off the shore, but if you want to go from Minnesota's lowest point to its highest, start at the lakeshore at Lutsen or Grand Marais and head on up to Eagle Mountain, 2,301 feet of erosion-resistant granite that withstood the force of glaciers. A drive of about 15 miles takes you to the head of a 3.5-mile root-covered and rocky hiking trail. The elevation rises gradually until the last half mile, which is considerably steeper and rougher.

Once at the top—a flat ridge—you'll find several excellent vistas of the Boundary Waters Canoe Area Wilderness and the Superior National Forest. Look to the west side of the ridge for a brass survey disk that marks the peak. Tread lightly: this is an environmentally sensitive area full of fragile plant life, so please stay on the main trail.

Eagle Mountain is part of the BWCAW, so you'll need a permit for a day trip. You can issue yourself a permit right at the trailhead—simply follow directions at the permit box. If you plan to stay overnight between May and September, you need an overnight permit. You can obtain one from a Forest Service office or outfitter.

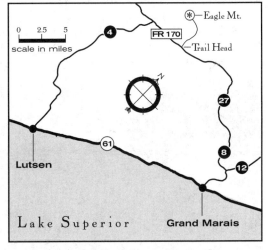

From Lutsen, take the Caribou Trail (County Road 4) to Forest Road 170. From Grand Marais, start on the Gunflint Trail (County Road 12) and connect to County Road 8, then 27 and finally FR 170.

The Stone Beach at Durfee Creek

North Shore • Lakeside at Milepost 115 on Highway 61

It's not an official beach, but the stretch of lakeshore along Highway 61 a mile or so north of Grand Marais is a stone-skipper's dream. The rocks that cover the beach have been worn smooth and flat by the waves of Lake Superior, and just about any stone found there makes a great skipper.

The stone beach at Durfee Creek: a rock skipper's paradise.

The site is also home to great scenic beauty for those who just want to sit on some of the large outcroppings (somewhat similar to those found at Stoney Point) and soak in the view. Five-Mile Rock (so named because it rests about five miles from the center of Grand Marais) lies off to the southwest, and the lake opens up before you. Signs of small fires indicate that the spot is used for nighttime outings as well.

There's a small wayside near a blue mailbox just before the highway crosses Durfee Creek. You can park there and easily walk to the lakeshore, where the rock beach stretches hundreds of yards in both directions. A few homes can be found farther along the shore, so be careful not to encroach on private property.

Twin Falls

South Shore · Two blocks west of Port Wing on Highway 13

Slow down just before you reach Port Wing as you drive east along the South Shore on Highway 13 and you'll see a large sign for Twin Falls Park—drive too fast and you'll miss it (when coming out of town from the east, the park is about two blocks west of Port Wing). Stop, back up if you missed it, and pull into the park. You'll find a circular dirt road to park along, a picnic area, and a trail leading a couple hundred yards up to a scenic overlook of the falls.

The falls are on a spring-fed creek that once must have been as big as a river, if the surrounding landscape is any testament. Spaced just a few feet apart, the falls cascade one atop the other and empty into an expansive cauldron. Part of the beauty of Twin Falls is that the erosion created by the running water has formed a cavern made of brown Lake Superior sandstone—a chance to see brownstone in its natural state and not as part of some historic building.

From the overlook you'll also see a flight of stairs on the western side of the creek leading down to an area below the falls and under the cavern. Tempting as it may be, please don't venture over to the western side of the creek—the land on that side is private property, and you'll be trespassing.

Twin Falls in late summer, as it trickles down brownstone steps.

Meyers Beach & Siskiwit Falls

South Shore • Beach: East of Cornucopia | Falls: Siskiwit Falls Road between Highway 13 and County 2

Looking for a spot to wear the kids out before expecting them to sit down and behave in a South Shore restaurant? Look no further than Meyers Beach, just outside of Cornucopia. The pristine, primitive beach, part of the Apostle Islands National Lakeshore, stretches for about a mile along Wisconsin's South Shore. Although a popular access site for kayakers, the beach is usually quiet and uncrowded. A nearby hiking trail leads to the Squaw Bay sea caves (see page 55).

The gentle cascade of Siskiwit Falls just east of Cornucopia.

The beach is located east of Cornucopia—take Highway 13 to Meyers Beach Road and head toward the lake. Parking is available, but there are no bathroom facilities, and camping is not allowed.

The Siskiwit Falls aren't much as far as dramatic descents are concerned. More of a gently flowing cascade—at least in late summer—the falls remind one of water running down a stairway rather than plunging down an elevator shaft. But they are quite lovely and provide a nice spot to rest and enjoy the outdoors accompanied by the sound of flowing water (and they make a great picnic spot.)

To find the falls, drive along Siskiwit Falls Road between Highway 13 and County Road C, about a mile east of Cornucopia, and look for the small bridge. Follow the footpath upstream 100 yards or so.

Squaw Bay Caves

South Shore • One mile east of Cornucopia's Meyers Beach

The Squaw Bay caves are a nearly mile-long string of structures carved into sandstone bedrock by wind, water, and ice. Part of the Apostle Islands National Lakeshore, the Squaw Bay caves can be found four miles east of Cornucopia. (Take Meyers Beach Road north off Highway 13; the caves are about one mile east of the beach.) Squaw Bay contains the largest sea caves on the Apostle Islands National Lakeshore, some up to 80 feet deep. The caves are best viewed from the lake, so if you don't kayak or canoe, you'll only find partial views from the hiking path. You can also look down onto some of the caves from a narrow footbridge that spans a deep crevasse.

If you visit during the winter, the ice will provide access to a much better view. Ice forms around the cave's sandstone bedrock of brown, red, orange, and yellow layers, creating unmatched winter beauty. You can get to the caves by taking the mainland trail on boots, snowshoes, or cross-country skis, but it's quicker to simply walk along the lakeshore. Whatever you do, be careful! Make sure the ice is thick enough to walk on—call the Apostle Islands Ice Line at (715)779-3398, extension 499. Conditions are best in January and February.

Many of the Apostle Islands are home to sea caves, but it's quite dangerous to trek to them during the winter and, naturally, you need a boat in the summer.

The Squaw Bay caves in winter: multicolored sandstone adorned with ice.

Sioux River: Big Rocks & a Big Beach

South Shore • Big Rock: Outside Washburn off County C | Beach: Between Bayfield & Washburn on Hwy. 13

The 13.3-mile Sioux River between Bayfield and Washburn offers outdoor enthusiasts a variety of sights. Upstream it runs over rocky terrain but as it nears the lake, the surroundings turn to wetlands.

If you enjoy rough terrain, you'll love Big Rock Park. The park has picnic and overnight campgrounds as well

as access to a rugged trail that runs along the Sioux. Many large rocks make the hike a challenge, but they also provide stunning natural beauty. This stretch of the Sioux is a popular fly-fishing spot, where brook, brown, and rainbow trout and coho salmon are often found deep below a layer of bedrock in a spot known as Big Rock Hole. To get to Big Rock Park from Washburn, take 10th Avenue out of town to County Road C, which connects to Big Rock Road, about two-and-a-half miles northwest of Washburn.

If you'd rather cool your heels than work your dogs, then the end of the Sioux is more for you. The mouth of the river is part of the Sioux River Coastal Wetlands, and alongside it you will find an expansive stretch of beach with views of Bayfield down the shore, Ashland up the shore, and the Apostle Islands across the water. The beach can be accessed from Friendly Valley Road off Highway 13.

Some of the big rocks at Big Rock Park on the Sioux River.

Stunning Views (often from unlikely places)

Duluth and the North Shore are home to some of the most scenic views found anywhere along the shores of Lake Superior. We've picked out twelve spots, many of which fall outside your typical idea of a scenic overlook.

Bardon's Peak

Bardon's (sometimes spelled "Barton's") Peak Forest Park is 2,775 acres of woodland west of Spirit Mountain. Skyline Parkway runs through the park as a dirt road and curves around Bardon's Peak. A stone wall keeps entranced motorists from plummeting over the side. The road is wide enough to pull off and either sit on the wall or scurry up the peak for a simply amazing look at the St. Louis River valley, Duluth, Superior, and the big lake. Besides the natural beauty, viewers can also see the entire neighborhoods of Morgan Park and Gary-New Duluth, the Oliver Bridge, and the abandoned U.S. Steel plant (as well as the scarred earth it has left behind). From Duluth, take Exit 249 off Highway 35, turn left onto Boundary Avenue and follow it to Skyline Parkway.

Thompson Hill Information Center

Folks entering Duluth from Highway 35 are always impressed with the view as they come over the ridge by Spirit Mountain—especially at night when the lights of Duluth and Superior seem to merge into one great city. That ridge is known as Thompson Hill, and it is home to one of the most scenic wayside rests anywhere. Its panoramic view can be enjoyed by the naked eye or through one of the center's view-finders. Large photos in the center itself show islands, points, lakes, and other landmarks in the St. Louis River valley. A stainless steel sculpture by David Von Scheggel titled *The Gate*, symbolizing Duluth as the gateway to the North Shore and the St. Lawrence Seaway, graces the center's grounds. From Duluth, take Exit 249 off Highway 35, turn right onto Skyline, and follow the signs.

Stunning Views, continued

Enger Tower: Sunrise, Sunset

Some think it was once an active lighthouse; others, a tribute from a grieving husband to his dead wife. Neither story is true. Sixty-foot-high Enger Tower was built in 1939 to honor Bert Enger, a prominent area businessman and Norwegian immigrant who came to this country penniless and made a fortune in furniture and real estate (see page 25 for more about the park). When the tower was finished, Crown Prince Olav of Norway visited Duluth to dedicate it. Since then, it has provided visitors with a great look at Duluth's harbor. Many people climb the tower, which stands 500 feet above the lake, during the day, but the great scenic advantage of the tower is that it's one of the few places on the Duluth hillside from which you can see the sunset. A gazebo in the park east of the tower makes a great place to watch the sun rise over Lake Superior.

The tower is located off Skyline Parkway between Enger Park Golf Course and Twin Ponds.

Central High School Parking Lot

When the Duluth School Board decided to close downtown's historic Central High School (see page 77) and build its replacement up over the hill, little did they know they'd be creating a scenic overlook. Though not as architecturally impressive as its brownstone predecessor, the new school is perched high above the city, and its lower parking lot provides a stunning view. Minnesota Point juts out almost directly below the parking lot, making it a great spot to watch ship traffic come and go.

The high school is located at 800 East Central Entrance. To get there, take Central Entrance to Pecan Street (the first lights past the junction of 6th Street, Mesaba Avenue, and Central Entrance), turn left, and follow the road to the high school. Time it right: it's hard to find a parking spot during school hours.

Stunning Views, continued

The "Coppertop Church"

It's almost a trend: abandon the old brownstone building near downtown and build something modern on top of the hill, turning your parking lot into a scenic overlook. Before school officials did it with Central High School in 1971, the good folks at First United Methodist moved up the hill in 1966. They tore down their towering church at 215 North Third Avenue West (see page 259) and built a more modern but no less impressive structure at the intersection of Skyline Parkway, Central Entrance, and Mesaba Avenue. The church's roof is made of copper, which has tarnished green over the years. Most Duluthians refer to it as the "Coppertop Church."

First United Methodist is located at 230 East Skyline Parkway, just east of where Mesaba Avenue and Central Entrance intersect (it has a big green roof, so you can't miss it).

Top of Chester

Ski jumpers claim the best view in Duluth is from the top of the Chester Park ski jump ramps—but you can't get there from here, unless you're willing to strap on some boards and finish with a leap. The rest of us will have to settle for the rock outcroppings found a few hundred yards behind the jumps. In summer the rocks are hidden by fields of wildflowers, and sometimes it's hard to see the lake for the trees, but on clear days the view is fantastic. If you follow one of the paths down from the rocks to a wide, grassy trail, you'll find a park bench next to a "Peace" signpost. Across from the bench, trees have been cleared to provide hikers with a place to rest and enjoy a look-see at the lake.

Chester Park is located at 1801 East Skyline Parkway. Parking is available near Upper Chester. Follow the road to the soccer fields and park, walk across the wide bridge beyond the picnic tables, then take the trails up.

Stunning Views, continued

Chi Chi's Deck / Back of Fitger's Complex
Let's face it: a Chi Chi's is a Chi Chi's is a Chi Chi's: Americanized Mexican food and mass-produced margaritas. But the Chi Chi's in the Fitger's Brewery Complex has something going for it most chain restaurants don't: two great decks just yards from shore. The main deck, accessible from the restaurant's bar, juts out from the top floor of the old brewery and offers the perfect place to watch the Wednesday night sailing regatta. The lower deck, made of iron, rises from the Lakewalk and stretches over the rails of the North Shore Scenic Railroad, with stairs providing a way for folks to get from the brewery to the shore (or vice versa). 600 East Superior Street.

Golf for the View
Golfers unwilling to shell out big bucks for an afternoon of self-torture will find two great public courses in Duluth. These aren't the worn-down and overcrowded courses you're likely to encounter in larger cities. In fact, in 1998 Golf Digest ranked Duluth #1 of 309 major cities based on access to good, affordable public and municipal golf. Lester Park and Enger Park both offer 27 holes punctuated by great looks at Lake Superior (you'll see more of the harbor at Enger, more of the lake at Lester). Remember, the greens always break toward the lake (well, almost always). For directions and tee times, call (218) 525-0828 (Lester Park) or (218) 723-3451 (Enger Park).

Rock Hill
The centerpiece of the Bagley Nature Center behind UMD, Rock Hill includes an observation deck that looks out over the UMD campus and Lake Superior and also offers a view of hardwood forest to the north—a particularly fine spot for watching the fall colors. The nature center is located northwest of UMD, off Buffalo Street. Park free in the lot during the summer and at meters during the academic year.

Stunning Views, continued

Park Point Beach: A View of Duluth
The previous eight overlooks offer views of Lake Superior from Duluth's hills. This one gives you a look at Duluth from next to the lake. Cross the Lift Bridge, drive a couple blocks, and pull into the parking area adjacent to the Tot Lot (a small playground; go straight when the road curves right). Walk toward the end of the Point for as long as you like. When you've had enough, turn back and head toward Duluth, but pause and take a good look at the buildings, homes, and trees that bloom from the city's hillsides. Makes you want to call it home. (Bring the kids and the dogs, but clean up after both.) The beach also makes a wonderful place to watch the sunrise.

Split Rock Lookout Station
At about Milepost 44 on Highway 61 (just past Gooseberry Falls State Park), you'll encounter the abandoned site of a commercial enterprise. It contains the charred remains of a building and the anchor from the *S.S. Medeira*, a ship that wrecked nearby in 1908. The area also has an abandoned "lookout" station with stairs you can climb for a view of the lake and Split Rock Lighthouse up the shore. **NOTE:** *This is not a state facility, and you may be trespassing* (although no signs are posted) *so try this at your own risk!* Next door you will find an official wayside, with a picnic table and trails leading toward the lake. The view's not as good, but it's a lot safer.

Palisade Head & Shovel Point
Although we've given an entire page to Palisade Head we could hardly have a section on "views" without mentioning it. The cliff stands 320 feet above the waters of Lake Superior, and you don't even have to get out of the car to enjoy a look. Shovel Point—formerly known as "Little Palisade"—is just down the road at Tettegouche State Park. (See page 43 for more information on Palisade Head and Shovel Point.)

Stunning Views, continued

Cutface Wayside

The Cutface Wayside is located at Highway 61's Milepost 104 on your way to Grand Marais. From the wayside's vantage point you can see Good Harbor Bay, Seagull Bay, and even Five-Mile Rock past Grand Marais. A marker at the site is dedicated in honor of S. Rex Green, an engineer who helped establish Highway 61 "for the public's full enjoyment of the glories of forests, streams, and lakes." After taking in the view, get back in the car and head toward Good Harbor Bay. At the mouth of Cutface Creek is a lakeshore wayside, where you can park and picnic and look for thompsonite, a semiprecious rock made of concentrically banded green, white, and pink stone. Outside of the privately owned Thompsonite Beach Museum and Gift Shop down the road (and spots in Australia and Scotland), the rock is found nowhere else in the world.

Mount Josephine Wayside & Overlooks

Mount Josephine is found just past Grand Portage and has three separate waysides on both the lake and inland sides of Highway 61 between Mileposts 146 and 148.

At Milepost 146 on the inland side, the winding Poplar Creek Road leads up to the Mount Josephine Wayside, a rest stop with bathrooms, picnic facilities, and a dog-walking area. It also has a few small trails and a great view of the lake and Wauswaugoning Bay.

Up the road from the wayside on the lake side of Highway 61 is a much closer view of the lake and the Susie Islands. You can also get a close look at the exposed stone of Mount Josephine where the highway cuts a path through its side.

Another stunning view of the lake is provided by an additional lakeside overlook at Milepost 148.

Architectural Adventures
(where to find great old houses & buildings)

Architectural Adventures

If you haven't noticed that Duluth is chock full of great old buildings, you're either not from around here or you spend most of your time above Skyline Parkway. Each time Duluth experienced an economic boom, the city saw some incredible structures rise from its streets. Buildings and houses constructed for lumber barons and mining executives dot downtown and the historic East End. Morgan Park, an entire community located about ten miles from downtown near Gary-New Duluth, was built to house workers at the nearby United States Steel plant, which has since closed its doors.

Duluth's structures exemplify a variety of architectural styles, from the ornate Queen Anne and Victorian to the utilitarian Arts and Crafts school. It includes examples of the Tudor Revival movement and the work of such prominent local architects as I. Vernon Hill, who introduced the "Ornamented Cube" to Duluth and influenced the city's architecture for decades after his death. Many houses and buildings, such as Old Central High School, feature the artistic flourishes of master stone carver O. George Thrana.

We've included some of the more stunning examples that still grace the city. Unfortunately, many of Duluth's finest buildings have gone. For a glimpse at some of Duluth's wonderful old buildings that have fallen victim to fire or the wrecking ball, see pages 237–266 in the "Local Lore and Places of Yore" chapter.

Certainly all the towns featured in *True North* boast some historic buildings—Ashland and Superior in particular. But Washburn—between Ashland and Bayfield—is perhaps the jewel of all the towns along Lake Superior's South Shore. The town's collection of brownstones,* constructed with stone quarried across the bay on the Apostle Islands, make it one of the most architecturally important and beautiful towns on our map. See page 90 for a description.

*"Brownstone" is actually sandstone and forms naturally in a variety of colors: brown, red, yellow, etc.

The Duluth Preservation Alliance

The Duluth Preservation Alliance was formed in 1978 to serve as a source of encouragement and technical advice for those who would undertake a restoration project and to help preserve Duluth's architectural heritage.

The DPA has advocated for the preservation of Glensheen Mansion (the Congdon estate), Old Central High School's Clock Tower, the Sacred Heart Music Center (see page 103), and St. Mark's African Methodist Episcopal Church at 530 North 5th Avenue East, and has made efforts to save Duluth's historic National Guard Armory. The DPA has also worked to preserve a specially paved street in Duluth's East End, a reminder of days when horses—not cars—dominated Duluth's streets.

The following seven pages make up the DPA's "East End Walking Tour," a guide to some stunning old houses all within a four-block area. Descriptions of the homes on the tour were researched by Maryanne C. Norton, coauthor of *Images of America: Duluth Minnesota* (and included here with permission from the DPA). Special thanks to residents of the East End Historic District for welcoming visitors to their neighborhood. Please, just enjoy the houses from the sidewalk.

To learn more about the Duluth Preservation Alliance, become a member, or make a donation to help save Duluth's historic homes and buildings, write to them at P.O. Box 252, Duluth, Minnesota 55801, or visit the Duluth Preservation Alliance Web site at www.duluthpreservation.org.

Duluth Preservation Alliance

The DPA's East End Walking Tour

The map below guides you to the 24 Duluth homes listed on the following six pages. Take Highway 35 North and exit at 21st Avenue East. Go up the hill a few blocks to Superior Street, turn right, and find a place to park near 24th Avenue East. Then use this book as your guide to some of the best examples of the variety of architectural styles that grace Duluth's historic neighborhoods. Information courtesy of the Duluth Preservation Alliance.

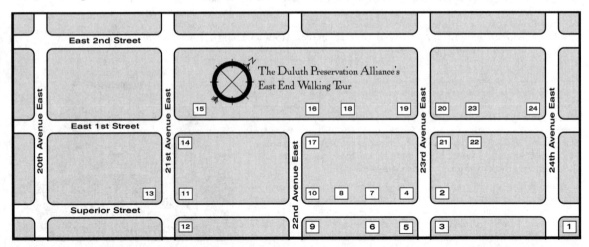

East End Walking Tour, continued

1. Alex and Katherine Hartman House • 1910 • 2400 E. Superior St.

(Frederick West Perkins, architect) Today this is the Duluth Woman's Club, but originally it was the home of Alex Hartman, president of the Duluth Edison Electric Company. The house was purchased and remodeled by the Woman's Club in 1936. The stucco and half-timbered Tudor Revival sits on a steep bluff overlooking Lake Superior.

2. Albert and Louise Ordean House • 1905 • 2307 E. Superior St.

(Emmet Palmer & William A. Hunt, architects) A prominent Duluthian at the turn of the century, Albert Ordean served as president of Merchants National Bank, a founder of First National Bank, and the director of the Great Northern Railroad. An example of Georgian Revival architecture, the formal red brick house features a centered gable, end chimneys, and an elaborate entrance.

3. Frederick and Katherine Patrick House • 1901 • 2306 E. Superior St.

(I. Vernon Hill, architect) Architect I. Vernon Hill was a gifted and innovative designer whose work influenced Duluth's architecture for years after his early death at age 36. In the Patrick house, he employed stone, half timbering, and steep gables in the Tudor Revival style. Carved eagle heads on brackets support the third-story gables. Patrick headed F.A. Patrick and Company, one of the country's foremost wool manufacturers.

4. Dwight Cutler House • 1906 • 5 N. 23rd Ave. E.

(William T. Bray & Carl Nystrom, architects) The stone facade facing Superior Street includes a three-story tower with battlements, suggesting the appearance of a medieval castle. The 23rd-Avenue facade features more battlements on the stone entrance as well as half timbering typical of the Tudor style. Cutler was president of a salt, lime, cement, and building materials firm.

East End Walking Tour, continued

5. George and Marion Stone House • 1901 • 2228 E. Superior St.

(P. Cooper and Son, architects) This large Renaissance Revival-style house with a red tile roof and a half tower on the front wall was built for the Stones in 1901. George Stone was an executive with Clyde Iron Works and the F.A. Patrick Company. From 1947 to 1977 the house served as a museum and offices for the Saint Louis County Historical Society. Today it is again a single-family residence.

6. I. Vernon Hill House • 1902 • 2220 E. Superior St.

(I. Vernon Hill, architect) As he did with the Patrick house, Hill decorated his own home with a carved head—this time a lion—under the corner eaves of the front porch. Built for $11,000 in 1902, the house's Tudor Revival design features half timbering, carved wood braces, and decorated steep gables, all of which create a delightful example of American picturesque architecture.

7. Warren McCord House • 1903 • 2219 E. Superior St.

(Architect unknown) This shingle-style house features a stone foundation, shingle wall cladding, and a center tower with a conical roof. It cost lumber executive Warren McCord just $8,000 to build.

8. Frank and Jennie Brewer House • 1902 • 2215 E. Superior St.

(Emmet Palmer, Lucien Hall, & William A. Hunt, architects) Duluth architects Palmer, Hall, and Hunt, who also designed the Irving School and Old Main, created a grand Georgian Revival house replete with classical ornamentation, columns, pilasters, and a porte cochere to protect visitors from unpleasant weather. It has been referred to as "the wedding cake house." Brewer was a partner in a lumber company and president of Great Northern Power Company.

East End Walking Tour, continued

9. Frank and Minnie House House • 1905 • 2210 E. Superior St.

(William T. Bray, architect) Another striking example of Tudor Revival architecture, this many gabled, half-timbered house features decorative wood carvings, stone trim, and stone projections on the chimneys. Frank House was president of the Duluth and Iron Range Railroad.

10. Charles and Belle Britts House • 1892 • 2201 E. Superior St.

(John J. Wangenstein & Ernest West Baillie, architects) This home was built in 1892 for $4,000. Its wrap-around porch and distinctive shingle work are typical of the Queen Anne style. Britts worked as a banker.

11. Marcus and Sarah Fay House • 1902 • 2105 E. Superior St.

(Edwin South Radcliffe, architect) Marcus Fay, who was involved in both copper and iron mining, once ran for mayor of Duluth. The Fays' eclectic house exhibits the massing of the Queen Anne style along with the detailing of the Colonial Revival style. An impressive iron fence surrounds the property.

12. Alfred and Jane McCordic House • 1891 • 2104 E. Superior St.

(Arthur Raeder, Henry Foccin, & Benjamin Crocker, architects) Duluth attorney Alfred McCordic and his family lived here very briefly. The house was originally built in the shingle style and was faced with wood shingles; stucco was added in the 1920s. Later owners, the Andreas Miller family, provided funds for what eventually became Miller-Dwan hospital.

East End Walking Tour, continued

13. George and Charlotte Crosby House • 1902 • 2029 E. Superior St.
(I. Vernon Hill, architect) The Crosby house is considered Hill's masterpiece, the one with which he introduced a new style of architecture to Duluth. Sometimes referred to as "Ornamented Cube," the style embellishes a square or rectangular box with flared dormers, gables, and classical detailing. The Crosby house's rectangle is of sandstone block with stone carvings by master stone carver O. George Thrana. The Cuyuna Iron Range was developed by Crosby, and he founded the town that bears his name.

14. Thomas and Martha Davis House • 1909 • 2104 E. 1st St.
(William T. Bray & Carl E. Nystrom, architects) This three-story brick Tudor Revival house features prominent chimneys, a Flemish gable, carved stone ornamentation on the entrance, and a tower with battlements. It cost Davis, a Duluth attorney, $21,000.

15. Zar and Frances Scott House • 1907 • 2125 E. 1st St.
(William A. Hunt, architect) This Tudor Revival house features half timbering, steep gable roofs, and finials on the gable and dormer peaks. Scott was a partner in the Scott-Graff Lumber Company of Duluth and a leader in the reforestation movement in Minnesota.

16. Alexander McDougall House • 1910 • 2201 E. 1st St.
(William T. Bray & Carl E. Nystrom, architects) Captain Alexander McDougall, master shipbuilder and inventor of the whaleback steamer, built this house when he was a widower in his sixties. Architects Bray and Nystrom were obviously influenced by I. Vernon Hill's Ornamented Cube designs. This yellow brick box has the same flared dormer gable that Hill employed on the Crosby house, along with classical columns and ornamentation.

East End Walking Tour, continued

17. William Cole House • 1908 • 2204 E. 1st St.
(Frederick German & A. Werner Lignell, architects) Another of the many East End Tudors, the Cole house was built for $16,000 in 1908, complete with matching carriage house. Cole was president of Northern Cold Storage and Warehouse Company.

18. Clinton and Katherine Markell House • 1908 • 2215 E. 1st St.
(Architect unknown) An early pioneer and Duluth's second mayor, Markell was instrumental in the development of grain shipping. The prominent feature of this shingle-style home is the curved entrance with decorative brackets.

19. Edwin and Lucretia Bradley House • 1904 • 2229 E. 1st St.
(William T. Bray, architect) This massive Georgian-style house has fluted columns and pillasters, Greek key designs over the windows, a classically decorated portico, and a gambrel roof. Bradley's wealth came from his lumber interests.

20. Joseph Bell and Louise Cotton House • 1906 • 2309 E. 1st St.
(Fred Kees & Serenus Colburn, architects) The restrained elegance of the Renaissance Revival style shows in the yellow brick Cotton house's classical brackets, dentils, and balustrades. A corporate-law attorney, Cotton represented John D. Rockefeller against the Merritt family in the latter's unsuccessful attempt to maintain ownership of mining lands in northern St. Louis County.

East End Walking Tour, continued

21. William and Fannie Olcott House • 1904 • 2316 E. 1st St.
(William T. Bray, architect) William Bray designed this impressive Georgian-style home and its matching carriage house for William Olcott, who was president of the Oliver Mining Company and later the Duluth Missabe and Northern Railroad. Architectural historian Roger Kennedy described the Olcott house, which reportedly cost $14,000 in 1904, as "a house carrying what surely must be the most overwhelming gambrel roof in the region."

22. George and Eleanor Swift House • 1894 • 2320 E. 1st St.
(Irving A. Spear, architect) This large Victorian house features dentils under the windows, square columns on the porch, and an interesting combination of colors. George Swift, an executive with the Oliver Mining Company, paid $6,000 in construction costs.

23. John and Caroline Richards House • 1894 • 2321 E. 1st St.
(Hugh Steele, architect) Hugh Steele added interest to this Queen Anne house through the use of a palladian window in the enormous front dormer, a decorative chimney, and an open front porch. Richards was a Duluth attorney.

24. Hugh Steele House • 1893 • 2327 E. 1st St.
(Hugh Steele, architect) Just as he did with the Richards' house, building contractor Hugh Steele built his own home in the popular Queen Anne style. The distinctive corner turret is covered with patterned shingles of many shapes and is crowned with a witch's hat roof.

These Old Houses

Oliver G. Traphagen House ("The Redstone") • 1892 • 1511 E. Superior St.
(Oliver Traphagen, architect) Architects tend to build the best for themselves, as was the case when Oliver Traphagen built his family a home. The house is quite impressive from the front, with its Flemish gable and ornate carvings in red sandstone, but take a peek around back and you'll see that most of the structure is simple red brick. Traphagen and his family abandoned the home in 1896 for the sun and surf of Hawaii, and Chester and Clara Congdon lived in it before building Glensheen. The building has since been used as a single-family home, was once divided into apartments, and is now the home of H.T. Klatzky advertising.

The Sellwood/Leithead House • 1902 • 16 S. 18th Ave. E.
(William A. Hunt, architect) In 1865 miner Joseph Sellwood set out from his home in Cornwall, England, for the copper mines in northern Michigan. After finding great success in various mining partnerships, he moved to Duluth and built three homes at the corner of 18th Avenue East and Superior Street, one for himself and two as wedding presents for his daughters. His daughter Ophelia and her husband Leslie Leithead—president of Leithead Drug Company—received this little beauty on the southeast corner. The house is a fine example of Romanesque Revival architecture, featuring towers and castle-like walls made of brownstone, that "Captain" Sellwood paid just $15,000 to build. The house at the southwest corner was Sellwood's wedding gift to another daughter, who married Larue Morshan.

These Old Houses, continued

Munger Terrace • 1871 • 405 Mesaba Ave.

(Traphagen & Fitzpatrick, architects) Almost immediately after Roger Munger's Chateauesque-styled townhouse rose out of the steep Hillside on Mesaba Avenue it became the place for wealthy Duluthians to call home. The original structure contained eight units of 16 rooms each, but tastes changed and as Duluth's affluent moved to the east end of town, the townhouse was converted into 32 much smaller apartments. Renovated in 1978, the building's towers and turrets still turn the heads of drivers heading up or down the hill on Mesaba Avenue.

Arthur P. Cook House • 1900 • 501 W. Skyline Pkwy.

(I. Vernon Hill, architect) Most Duluthians know the Cook home as the "House of Rock" both for the rocky lot it sits on and the incorporation of the same stone by architect I. Vernon Hill, who was just 31 years old when he designed it. With arguably one of the best views of the Duluth-Superior harbor, the house was built of stone and timber for just $5,000. It became the most photographed house in Duluth and in 1931 was featured in an advertisement for the Duluth Builders' Exchange touting the future of Duluth as a "metropolis serving the great Northwest Empire and its Atlantic Gateway." Those cruising Skyline Parkway (Boulevard Drive at the time the house was built) will be remiss if they don't pull over for a long look at this much-coveted home.

Opulent Old Churches

First Unitarian Church • 1910 • 1802 E. 1st St.
(Anthony Puck, architect) Radio humorist and Minnesotan Garrison Keillor has made a living peppering his stories with good-natured fun at the Unitarians' expense. Perhaps their emphasis on democracy and freedom is too much for Minnesotans steeped in Lutheran doctrine, but Duluth has welcomed them since 1877. Their incredible Tudor Revival church was built in 1910 and held Unitarian services until 2001, when it was sold. It is now home to a Quaker congregation.

St. Paul's Episcopal Church • 1913 • 1710 E. Superior St.
(Bertram Goodhue, architect) In 1913 the congregation at the first church built in Duluth—an 1869 Episcopalian structure located on the northwest corner of Lake Avenue and 2nd Street—chipped in to build a new one. Bertram Goodhue designed the church in the English Gothic style, very like an English country parish church. The church was built at a cost of $72,000. In 1929 a simple timbered parish hall was added for $105,000. In the 1990s, the roof's blue-gray slate was repaired, complete with copper flashing. Get in close for a look at the carvings. The original church was often called "Jay Cooke's Church" because the financier made a major contribution to its building finances. A statue of Cooke and his dog stands across from the Kitchi Gammi Club (see page 84).

Opulent Old Churches, continued

Sacred Heart Cathedral • 1898 • 201 W. 4th St.

(Architect unknown) Once the home of the archdiocese of Duluth, Sacred Heart Cathedral served Catholics in Duluth for 87 years. Inside the church you'll find an Italian marble altar and the original pipe organ (unfortuntely, the church's wooden pews have been replaced by cheap purple chairs that distract considerably from the building's beauty). Although it was replaced as the seat of the archdiocese in 1957 when the Cathedral of Our Lady of the Rosary opened its doors, masses were held here until Sacred Heart merged with St. Mary Star of the Sea in 1985. The church is now the home of the Sacred Heart Music Center, which presents a wide variety of concerts (see page 103).

First Presbyterian Church • 1891 • 300 E. 2nd St.

(Traphagen & Fitzpatrick, architects) The area in and around downtown Duluth once included large churches representing every denomination that had a parish inside the city. First Presbyterian is the last standing representative of that era. The Romanesque building, constructed of varied shades of brown Lake Superior sandstone blocks and adorned with carvings and stained-glass windows, seems to erupt from the steep hillside of 3rd Avenue East. Its corner bell tower reaches 125 feet above 2nd Street, and inside the church there's room enough for 1,000 parishioners. At the time it was built, the church was at the heart of Duluth's most affluent neighborhood. When parishioners moved east, attendance declined.

Old-School Schools

Old Central High School • 1891–1892 • Lake Ave. & 2nd St.
(Emmet S. Palmer & Lucien P. Hall, architects) Most everyone who has ever been to Duluth has seen Old Central—its 230-foot clock tower rises above downtown and simply cannot be ignored. The Romanesque building is made of locally quarried brownstone and is modeled after the Allegheny Courthouse in Pittsburgh, Pennsylvania. In his description of Old Central's stone gargoyles, architectural historian James Allen Scott wrote that "about the cavernous entrance in the tower angelic cherubs lovingly smile while overhead grotesque animal figures leer their prurient intents." The building ceased operating as a school in 1971 and is now home to the Duluth School District's administrative offices.

Denfeld High School • 1925–1926 • 4405 W. 4th St.
(Abraham Holstead & William J. Sullivan, architects) Built in a style dubbed Collegiate English Gothic, Denfeld High School (home of the Hunters) reflects Renaissance ideals. The building is shaped like an H with a rising clock tower that stands for "aspiring idealism." The building's eight buttresses were intended to represent "the eight types of human beings who supported the human kingdom: masters, rulers, philanthropists, philosophers, magicians, scientists, devotees, and artists." Stone carvings of Renaissance symbolism adorn the school. The building is still in use as a high school today; it takes its name from Robert E. Denfeld, Duluth's superintendent of schools for over 30 years beginning in 1885.

Old-School Schools, continued

Jefferson School • 1890 • 916 E. 3rd St.
(McMillan & Radcliffe, architects) When Jefferson School first opened its doors in 1893 it was called "undoubtedly one of the finest ward school structures in the country." The Neo-Classical Colonial structure cost $84,000 and boasted toilets (or "water closets" at the time) with "automatic flush." After closing in the mid-1980s, the school was converted into the Jefferson Square Apartments (many boasting lake views); it also houses the Jefferson Children's Center.

Endion School • 1890 • 1801 E. 1st St.
(Adolph F. Rudolph, architect) Built in the Romanesque Revival style of red pressure brick, the Endion School hosted students from Duluth's Endion neighborhood for 87 years until closing its doors in 1977. A belfry once sat atop the building, but in 1970 it was victimized by vandals and had to be taken down. Today the building houses the Endion School Apartments.

The name "Endion" comes from a town site registered in 1856 and is Ojibwe for *My, Your*, or *His Home*. When the town was absorbed by a growing Duluth, it became a neighborhood. Endion Station, now found along the Lakewalk, once stood at 15th Avenue East & South Street, but was relocated when Interstate 35 was extended through Duluth to 26th Avenue East.

Boomtown Buildings

Civic Center • 1909, 1923, 1928 • 5th Ave. W. & 1st St.
(Daniel H. Burnham & Company, *et. al.*, architects) Your one-stop shopping spot for some impressive Classical/Renaissance architecture, the Civic Center in Duluth includes the St. Louis County Courthouse, Duluth City Hall, and the U.S. Federal Building as well a county jail, the "Fortitude Defending the Flag" monument, and a fountain. The courthouse was designed by D.H. Burnham and went up in 1909; other architects designed City Hall and the Federal Building, but did so in a manner in keeping with Burnham's original idea. The whole complex was part of the "City Beautiful" movement of the early 20th century.

The fountain outside the St. Louis County Courthouse, the centerpiece of Duluth's Civic Center.

Duluth Union Depot • 1892 • 5th Ave. W. & Michigan St.
(Robert Swain Peabody & John Goddard Stearns, architects) Designed by Boston architects Peabody and Stearns to resemble a French Norman chateau on a grand scale, Duluth's Union Depot–including a track, roundhouse, and a shed system–was built for a cost of $615,000. At one point, it serviced over 60 trains a day from the St. Paul & Duluth Railways, Northern Pacific, and others. It closed as a railroad depot in 1969 and is now home to the St. Louis County Heritage and Arts Center, housing museums and performance stages (see pages 97 and 98). In 2001 its bricks were cleaned and the roof was replaced. (The photo at left was taken c. 1970.)

Boomtown Buildings, continued

Alworth Building • 1910 • 306 W. Superior St.

(Daniel H. Burnham, architect) Sixteen stories of concrete and steel covered in buff-colored brick and terra cotta make the Alworth building the tallest in Duluth. You have to have a good eye to see the structure's ornamental features, most of which appear at the top few floors. The building is crowned with an ornate cornice and oval window openings on the top floor and features lion heads carved in stone. The cost to construct what the *Duluth News-Tribune* once called "a cosmopolitan office building, one that dwarfs the Tower of Babel" and "an epoch in the architectural history of Duluth"? A mere $500,000. It took workers nine months to build Duluth's "skyscraper," as much a feat today as it was in 1910 (and much of the work was done during winter months).

Board of Trade Building • 1895 • 301 W. 1st St.

(Traphagen & Fitzpatrick, architects) Fire has shaped the history of this great old building. It was built after the original Board of Trade building burned in 1894, and its cornice was removed after another fire in 1948. Built of steel, stone, brick, and marble, the ornate Romanesque structure with a two-story entrance and elaborate O. George Thrana stone carvings cost $350,000. Today the building is used as office space for attorneys and architects. The Minnesota Ballet also makes its home here and recently renovated the trading floor for use as rehearsal space. The company's efforts won it an award from the Duluth Preservation Alliance. If you ask nicely and don't interrupt rehearsal, the folks in charge will let you go up to the balcony and have a look around.

Left: The Board of Trade building's ornate two-story entrance.

Boomtown Buildings, continued

Wirth Building • 1886 • 13 W. Superior St.
(George Wirth, architect) When St. Paul architect George Wirth was asked by his brother Max W. Wirth to design a combination drug store and family residence, he chose to work in the Romanesque Revival style, leaving downtown Duluth with an architectural beauty that remains the jewel of West Superior Street. The facade is made of a combination of brown- and buff-colored sandstone and features ornate carvings, arched window casings, and a projecting bay on the second floor to help flood the residence with natural light. Today the renovated building is home to the building's current owner, an antique shop, and other businesses in the upper offices.

Masonic Temple • 1904 • 4 W. 2nd St.
(C. H. Smith, architect) Mystery surrounds the Masons. George Washington was a Mason, and some say they remain a force behind global politics. Whatever the truth, they've left quite a few interesting buildings in their wake. Home to the "Palestine Lodge #79," first established in 1869, the Masonic Temple is one of many buildings the Masons have constructed in Duluth (their first permanent home was the ornate Temple Opera Building, see page 264). It once boasted Moorish onion-shaped domes at each corner of the roof, but they have since been destroyed (and an elevator has been added). Its cornerstone was laid August 10, 1904, by Masonic Grand Master of Minnesota William A. McGonagle. Joshua B. Culver, Duluth's first mayor, was the first Master of Palestine Lodge...coincidence?

Left: Columns support the Masonic Temple's Second Street entrance.

Boomtown Buildings, continued

Old Jail (& City Hall) • 1889 & 1891 • 126 & 132 E. Superior St.
(Oliver G. Traphagen, architect) After Duluth pulled itself up by the bootstraps following a recession in the 1870s, the town was rechartered in 1887. A seat of government was required, and by 1889 City Hall sat at the corner of 2nd Avenue East and Superior Street. It filled up quickly, requiring a separate jail and police headquarters, which opened next-door in 1891 complete with carvings and a Flemish gable. Replaced by new buildings in 1929, the old City Hall has since had its lower facade covered by short-sighted property owners. The jail, however, was restored in 1968 and is now home to Architectural Resources, Inc.

Hotel Duluth (Greysolon Plaza) • 1925 • 227 E. Superior St.
(Martin Tullgren & Sons, architects) The compass embedded in the sidewalk outside the Hotel Duluth inspired this book's title and logo, so we're a bit partial to it. The hotel, now named Greysolon Plaza, was built in 1924 for a cost of $2.4 million. Made of reinforced steel and concrete, the hotel boasts many wonderful architectural features, such as a Classic-Revival facade, a lobby and mezzanine designed in the Italian-Renaissance style (pictured), and what its builders called a "typical Spanish dining room." Today its rooms are dedicated to senior housing while its ballroom plays host to wedding receptions, proms, and other large gatherings. It is also home to the Chinese Garden restaurant (see page 147) and Romano Grocery (see page 157). President John F. Kennedy stayed in the hotel in the summer of 1963. See page 246 for a story of the hotel's early years and how its now-closed Black Bear Lounge got its name.

Boomtown Buildings, continued

Engine House #1 • 1889 • 101 E. 3rd St.
(Oliver G. Traphagen, architect) Just above and across the street from Old Central High School (or directly true north) sits Engine House #1, the ironically named third firehouse in Duluth. The first, a wooden building near Minnesota Point, burned to the ground. The second, run by volunteers, remains at 22 East 2nd Street, but most of its decorative features are gone. Built in 1889, the stone and brick Engine House #1 was once crowned with an impressive bell tower; the tower was removed in 1910 and the firehouse closed in 1918. It is now used as a maintenance garage by the city school district.

Carnegie Library • 1902 • 101 W. 2nd St.
(Adolph F. Rudolph, architect) When Duluth began to outgrow its first library (housed inside the Temple Opera Building, see page 264), it used a $25,000 donation from Andrew Carnegie to help build a brick sandstone structure in a Neo-Classical design that ultimately cost $65,000. The building includes a central dome and two Tiffany windows depicting the area's history. The library was converted to office space in the 1980s. Visitors can stop in and check out the public space (but please don't interrupt the work going on behind closed doors). The current Duluth Public Library is that ore-boat-like structure across from the Depot.

Boomtown Buildings, continued

Duluth National Guard Armory • 1915 • 1305 London Rd.
(Kelly & Williams, architects) Besides acting as headquarters for Duluth's Minnesota National Guard, the Duluth Armory also hosted hundreds of cultural events. A young Bob Dylan sat among the Armory's audience when Buddy Holly, Richie Valens, and the Big Bopper played here just days before taking the fateful flight that claimed their lives and inspired Don McClean's "American Pie" ("The day the music died..."). The Guard moved to new headquarters in 1977.City leader are seeking ways to save the old building, which has been neglected for yars.

Kitchi Gammi Club • 1912 • 831 E. Superior St.
(Bertram Goodhue, architect) In 1883 sixteen Duluth men—including Chester Congdon and Guilford Hartley—formed the Kitchi Gammi Club, the first men's club in the state (female guests used a side entrance as late as the 1980s). After renting several locations, the club built itself a $304,000 home in 1912. The building features elements of Gothicism mixed with Georgian pilasters and Tudor details and the stone carvings of O. George Thrana. Many wealthy men from out of town were members so that they could stay at the Kitch when in town on business. One, Andrew Carnegie, was expelled for not paying his dues.

Morgan Park

Folks unfamiliar with the history of Morgan Park are often taken aback the first time they encounter its concrete houses. At the turn of the 20th century, U.S. Steel decided to build a steel mill in the vicinity of Duluth to save on transportation costs (its ore came from Minnesota's Mesabi Iron Range). After Minnesota threatened to tax iron ore that crossed the state line—unless the plant was located in the state—a site near Gary-New Duluth was chosen. U.S.S. built Morgan Park (named for U.S. Steel founder J.P. Morgan; it was originally to be named "Model City") to provide nearby housing for its employees. Construction began in 1913 and by 1915 the plant was producing steel. At the time, Morgan Park had the most modern school, hospital, and community facilities in the nation. The steel plant shut down in the 1970s, but Morgan Park remains a thriving community.

All the company's buildings were made chiefly of concrete block produced at the company's own cement plant because the material needed little maintenance. The somewhat harsh look of concrete was softened by gables, eaves, and rooflines that concealed the appearance of monotonous regularity.

The heart of the community was the Goodfellowship Club, a workers' association dedicated to serving sick or needy fellow employees. The club was housed in a large, multi-use building (pictured) that included a gymnasium with a running track, an auditorium, an indoor swimming pool, and a bowling alley. It was torn down in 1981 when a more fuel-efficient building was built to replace it.

Small Yet Significant

Finnish Immigrant Home (Harbor House) • c. 1870 • 329 Canal Park Dr.

(Architect unknown) This tiny home was built in about 1870, probably by sawmill owners after a land grab made possible by the Treaty of LaPointe—you needed merely to stake a claim and the land was yours. It served as the home of Harry and Maria Hill, poor immigrants from Finland who arrived in 1880. In fact, most of Canal Park was settled by Finns. The Hills helped by bringing family and fellow townspeople from Finland, building a Finnish church, one-room school, and sauna—and by adding their own seven children to the population. They also owned

the red brick store and boarding house next-door. The store was called the Harry Hill Store and Lunch Counter, but was often referred to as "The Little Red Hotel."

Between 1885 and 1895, Canal Park was Duluth's Bowery—a legal red light district—and the boarding room was thought to have been used for prostitution. Later, during prohibition, a secret passageway was employed to sneak between the Hill home and the boarding house—you can still see the doorway if you visit it today (the house, now a retail shop, is still 95 percent intact). It is now the Harbor House (see page 217).

The Hill family owned the house until 1976, using it as a residence until some time in the 1960s. The lunch counter stayed open until 1974, operated by Sophie and Ann Hill. Maria Hill, by the way, was the first woman in Duluth to own a car.

Ruins of Duluth, Part One:
Duluth Normal School (a.k.a. "Old Main")

"Old Main" (DSTC Normal School) • 1898 • 2205 E. 5th St.

(Palmer, Hall, & Hunt, architects) In 1895 the State of Minnesota created the Normal School at Duluth. It was damaged by fire while under construction and opened in 1902. In 1905 it became the Duluth State Normal School. A west wing was added in 1909, an east wing in 1915. Its name was changed to the Duluth State Teachers' College in 1921, and finally, in 1947, to the University of Minnesota, Duluth Branch ("Branch" was dropped in 1959). In 1948 ground was broken for the first building of the new campus. The old campus continued to serve UMD students for years. Its central building, "Old Main," was used as a theater (performances are now held at the University's Marshall Performing Arts Center, built in 1974).

Old Main was consumed by fire in February, 1993. The building was once an architectural hybrid of Romanesque and Renaissance features, but today only its arches stand preserved as a monument—the site has become a Duluth city park. Most of the buildings that surrounded Old Main are still in use by the university as research facilities. Torrence Hall, a former dormitory, has been converted into apartments.

Ruins of Duluth, Part Two:
Minnesota Point Lighthouse

(Architect unknown) Lake Superior's first lighthouse once stood 50 feet tall and served mariners for 20 years, from 1858 to 1878. R.H. Barrett, its first and only keeper, and his family lived in a simple cottage next to the tower of red Ohio brick wrapped in lime-stone. Barrett kept the light burning and, when the fog became thick, actually used his own lungs to blow a warning through a logging camp dinner horn. Local residents called the horn "Barrett's Cow."

The lighthouse was abandoned in 1878. The keeper's cottage was destroyed, and the tower now stands barely 30 feet high and has to be protected by a fence, but its French lenses are still used in the west pier-head light of the Superior Entry. (See page 31 for directions to the lighthouse.)

Nearby, you'll also find the empty hull of a concrete building. It is the remains of the U.S. Lighthouse Station Depot, which was used to store buoys and acetylene used in the batteries that powered the lighthouse at Canal Park. The vessels *Amaronth* and *Marigold* loaded and unloaded acetylene and other supplies at the building from 1905 until World War II. The Corps of Engineers did not want to store the potentially dangerous gas too close to Canal Park and the Aerial Lift Bridge.

Ruins of Duluth, Part Three:
Uncle Harvey's Mausoleum (a.k.a "The Cribs")

(Architect unknown) Many dramatic theories have been proffered about the original use of the concrete ruins that lie about thirty yards into Lake Superior just off the Lakewalk behind some of Canal Park's hotels. One story claims it was a prohibition-era gambling house. Federal lake charts identify the ruins as "the cribs," but it is more popularly known as "Uncle Harvery's Mausoleum." The truth is neither glamorous nor grim.

"Uncle Harvey" was Harvey Whitney, one of the Whitney brothers of Superior. Built in the winter of 1919, the "mausoleum" was no burial site but rather a sand and gravel hopper that was abondoned in 1922 after another of Duluth's building booms reached its end. Harvey Whitney had gambled that the city of Duluth would revive efforts to build an outer harbor breakwater, and he hoped to provide the materials. Unfortunately for Whitney, the plan was scrapped. Since demand never materialized, the operation shut down.

The hopper operated by taking sand from the Apostle Islands and gravel from Grand Marais, which was loaded from the scow Limit using steam-powered clam-shell cranes. A conveyer belt then carried the sand and gravel to shore where it was sent through a tunnel into trucks. (The tunnel was the alleged site of the "casino.")

Today, the cribs are used by scuba divers and adventurous folks who swim out to the concrete ruin and use it as a diving platform. It is also home to nesting ducks.

Washburn's Brownstones

The town of Washburn, Wisconsin, is the seat of Bayfield County and home to some of the finest examples of buildings encased in Lake Superior brownstone you'll find along the shore of the big lake. The town is so proud of its architectural heritage that it honors the buildings each year on the last weekend of July during its Brownstone Days festival.

Much of the red Lake Superior brownstone used in Washburn's historic 19th-century buildings was quarried locally, some of it right across the bay on the Apostle Islands. Prominent structures include the current home of Chequamegon Book & Coffee (left, see page 194), the Iron Works (center), whose stone facade is also adorned with a painting, the Washburn Cultural and Art Museum (right), and the county courthouse and library.

A few of Washburn's brownstones: Chequamegon Book & Coffee, the Iron Works, and the Washburn Cultural & Art Museum (former home of the town's bank).

Arts & Culture

(museums, galleries, theatre,
ballet, symphony, etc.)

Arts & Culture

While the Twin Ports certainly don't rate as a major metropolitan area, they hold their own when it comes to the arts. It seems that souls hearty enough to inhabit what some folks might deem a hostile environment tend to be a bit more creative and expressive (or perhaps crazy?) than those who live in climates that don't require furnaces or basements or window screens. The population may be relatively small and we may never get a traveling Monet or Van Gogh exhibit to stop by, but we still have our own orchestra and a first-rate ballet company, as well as a variety of smaller theatre and comedy groups, musical groups, art museums, galleries, and artist cooperatives.

The Twin Ports, along with the North and South Shore communities, also give no short shrift to history and regional culture, evidenced by the wide variety of museums throughout the area. There are a number of active historical societies eager to share what they know about the people who first settled the region and the industries that sustained them (and made some of them ridiculously wealthy).

The region is home to writers working in a wide variety of styles. It supports a thriving community of essayists, fiction writers, poets, and playwrights, including Anthony Bukoski, Nancy Fitzgerald, Louis Jenkins, Milan Kovacovic, Joseph Maiolo, Patrick McKinnon, Margi Preus, Barton Sutter, and Connie Wanek, among many others. The Twin Ports are also home to Holy Cow! Press, the Lake Superior Writers Group, Poetry Harbor, and *North Coast Review*. While you're in the area, make sure to check local newspapers for special events and readings involving our homegrown wordsmiths.

While this chapter highlights permanent homes of the arts, keep in mind that art can be found (and cultural events take place) just about any time and anywhere. Live music is available somewhere every night of the week (check the "Nightlife" chapter for likely spots), readings take place at colleges and local book stores, and many of the listings in the "Annual Events" chapter center around the region's rich and varied ethnic heritage.

Art Galleries

Washington Galleries

Central Hillside, Duluth • 315 Lake Ave. N. • (218) 722-3131 • Sat.–Sun. 1 P.M. - 5 P.M. / Special events

The story of Washington Galleries begins in 1911 when the building it occupies was erected just up the street from Duluth's historic Central High School. The structure served as Washington Junior High School until 1992 when it was purchased by Artspace, a Minneapolis-based non-profit developer taking on its first project outside the Twin Cities area. Since that time, Artspace has completed similar projects in major cities around the country. Renovations converted the classic old school's six stories and 44,000 square feet into 39 apartments as well as gallery space, two dance studios, three musical rehearsal rooms, and other meeting rooms. Washington Studios, as the building is now known, functions as a cooperative, providing living and working space for its artist members. Artists have the opportunity to show their works in the on-site gallery. Since the gallery has somewhat limited hours, be sure to check local newspapers for special events and openings.

Dirtygirlz Cooperative

Downtown, Duluth • 114 N. 1st Ave. W. • (218) 733-9595 • F & Sat. 10 A.M. - 6 P.M. / Sunday hours vary (call ahead)

When ceramics students at Lake Superior College, a Duluth technical college, found that they were losing badly needed work space, Mary Pechacek and some other "dirty girls" (so called because they tended to leave clay footprints around) decided to take matters into their own hands. They searched for and found space, not only to work in, but also to display and sell their creations. Now at its second location, the cooperative is open to both men and women artists and is not restricted to those who play with clay. Members have access to the cooperative's workspace—which includes two kilns, tables for potters, and lots of open space for easels and other equipment—24 hours a day, seven days a week. In exchange, members keep the studio space clean and help staff the gallery. The gallery's hours can fluctuate throughout the year, so it's not a bad idea to call before you visit.

Art Galleries, continued

Duluth Artist Guild's Limbo Gallery
Downtown, Duluth (inside the NorShor Theatre) • 211 E. Superior St. • (218) 727-7585 / Call for hours (open randomly)

DAG strives to support the community through the arts and to make art accessible to everyone. Its Limbo Gallery is home to works by new and established area artists, from painters and scultpors to cartoonists and digital photgraphers. The works are often off-beat: an installment by artist Jim Richardson included a Lego reen-actment of the JFK assassination. The gallery doesn't keep regular hours, so call ahead.

Lizzard's Art Gallery & Framing
Downtown, Duluth • 38 E. Superior St. • (218) 722-5815 • M–Sat. 10 A.M. - 5 P.M.

Lizzard's features works from local, regional, and national artists and a full-service frame shop. The gallery's high tin ceilings, glossy wood floors, and ample windows create a welcoming environment. Inside its two large, bright rooms you'll find paintings, prints, sculpture, pottery, photography, jewelry, glassware, and textile works.

The Frame Corner & Gallery
Downtown, Duluth • 323 W. Superior St. • (218) 218-722-7174 • M–F 9 A.M. - 5:30 P.M. / Sat. 10 A.M. - 4 P.M.

Besides full-service framing and a fine selection of prints and photographs from regional and international artists, the frame corner also features some fun stuff, like renderings of the Peanuts characters and the art of Dr. Suess.

Art Options Gallery & Framing
Downtown, Duluth • 132 E. Superior St. • (218) 727-8723 • Opens M–Sat. at 10:30 a.m. / Closed Sundays

Art Options' tiny space in Duluth's old City Hall (built in 1891) is packed to the rafters with images of Duluth both old and new as well as a variety of art by a variety of regional artists.

Art Galleries, continued

Alternative Outlets for Local Art

The establishments listed below also display and sell original art by local artists.

Beaner's Central • 324 N. Central Ave. • (218) 624-5957 • opens M–F 6:30 A.M., Sat. 8 A.M., Sun. 10 A.M. / closes 9 - 11 P.M.

Coco's to Geaux • 324 W. Superior St. • (218) 740-3039 • M–F 7 A.M. - 5 P.M. (lunch 11 A.M. - 1:30 P.M.)

Lakeview Coffee Emporium • 600 E. Superior St. • (218) 720-4464 • M–Sat. 7 A.M. - 8 P.M. / Sun. 8 A.M. - 6 P.M.

Pepper McGregor's • 4721 E. Superior St. • (218) 525-5016 • M–Th. 6 A.M. - 8 P.M. / F & Sat. 6 A.M. - 10 P.M. / Sun. 7 A.M. - 3 P.M.

A Sampling of Duluth's Outdoor Public Art (mostly sculpture)

Sculpture Garden: Above the Lakewalk at the "corner" of Lake Superior. A variety of fine works.

Canal Park: A variety of sculptures line Canal Park Drive, including one of Albert Woolsen (see page 248) near the Lake Superior Maritime Museum and a whimsical fountain/sculpture across from Little Angie's Cantina.

Lake Avenue & Superior Street: The abstract North and South Shore of Lake Superior becomes a fountain in a stunning piece by local artist Ben Effinger.

Leif Erickson Park: Leif himself—proclaimed as "Discoverer of America"—stands next to the Rose Garden. (A replica of a Viking ship can be found closer to the lake.)

UMD: Jacques Lipschitz's statue of Daniel Greysolon Sieur du Lhut—Duluth's namesake—stands in Ordean Court.

Thompson Hill Information Center: David Von Scheggel's "The Gate," a symbolic piece in stainless steel.

Lakewalk: A mosaic mural depicting Duluth's waterfront lines the wall just below the Sculpture Garden.

Museums

Tweed Museum of Art

UMD Campus, Duluth • 10 University Dr. • (218) 726-8222 • T 9 A.M. - 8 P.M. / W–F 9 A.M. - 4:30 P.M. / Sat.–Sun. 1 P.M. - 5 P.M.

The Tweed Museum of Art on the University of Minnesota Duluth campus houses nine galleries and displays works in all media. The museum strives to represent the history of art as well as contemporary trends, and to present artwork from various world cultures. To that end, each year the Tweed organizes eight to ten major exhibitions and presents rotating exhibits from its permanent collection. The permanent collection includes works from the 14th century to the present, with strong representations of 16th- to 19th-century European painting, 19th- and 20th-century American painting, and modern and contemporary art. The Tweed's museum store is a great place to find quality gifts like posters, art books, and unique jewelry. Closed university holidays.

Graffiti Graveyard

Between Downtown and Bayfront Park • Always Open

Graffiti Graveyard is the unofficial name of an area underneath Interstate 35 between Bayfront Park and the Depot (park near Bayfront and walk across Railroad Street and a set of tracks, then follow the wall that passes below the highway until you find the entrance—watch out for the water). Wide as four lanes of highway and nearly a half mile long, the Graveyard has become a haven for graffiti artists. Every wall and pillar has been hit with paint, some of it amateur scribblings, some of it well-executed works of art. From original creations to your favorite Warner Brothers cartoon characters, you'll find miles of self-expression and slogans along with the typical declarations of who was here and who loves whom. Another local site for graffiti artists is found under the Eighth Street bridge that crosses over Chester Creek. As you walk under the bridge, look up: directly under the midpoint of the arch you'll see the words "Beat This! 10-2-91." You'll wonder how it got there. That is, if it's still there. The bridge recently underwent renovations and may have received a fresh paint job by the time you read this.

Museums, continued

The Depot

Downtown, Duluth • 506 W. Michigan St. • (218) 733-7500 • Summer: Daily 9:30 A.M. - 6 P.M. Winter: M–Sat. 10 A.M. - 5 P.M. / Sun. 1 P.M. - 6 P.M.

Technically, the Depot is actually the St. Louis County Heritage and Arts Center, but local residents call it the Depot for obvious reasons: it's a whole lot easier to say, and the building once functioned as a railroad depot. Built in 1892, the building was a Union Railroad depot that by 1910 served seven lines with as many as 5,000 passengers per day passing through its doors until it closed as a railroad depot in 1969 (see page 79). In 1971 the building earned a spot on the national register of historic places, and in 1973 it began operating as a cultural center. Today the Depot is home to four museums and provides office, theater, and studio space for five performing arts organizations including the Duluth Art Institute, Duluth Children's Museum, Minnesota Ballet, and Duluth Playhouse.

Given the range of organizations it hosts, the Depot is a sort of cultural one-stop shop, offering something to interest just about anyone. The main entrance, located at street level, leads to The Great Hall, an impressive open area where travelers once bought tickets, waited for trains, and perhaps grabbed a quick meal and a shoe shine. Make sure to pause here and check out the vaulted ceiling on your way through to the St. Louis County Historical Society's (SLCHS) exhibits. Up one floor you'll find the Lake Superior Ojibwe Gallery, also operated by the SLCHS, and the Duluth Art Institute. Down one floor from the Great Hall, you'll find the Duluth Children's Museum, which continues down yet another level. The best way to get to there is through the Children's Tree, a spiral staircase that wends its way through a life-sized diorama of a tree's interior. The lower level, called the Track Level since this was the actual train arrival and departure area, holds what is indisputably the Depot's finest exhibit: the Lake Superior Railroad Museum. Plan to spend a lot of time here and expect to feel about ten years old by the time you leave. If you're not convinced yet, read more about the Railroad Museum on page 98.

Museums, continued

Lake Superior Railroad Museum

Downtown, Duluth • 506 W. Michigan St. • (218) 733-7590 • (Same operating hours as the Depot, previous page)

Located on and around the original tracks that used to service trains coming in and out of the Duluth Union Depot, the Lake Superior Railroad Museum is more than a museum, it's a trip back in time. As you descend the wide, crowd-accommodating staircase from the Depot's Great Hall you begin to detect the aroma of old trains: oil and grease and soot and who knows what else, all comingling to form the smell of history. Along six tracks, the museum displays carefully restored train cars of all types, including plows, steam locomotives, and passenger and dining cars. Some can be viewed from platforms, others you can actually walk through to get a closer look. To further enhance your time travel, the trains are surrounded by Depot Square—a meticulous recreation of turn-of-the-century shops and offices that could be a museum unto itself. Each building is outfitted with period-appropriate signage, window-dressing, furniture, wares, etc. The Railroad Museum is simply not to be missed. (And if you have the time, you can take the North Shore Scenic Railroad to Two Harbors and back.)

Old Fire House & Police Museum

East End, Superior • 402 23rd Ave. E. • (715) 398-7558 • Open seasonally (call ahead)

The last of Superior's turn-of-the-century fire houses, the museum was originally the East End Fire Hall, built to replace an old wooden firehouse that stood on the same spot until, ironically, it burned down in 1896. In 1982 the old fire hall became a museum dedicated to firefighters and police officers, and in 1996 it became the home of the Wisconsin State Fire and Police Hall of Fame, honoring the heroic deeds of firefighters and police officers throughout the state's history. Visitors will find vintage firefighting and police memorabilia, including several old firefighting rigs. The museum is open seasonally for self-guided tours at the cost of a small donation.

Museums, continued

Karpeles Manuscript Library Museum

Duluth • 902 E. 1st St. • (218) 728-0630 • Daily 12 P.M. - 4 P.M. / Closed Holidays & Mondays from Labor Day to Memorial Day

This Duluth museum is one of seven Karpeles sites located throughout the U.S. Together, the libraries house the world's largest private holding of important original manuscripts and documents from the fields of literature, science, religion, history, art, and even popular culture. Every three months a new exhibit is featured, along with the museum's ongoing displays. Recent featured exhibits traveling among the Karpeles libraries included, early baseball documents, original nursery rhyme illustrations, and a collection of Eva Peron material. Free admission.

Museums on the Beaten Path

Fairlawn Mansion (Pattison estate) • 906 E. 2nd St., Superior • (715) 394-5712 • Tours: M–Sat. 9 A.M. - 5 P.M. / Sun. 12 P.M. - 5 P.M.
Tours of a 42-room Queen Anne-style house built by Superior's three-time mayor Martin Pattison in 1891.

Fitger's Brewery Museum • 600 E. Superior St. • (218) 722-0410 • Hours vary
Brewery equipment and memorabilia help tell the tale of Duluth's most successful brewery.

Glensheen Mansion (Congdon estate) • 3300 London Rd. • (218) 726-8910 • Tours: M–F 9:30 A.M. - 4 P.M., May–October
Tours of the house Chester and Clara Congdon finished in 1908, modeled after an early 17th-century English country estate.

Great Lakes Aquarium & Freshwater Discovery Center • 353 Harbor Dr. • (218) 740-3474 • M–Sun. 10 A.M. - 6 P.M.
Fresh water fish and marine life.

Lake Superior Maritime Museum • Canal Park • (218) 727-2497 • Summer: Daily 10 A.M. - 9 P.M. / Winter: F–Sun. 10 A.M. - 4:30 P.M.
History of the Duluth-Superior harbor and shipping and shipwrecks on the Great Lakes.

Richard I. Bong World War II Heritage Museum • 305 Harbor Dr., Superior • (715) 392-7151 • Daily 9 A.M. - 5 P.M. • See page 250.

***S.S. Meteor* Museum • 300 Marina Dr., Superior • (715) 392-5742 •** Tours of the *S.S. Meteor* whaleback and *Col. D.D. Gaillard* dredger.

***William A. Irvin* • 350 Harbor Dr. • (218) 722-7876 • Tours: Sun.–W 9 A.M. - 6 P.M. / Th.–Sat. 9 A.M. - 8 P.M. •** Ore boat tour.

Theatre

Manion Theatre & University Experimental Theatre (UWS)
UWS Campus, Superior • Belknap St. & Catlin • (715) 394-8380 • Call for performance schedule

The University of Wisconsin-Superior's 237-seat Manion Theatre offers a wide range of theatre—from musical to drama to opera—produced by the school's theatre department and occasionally involving guest directors and performers. The University Experimental Theatre is home to department productions as well as shows produced entirely by students

Mitchell Auditorium & the Little Theatre (CSS)
St. Scholastica Campus, Duluth • 1200 Kenwood Ave. • (218) 723-5900 • Call for performance schedule

Theatre students at College of St. Scholastica have two venues on campus in which to showcase their talents: Mitchell Auditorium, seating 500 (also home to musical performances, lectures, and concerts) and the Little Theatre, a 150-seat "black box." The Theatre Department stages three professionally directed productions each year.

Marshall Performing Arts Center & Dudley Experimental Theatre (UMD)
UMD Campus, Duluth • 10 University Dr. • (218) 726-8561 • Call for performance schedule

MPAC is the home of the University of Minnesota Duluth's award-winning theatre department, which has sent several plays to the Kennedy Center as part of the American College Theatre Festival since 1987. Each year the UMD Theatre Department stages several productions, including a musical, a modern drama, and a classic Greek or Elizabethan play, as well as plays written and produced by students. The main theater seats 700 people; Dudley Experimental Theatre holds about 100.

Theatre, continued

Renegade Comedy Theatre
Downtown, Duluth • 404 W. Superior St. • 800-722-6627 or (218) 722-6775 • Call for show times

Since 1991 Renegade Comedy Theatre has been producing and performing original material as well as the works of other writers. Each year, the troupe puts together several shows, including Halloween- and holiday-themed sketch programs. Renegade also produces works for kids through the Renegade Children's Theatre. But even if there's not a show running, you can always catch the Renegade folks in action at the Comedy Olympics every Friday and Saturday night at 9:30 P.M. The Comedy Olympics is a show structured like television's *Whose Line is it Anyway* in which two teams of two troupe members compete to come up with the best improvisational response to audience suggestions while a referee officiates. To find out if a regular show is running, check local newspapers or call the Renegade box office.

Colder by the Lake
Duluth • No permanent address • www.colderbythelake.com • Check Web site for show times and locations

Colder by the Lake is the area's oldest surviving comedy theatre troupe, entertaining Duluth audiences since 1983. Throughout the '80s, Colder performed several sketch-based revues each year, but of late they have focused on producing one or two full-scale shows per year based on original material or well-known works such as Shakespeare's *A Midsummer Night's Dream*. They last entertained local audiences in January 2002 with a revival of their highly acclaimed and downright hilarious 2001 production *Les Uncomfortables*, an original comic opera about Duluth's founder, Daniel Greysolon Sieur du Lhut, written by Colder founder Margi Preus and long-time Colder writer/performer Jean Sramek. It's difficult to predict when the Colder crew will stage another show, so check their Web site or the entertainment calendars in local newspapers when you're in the area.

Theatre, continued

Duluth Playhouse

Downtown, Duluth • 506 W. Michigan St. • (218) 733-7555 • Box Office: M–F 9 A.M. - 5 P.M. / Sat. 12 P.M. - 6 P.M.

The Duluth Playhouse, staging musical and nonmusical productions since 1914, bills itself as "excitement for the whole family" and reflects this motto in its choice of material. Recent seasons featured titles such as *Annie*, *The Miracle Worker*, and *The Adventures of Tom Sawyer*—all suitable for theater-goers of all ages. But for those who might find these choices a bit too advanced, the Playhouse also has a children's theatre that puts on shows performed by children for children, based on material that most kids will find familiar and entertaining. Performances take place Wednesday through Saturday with matinees on Saturday and Sunday.

Minnesota Ballet

Downtown, Duluth • Box Office: 301 W. 1st St. • (218) 529-3742 • M–F 9 A.M. - 4 P.M.

The Minnesota Ballet is a professional company of 12 dancers that makes its home in Duluth's historic Board of Trade building (see page 80). The company tours internationally and throughout the U.S. and performs each season in Duluth and the Twin Cities. The Ballet performs a variety of works from both classical and modern ballet, as well as theatrical ballroom and jazz styles. It also conducts residency, outreach, and education programs to teach the art and history of ballet to area students and residents through lectures and demonstrations, and offers classes to all age groups and to people with physical challenges.

Music*

Duluth–Superior Symphony Orchestra

Duluth • Box Office: (218) 733-7579 • M–F 8:30 A.M. - 5 P.M. • Performances: DECC Auditorium, 350 Harbor Dr.

The Duluth–Superior Symphony Orchestra got its start in 1931, though it was then called the Duluth Civic Orchestra, performing in the historic Duluth Armory building (see page 84). In 2001 the DSSO celebrated its 70th year and the addition of its new conductor, Markand Thakar. The orchestra performs 20th-century American and contemporary works along with classical works of the Western European symphonic tradition. Each season features ten regular performances (some with classical programs, some pops) as well as a performance of Handel's *Messiah*.

Sacred Heart Music Center

Central Hillside, Duluth • 201 W. 4th St. • (218) 723-1895 • Open for performances and tours (call for schedules)

The former Sacred Heart Cathedral (see page 76) was completed in 1896 and is now managed by a non-profit organization. The group is dedicated to the preservation and renovation of the 100-year-old landmark and to providing a venue for the performing arts in Duluth by regional, national, and international artists. From the early music of the Twin Cities' renowned Rose Ensemble to the modern, ethereal sound of Duluth's own Low, the Music Center's architectural features and superb acoustics provide a unique setting for a wide variety of aural entertainment. The former cathedral has also retained its historic 1898 Felgemaker pipe organ. The center often provides visitors opportunities to hear (and even play) the organ. Self-guided and group tours are available; contact the Music Center for schedule and details.

*For additional live music venues, see pages 118–120.

North Shore Galleries & Museums

J. Pepper Inn
Knife River • 243 Riverview St. • (218) 590-3839 • F–Sun. 12 P.M. - 6 P.M.

Work by local and national artists; mostly paintings and sculpture.

3M/Dwan Museum
Two Harbors • 201 Waterfront Dr. • (218) 834-4898 • May–October: Daily 9:00 A.M. - 5 P.M.

Displays and interactive programs on the history of 3M in the building where it all started in 1902.

Two Harbors Lighthouse
Two Harbors • 1 Lighthouse Point • (218) 834-4898 • May–October: Daily 9:00 A.M. - 5 P.M.

Built in 1892, oldest continuously operating lighthouse on the north shore. Shipwreck exhibits, tours.

Lake County Historical Museum
Two Harbors • 520 South Ave. • (218) 834-4898 • M–Sat. 9 A.M. - 5 P.M. / Sun. 10 A.M. - 3 P.M.

Exhibits on the pioneering history of Lake County, North Shore dogsled mail delivery, logging, and more.

North Shore Commercial Fishing Museum
Tofte • Highway 61 & County Rd. 2 • (218) 663-7804 • Summer: Daily 9 A.M. - 7 P.M. / Winter: Daily 9 A.M. - 5 P.M.

Displays on commercial fishing, Lake Superior, and the people who settled the area.

North Shore Galleries & Museums, continued

Thomsonite Beach Gemstone Museum
2920 W. Highway 61 • (218) 888-387-1532 • Open daily during the summer

Part museum, part giftshop—and one of only two places in the world this "Lake Superior" gemstone is found.

Johnson Heritage Post Art Gallery
Grand Marais • 115 W. Wisconsin • (218) 387-2314 • Summer: M–Sat. 10 A.M. - 5 P.M. / Sun. 12 P.M. - 4 P.M. / Winter: T–Sun. 12 P.M. - 4 P.M.

Revolving exhibits, plus a permanent collection of paintings by Anna Johnson, a regional pioneer.

Sivertson's Gallery
Grand Marais • 14 W. Wisconsin • (218) 387-2491 • Open daily at 10 A.M.

Local and regional art from local and regional artists—painting, photography (including Jim Brandenberg), sculpture—as well as Inuit art from Alaska and Canada. There's another Sivertson's Gallery in Duluth's Canal Park.

Waters of Superior
Grand Marais • 501 W. Highway 61 • (218) 387-9766 • Open daily

Features the photography of Craig Blacklock, famous for his nature shots of Lake Superior. It also offers jewelry, home furnishings, clothing, and art. (Blacklock also has galleries in Duluth and Moose Lake).

Grand Portage National Monument
Grand Portage • 211 Mile Creek Rd. • (218) 378-2788 • May–October: Daily 9 A.M. - 4:30 P.M.

Exhibits on the fur trade and area history, craft and cooking demonstrations, American Indian artifacts, and more.

South Shore Galleries & Museums

Bayfield Maritime Museum
Bayfield • 131 S. 1st St. • (715) 779-9919 • July–Aug.: Daily 10 A.M. - 7 P.M. / June, Sept., Oct.: Daily 10 A.M. - 5 P.M.

Displays on commercial fishing, lighthouses, sailor crafts, shipwrecks, and more.

Native Spirit Gifts and Gallery
Bayfield • 14612 Highway 13 • (715) 779-9550 • May–Oct.: M–Sat. 10 A.M. - 5 P.M. / Sun. 12 P.M. - 5 P.M. / Wknds. until Christmas

Cultural displays, American Indian art from the Great Lakes region, craft demonstrations, and birch bark canoes.

Apostle Islands National Lakeshore Museum
Bayfield • 415 Washington Ave. • (715) 779-3397 • Mem. Day–Labor Day: Daily 1 P.M. - 4 P.M. / After Labor Day: wknds. only

Exhibits on logging, lumbering, agriculture, and more, plus an extensive collection of historic photographs.

Washburn Historical Museum and Cultural Center
Washburn • 1 E. Bayfield St. • (715) 373-5591 • April–December: Daily 10 A.M. - 4 P.M.

Local and regional history exhibits, dioramas, and fine art.

Northern Great Lakes Visitor Center
Ashland • 29270 Highway G • (715) 685-9983 • Summer: Daily 9 A.M. - 7 P.M. / Winter: Daily 9 A.M. - 5 P.M.

Observation tower, interpretive and historic exhibits, boardwalk trail, visitor information, and trip planning.

Nightlife
(libations, live music, dancing, etc.)

Nightlife

You can find just about anything to do in the Twin Ports on a weekend night (and most weeknights). Both Duluth and Superior have plenty of watering holes, but Superior in particular offers many places to drink. They say "Soup Town" has more bar stools than church pews, and they might be right: Twenty-six bars operate along one 10-block strip of Tower Avenue, and nine more can be found a block or less from the Tower Avenue strip.

With that many bars on one Superior street, we couldn't do a fair job describing each and every bar in Superior and Duluth without developing a serious drinking problem, so we've hand-selected a number of places because of their authentic atmosphere or specialty. We also profiled some neighborhood taverns in case you find yourself on an unfamiliar side of town and want to stop for a cold one in a comfortable setting. We tried to avoid places you could find anywhere—in other words, no chains, sports bars, or typical college bars.

For those who like to do more than just drink, we've listed Twin Ports dance clubs, bowling alleys, pool halls, and live music venues. The Twin Ports enjoys an eclectic music scene and has recently seen some of its local musicians achieve regional, national, and even international acclaim. Check the local arts & entertainment papers to find out where you can see college "slow core" chart-toppers Low, the Black-Eyed Snakes's power blues, singer-songwriter Haley Bonar, slide-steel guitar folk blues master Charlie Parr, and literally dozens of other bands whose range runs from reggae-fusion to alt-country and from to punk to jam bands.

Check out the end of this section for some great places to enjoy a drink along the shores. Be aware that the Duluth Smoking Ban includes billiard parlors and bowling alleys. By the way, Wisconsin bars serve until 2 A.M. weeknights and 2:30 A.M. weekends. Duluth bars are open until 1 A.M., but recent changes in the law may allow them to stay open until 2 A.M. by the time you read this. And if you're out at a Superior nightspot and think you've spotted Rod Stewart slumming it, you're wrong—but you're not the only person to make that mistake. That's just Rod's local doppleganger.

Authentic Atmosphere

The Anchor Bar
North End, Superior • 413 Tower Ave. • (715) 394-9747 • Sun.–Th. 'til 2 A.M. / F & Sat. 'til 2:30 A.M. • Full bar

If you're looking for a place with character, the Anchor has it in spades. No fake antiques or sports memorabilia here, just real things from real ships in a real harbor town: diving suits, flags, life rings, etc. If you're lucky, the barber chairs will be unoccupied when you get there. Besides that, beer is inexpensive and the Anchor boasts one of the best selections of imports and microbrews in the Twin Ports—and the best burgers and fries, hands down.

Molly's
North End, Superior • 411 Tower Ave. • phone number unavailable • Sun.–Th. 'til 2 A.M. / F & Sat. 'til 2:30 A.M. • Full bar

From its pressed tin ceiling to the Tiffany-esque stained glass lamps behind the bar, Molly's has about the best décor you're likely to find in a dive. Molly's son Oscar has decorated the bar with great old memorabilia, including antique signage such as an advertisement for land at Tower and Belknap—now the heart of downtown—at just $1 an acre. Leinies cost a buck, and Molly's has the best classic R & B jukebox in the midwest. Molly's was once considered a GLBT bar, but these days you'll find all kinds of folks enjoying themselves under its roof.

Choo Choo Bar
Itasca, Superior • 5002 E. 3rd St. • (715) 398-3788 • Sun.–Th. 'til 2 A.M. / F & Sat. 'til 2:30 A.M. • Full bar

Structure sets the Choo Choo apart from any other bar in the Twin Ports. Made from old railroad cars (it sits along the tracks in Superior's Itasca neighborhood), the Choo Choo's ceilings are low and curved, and the bar itself is quite narrow, creating a cozy atmosphere. Not much of a choice in beer, just a few domestic taps, cans, and bottles. You can play pool or darts, and the jukebox selection runs from Johnny Cash to the Backstreet Boys.

Authentic Atmosphere, continued

Kom-On-Inn
Spirit Valley (West Duluth), Duluth • 332 N. 57th Ave. W. • (218) 624-3385 • Open 'til 1 A.M. • Full bar

For a glimpse of what West Duluth once looked like, all you need do is step inside the Kom-On-Inn. The highlight of this long, narrow drinking hole is the line of wooden booths, each sporting an original oil painting by Art Fleming depicting the mills and factories that flourished in this once-industrial end of town. The Kom-on-Inn has been open since Prohibition ended, and it hasn't raised its prices much since. A must stop in West Duluth.

NorShor Theatre
Downtown, Duluth • 211 E. Superior St. • (218) 727-7585 • Open 'til 1 A.M. • Full bar

Duluth's historic Orpheum Theatre (see page 264) was renovated in the late 1930s, transforming the vaudeville house into an art-deco movie theater. It is now a bar/nightclub that shows independent and foreign films and acts as the epicenter of Duluth's ever-growing live music scene. Three-dimensional art deco reliefs decorate the stairway walls and those adjacent to the main stage. The mezzanine lounge features a classic wooden bar where you can choose from a good selection of imports and microbrews—or ask Rick to twist you up a martini.

Sir Benedict's Tavern
Brewer's Creek, Duluth • 805 E. Superior St. • (218) 728-1192 • Open 'til 11 P.M. • Beer & wine only

Sir Ben's strives to be an authentic British pub, and while it's not exactly what you'd find in the U.K., it does have a warm, comfy feel and an incredible selection of imported beers from around the globe. The pub hosts live music on weekends and a bluegrass jam every Wednesday night. In the summer, Sir Ben's patio makes a great spot to enjoy a beer and gaze at the big lake. If you're hungry, Sir Ben's also serves soups and sandwiches.

Under the Rainbow (GLBT Establishments)

Bev's Jook Joint

Downtown, Superior • 820 Tower Ave. • (715) 392-5373 • Sun.–Th. 'til 2 A.M. / F & Sat. 'til 2:30 A.M. • Full bar

Bev's is about the friendliest place in downtown Superior. People of all orientations gather to listen—and some-time join in on—live music performances from local and national acts (primarily blues). A variety of instruments adorn the walls, and all may be taken down and played if you care to jam with the band (and if the band's into it). In the summer, step out back for some fresh air when the band takes a break. Good beer selection.

J.T.'s

North End, Superior • 1506 N. 3rd St. • (715) 394-2580 • Sun.–Th. 'til 2 A.M. / F & Sat. 'til 2:30 A.M. • Full bar

One of three remaining bars along Superior's once notorious 3rd Street (filled with speakeasies and brothels during Prohibition), J.T.'s erupts on weekend nights as the dance floor fills with folks of all ilks who just want to shake their groove thang. If you're not into dancing, J.T.'s has a couple of pool tables to keep you busy, and they open the grill in the afternoon. Good selection of beer and wine, and the bar occasionally hosts drag shows.

The Main Club

Downtown, Superior • 1217 Tower Ave. • (715) 392-1756 • Sun.–Th. 'til 2 A.M. / F & Sat. 'til 2:30 A.M. • Full bar

If you've come back for a visit, don't look for the Main in its old location in the North End—that burned to the ground. Now located next to the Androy Hotel on Tower, the Main has long served the Twin Ports' GLBT com-munity and plays host to an annual ball and Gay Pride celebration. The Main has a small dance floor with music spun by a DJ and its bar offers a fine selection of beers.

Brewpubs

Fitger's Brewhouse

Brewer's Creek, Duluth • 600 E. Superior St. • (218) 726-1392 • M–Sun. 11 A.M. - 1 A.M. • Beer & wine only • Smoke free

Hands down, the best beer you'll find in Duluth or up the North Shore (maybe even Minnesota). From the Witch Tree ESB to the Bigboat Oatmeal Stout, master brewer Dave Hoops and his crew cook up an excellent assortment, including seasonal beers. (In honor of the annual Home Grown Music Fest, the Brewhouse offers "Home Grown Hempin' Ale.") You can enjoy live music from local and national singer/songwriter acts most weekends, and Thursday night is home to Starfire Lounge: inexpensive pitchers and an eclectic mix of music. The Brewhouse also makes great food, from gourmet sandwiches and burgers to vegetarian entrées, including a portabella burger and a HUGE black-bean burrito.

Twin Ports Brewing Company

Downtown, Superior • 1623 Broadway St. • (715) 394-2500 • Sun.–Th. 'til 2 A.M. / F & Sat. 'til 2:30 A.M. • Beer only

The Twin Ports Brewing Company features the handcrafted brews of Rick Sauer and the only hand-poured beer north of the Twin Cities, thanks to its Victorian beer machine. (It pulls the beer out of the cask the old way, without the aid of carbon dioxide.) Sauer puts up a regular line of brews such as the Derailed Ale, Burntwood Black, and Twin Ports ESB as well as seasonal brews like the Apple Harvest Ale, which isn't overly fruity despite its name. Located inside the old Russell Creamery, Twin Ports's glazed-tile walls are adorned with old signs from Superior's brewing history, especially those advertising the Northern Brewing Company. Limited food available, including a smoked salmon platter. Wednesdays after 9 P.M., pitchers are just $7, and weekdays from 4 to 6 P.M., pints are only $2.50. If you're bored with pool or darts, ask for a cribbage board, chess set, or Yahtzee game.

Neighborhood Saloons

The Reef

Endion, Duluth • 2002 London Rd. • (218) 724-9845 • Open 'til 1 A.M. • Full bar

Besides Black Woods restaurant, The Reef is the only place you can get a drink east of downtown. Its clientele ranges from neighborhood regulars to UMD and St. Scholastica students. The Reef has lots of games to play (pool, darts, foosball, video games) and plenty of TVs to stare at, including a couple big screens (and they're not always tuned to sports). A limited number of imports and microbrews. Live music on weekends.

The North Pole

Irving (West Duluth), Duluth • 5606 Raleigh St. • (218) 624-9623 • Open 'til 1 A.M. • Full bar

The North Pole is a classic neighborhood saloon. Its west wall is dominated by a superb wooden bar with wooden coolers and a modestly ornate back covered with years of memorabilia, Swisher Sweet cigars, Hav-A-Hank handkerchiefs, and Ronson lighter flints. Tap beer (domestic only) sells for $1.25, but 20-ouncers go for $1.50 during NFL games. The only jukebox anywhere that still has Boyce & Hart's "I Wonder What She's Doing Tonight."

Buena Vista Lounge

Central Hillside, Duluth • 1144 Mesaba Ave. • (218) 722-1371 • Open 'til 1 A.M. • Full bar

Located where the 'Heights meets the Hillside, the Buena Vista Lounge is the last non-chain drinking establishment in Duluth until you near the outskirts of Hermantown out past the Miller Hill Mall shopping corridor. The Buena's simple décor is dominated by a large, rectangular bar—nothing fancy here, just a good, comfy spot for a drink. Domestics and a couple microbrews on tap; many TVs, dartboards, and video games to entertain you.

Neighborhood Saloons, continued

Alpine Bar & Lounge

Gary-New Duluth, Duluth • 1308 Commonwealth Ave. • (218) 626-9979 • Open 'til 1 A.M. • Full bar

Although the bar is topped in Formica, the rest of the Alpine has an authentic touch, from the mosaic tile floor to the bar's brass rail—they even sell pork rinds, pickled eggs, and pickled turkey gizzards. And although a sign proclaims "Alpine Proudly Serves Pabst Blue Ribbon on Tap," it actually sells no tap beer. Plenty of domestic bottles and cans, though, and everything from Buddy Holly to Duran Duran on the jukebox. Karaoke on weekends.

Congress Bar

Gary-New Duluth, Duluth • 1334 Commonwealth Ave. • (218) 626-9967 • Open 'til 1 A.M. • Full bar

The centerpiece of the Congress is its classic wooden bar and bar back, complete with a mirror held in place by tufted leather (which, sadly, has been covered over). In the summers, an outdoor beer garden opens out back. You'll find Old Style, Killian's, and MGD on tap plus domestic and a few Mexican imports in the cooler. Register to win the "Customer of the Week" drawing for free drinks every night for a week.

The Wabegon Inn (and Last Chance Café)

Fond du Lac, Duluth • 14030 W. Highway 23 (keep driving past Fond du Lac) • (218) 636-1700 • Open 'til 1 A.M. • Full bar

If you've spent the day in Jay Cooke or are heading down to the 'Cities on Scenic Highway 23, the Wabegon makes a great spot to wet your whistle. Small and simple, the Wabegon has darts, a pool table, and a juke box (mostly new country). You'll find Bud and Miller on tap for just $1.50. You'll also find an anomaly in this place so close to where Packerland intersects with Vikingland: a Tampa Bay Buccaneers mirror. The Wabegon also sells off-sale liquor and houses the Last Chance Café (burgers, steaks, barbecued ribs, spaghetti). Don't drink and drive!

Neighborhood Saloons, continued

El Dorado
Oliver, WI • 2110 E. Union St. • (715) 392-3717 • Sun.–Th. 'til 2 A.M. / F & Sat. 'til 2:30 A.M. • Full bar

Before the El Dorado changed hands in 1999, it looked like a hybrid saloon/thrift store—you could get a beer and a ceramic trout-shaped flower pot. Today the knick knacks are gone, but the El Dorado still makes a great place to have a beer, shoot a game of pool, or play one of their many video-gambling machines. Named by its original owner, who had made his fortune in a silver mine, the El Dorado is decorated with authentic wagon wheels and oxen harnesses. You can enjoy a can of domestic beer for $1.50. Some food and off-sale available.

Charlie Brown's
Billings Park, Superior • 1828 Iowa Ave. • (715) 394-5295 • Sun.–Th. 'til 2 A.M. / F & Sat. 'til 2:30 A.M. • Full bar

Next door to the antique shop, across the street from the bakery, and a few doors away from the café, Charlie Brown's helps make up "downtown" Billings Park. This tiny corner bar is decorated with an array of beer steins and—because of its name—Peanuts memorabilia. Where else can you get drunk while staring at Snoopy and Woodstock without feeling like some kind of creep? Pool table in back, and domestic taps are just $1.

The Office
East End, Superior • 2129 E. 5th St. • (715) 398-7536 • Sun.–Th. 'til 2 A.M. / F & Sat. 'til 2:30 A.M. • Full bar

Another great neighborhood saloon with an old wooden bar and coolers, The Office is located in the heart of Superior's East End business district. The walls are covered with photos of patrons from days gone by, and you'll find everything from Patsy Cline to the Beatles on the jukebox. It will cost you $1.25 for a domestic tap, and don't bother asking if they have imports or microbrews. Limited off-sale liquor and beer available.

Bowling Alleys*

Incline Station Bowling Center
Downtown, Duluth • 601 W. Superior St. • (218) 722-0671 • Every day 9 A.M. - 12 A.M.

Features Atomic Bowling (disco music and black lights) and bumper bowling. Attached bar & grill.

Landmark Lanes
Downtown, Superior • 1914 Broadway St. • (715) 394-4422 • Every day 11 A.M. - 12 A.M.

Bumper bowling and birthday party reservations available.

Stadium Lanes
Lincoln Park, Duluth • Grand Ave. at 34th Ave. W. • (218) 628-1071 • Sun.–Th. 12 P.M. - 12 A.M. / F & Sat. 'til 1:30 A.M.

Bumper bowling available. Leagues from 5 P.M. to 9 P.M. Monday–Thursday. Attached bar (Mary's Place).

Tanski's Ridgeview Lanes
Woodland, Duluth • 3930 E. Calvary • (218) 728-3614 • M–F 3 P.M. - 12 A.M. / Sat. & Sun. 12 P.M. - 12 A.M.

A great old bowling center. Call ahead for bumper bowling. Full bar and pizza available.

Village Lanes
South End, Superior • 6419 Tower Ave. • (715) 394-4436 • M–Th. 10 A.M. - 12 A.M. / F & Sat. 'til 2:30 A.M. / Sun. 'til 12 A.M.

Bumper bowling available; full bar and grill.

*Call ahead to make sure it's not league night! (Note: Duluth bowling alleys are smoke free.)

Billiard Parlors

Horseshoe Billiards

Lincoln Park, Duluth • 2415 W. Superior St. • (218) 727-5144 • Sun.–Th. 10 A.M. - 2 A.M. / F & Sat. 10 A.M. - 3 A.M.

You'll find twenty pool tables at Horseshoe's: ten bar-sized (7-foot), nine 9-foot, and one snooker table (6 x 9 feet). You'll also find several dart boards. Beer and soft drinks available. **(Note: Duluth billiard parlors are smoke free.)**

Mr. Lucky's

Downtown, Superior • 1022 Tower Ave. • (715) 395-9789 • Sun.–Th. 'til 2 A.M. / F & Sat. 'til 2:30 A.M.

Mr. Lucky's, a self-proclaimed "modern, upscale billiards parlor," has thirteen bar-sized pool tables, four 9-foot tables, and one snooker table. Mr. Lucky's also has a full-service bar, serves pizza, and sells pool cues and tables.

Shark's Billiards

Downtown, Duluth • 327 W. Superior St. • (218) 529-1626 • Sun.–Th. 11 A.M. to 3 A.M. / F & Sat. 11 A.M. to 4 A.M.

Located at the former site of Gold's Gym, Shark's is loaded with about two dozen billiard tables, including one snooker table and a combination of 7- and 9-foot tables. Plenty of other games as well. Shark's serves beer (until 1 a.m.) but caters to a younger crowd. **(Note: Duluth billiard parlors are smoke free.)**

Bars with Above-Average Billiard Facilities

Capri Bar • Downtown, Superior • 1224 Tower Ave. • (715) 395-1908 • Sun.–Th. 'til 2 A.M. / F & Sat. 'til 2:30 A.M.
The Palace • Downtown, Superior • 1108 Tower Ave. • Sun.–Th. 'til 2 A.M. / F & Sat. 'til 2:30 A.M.
The Pioneer • Downtown, Duluth • 323 W. 1st St. • Open 'til 1 A.M.
The Reef • East End, Duluth • 2002 London Rd. • (218) 724-9845 • Open 'til 1 A.M. • (see page 113)

Live Music Venues

Amazing Grace Bakery & Café
Canal Park • 394 S. Lake Ave. • (218) 723-0075

Folk, Celtic, singer-songwriter in the basement of the DeWitt-Seitz building, plus a summer music fest, and an annual jug band competition.

Beaner's Central
Spirit Valley, Duluth • 324 N. Central Ave. • (218) 624-5957

Eclectic: singer-songwriter, reggae, rock, country, etc. (see page 138 for details). Closes early (Beaner's is a coffeeshop, but beer is available).

Bedrock Bar
Lincoln Park, Duluth • 2023 W. Superior • (218) 720-4755

Mostly hard rock and heavy metal cover bands in a sports bar-like setting.

Blue Note Café
Canal Park, Duluth • 357 Canal Park Drive • (218) 727-6549

Live music (usually jazz) on Friday and Saturday nights in a Canal Park coffee house/sandwich shop.

Bev's Jook Joint
Downtown, Superior • 820 Tower Ave. • (715) 392-5373

All kinds of blues and much more for a predominantely GLBT crowd (everyone's welcome—see page 111 for details).

Charlie's Club
Spirit Valley, Duluth • 5527 Grand Ave. (218) 624-3150

Mostly hard rock and heavy metal cover bands, usually only on weekends.

Club Saratoga
Canal Park, Duluth • 331 Canal Park Drive • (218) 722-5577

Jazz jam on Saturday starting at 3:00 in the afternoon. (Keep the kids at home—all other times, the 'Toga is a "gentlemen's club.")

Fat Daddy's Live
Downtown, Superior • 705 Tower Ave. • (715) 394-2892

All sorts of live music, from blues to punk (you might remember this place as the Cove Cabaret or Club Key West; the leaking bathroom has been fixed).

Live Music Venues, continued

Fitger's Brewhouse
Brewer's Creek, Duluth • 600 E. Superior St. • (218) 726-1392

Singer/songwriters on weekends and a taste of recorded local music Thursdays at the Starfire Lounge (see page 112 for details).

The Limit
Gary-New Duluth • 1426 Commonwealth Ave. • (218) 626-3398

Local and regional country and top 40 pop cover bands near Jay Cooke State Park.

Mama Gets
Downtown, Superior • 525 Tower Ave. • (715) 395-6030

Singer/songwriters perfom Thursday through Saturday nights in the former Berger Hardware building (see page 139).

Norm's Beer & Brats
Downtown, Superior • 1901 Broadway St. • (715) 394-9689

Local and sometimes national rock acts (original and cover bands) for a predominantely college crowd (backward baseball caps not required).

NorShor Theatre
Downtown, Duluth • 211 E. Superior St. • (218) 727-7585

The epicenter of the Twin Ports's live music scene located in a historic art-deco theater, featuring local, regional, and national acts on the 1500-seat Main Stage or the more intimate Mezzanine Stage (see page 110).

Pizza Lucé
Downtown, Duluth • 11 E. Superior St. • (218) 727-7400

Live local music almost every night, plus a bloody mary brunch on Sunday mornings. And "The Looch" has a caberet license that allows music until the wee hours.

Red Lion
Downtown, Duluth • 220 E. Superior St. • (218) 722-9440

During most of the week, The Lion is a popular watering hole for folks who live near downtown, but on weekends and Wednesdays the stage offers live music. Home of Duluth's best standing gig, the Black Labels on Wednesday nights.

Live Music venues, continued

The Reef

Endion, Duluth • 2002 London Rd. • (218) 724-9845

Local and regional original and cover bands on weekends (see pages 113 and 117 for details).

Schooner's Beach Club

Canal Park, Duluth • 250 Canal Park Dr. • (218) 727-8821

Local, regional, and national blues acts on weekends in the lounge attached to the Canal Park Inn.

Sir Benedict's Tavern

Brewer's Creek, Duluth • 805 E. Superior St. • (218) 728-1192

Bluegrass jams and singer/songwriters (see page 110 for details).

Tap Room

Brewer's Creek, Duluth • 600 E. Superior St. • (218) 722-0061

College crowd and a DJ on weeknights; live local and national acts on weekends. (Where the dinosaur acts and hair bands from the past play in Duluth.)

Third Rock

Downtown, Superior • 1201 Tower Ave. • (715) 394-7171

Hard rock; occasional national acts. (Where the dinosaur acts and hair bands from the past play in Superior.)

Tyomie's Bar

Downtown, Superior • 601 Tower Ave. • (715) 392-1197

Cover bands in what many consider a "biker" bar.

Western Tavern

Lincoln Park, Duluth •2801 W. Superior St. • (218) 624-7742

Modern country cover bands and line dancing.

Dance Clubs

Stargate

Downtown, Superior • 619 Tower Ave. • (715) 395-2222 • Sun.–Th. 'til 2 A.M. / F & Sat. 'til 2:30 A.M.

DJ spins top 40 dance, rap, and hip hop.

Grandma's Sports Garden

Canal Park, Duluth • 425 S. Lake Ave. • (218) 722-4724 • Nightly 'til 1:00 A.M.

DJs play top 40 dance to a mostly college-aged crowd.

Hall of Fame

Downtown, Superior • 1028 Tower Ave. • (715) 394-4225 • Sun.–Th. 'til 2 A.M. / F & Sat. 'til 2:30 A.M.

DJs play top 40 dance, rap, and hip hop.

The Saloon

Downtown, Superior • 1807 N. 11 St. • (715) 392-6400 • Sun.–Th. 'til 2 A.M. / F & Sat. 'til 2:30 A.M.

DJs—including guest DJs from Minneapolis, Madison, and Chicago—spin underground house music on weekends.

J.T.'s

North End, Superior • 1506 N. 3rd St. • (715) 394-2580 • Sun.–Th. 'til 2 A.M. / F & Sat. 'til 2:30 A.M.

Gay, straight, or anywhere in between—you're welcome on the dance floor (see page 111 for details). Top 40 dance. (The Main Club—page 111—also offers dancing for the "alternative" crowd.)

North Shore Nightspots

The Landing
Two Harbors, MN • 621 7th Ave. • Open 'til 1 A.M.

Housed within the historic Pearson Motors building that dates back to 1920, The Landing is a combination small-town tavern and sports bar. Inside you'll find high ceilings, pine walls, and a large wrap-around bar, behind which bartenders pour plenty of domestic beers and a limited number of imports. The Landing has two pool tables, foosball, and darts, and you can order a Shirk's pizza or Asian food from the Vietnamese Lantern, next door.

The Green Door
Beaver Bay, MN • Highway 61 • Open 'til 1 A.M.

The Green Door was once the Beaver Bay schoolhouse, and not much has changed inside—the blackboards are still in place, and some of the regulars at the Thursday afternoon cribbage matches attended grammar school there. A standard domestic beer selection and few imports; off-sale available as well. You can play pool, foosball, and darts and dance to live music on weekends. Look for the giant beer keg as you drive through town.

Gunflint Tavern
Grand Marais, MN • 111 W. Wisconsin • M–Sun. 'til 12 A.M. / F & Sat. 'til 1 A.M.

We weren't sure whether to put the Gunflint under "Eats" or "Nightlife," but since it has arguably the best beer selection on the North Shore, nightlife got the nod. You'll find selections from Ireland's Guinness to Duluth's Lake Superior Brewing Co. and just about everything in between. They also have great food for meat-eaters (Jamaican jerk tuna steak) and for veg heads (too many selections to mention). As if that weren't enough, the Gunflint is housed inside the historic Grand Marais State Bank—the vault is behind the bar.

South Shore Nightspots

Rum Line Tavern
Bayfield, WI • 31 S. 1st St. • Sun.–Th. 'til 2 A.M. / F & Sat. 'til 2:30 A.M.

Housed in an unassuming blue brick building shaped somewhat like a quonset hut and sporting a cow weather vane, the Rum Line is found just off Bayfield's beaten path of often overly quaint "shoppes." The Rum Line helps keep the Caribbean in the booze business by offering 24 varieties of rum. On tap you'll find seasonal Leinenkugel's and Summit Pale Ale, plus the usual suspects of imports in bottle. Bloodies on Sunday for $3.

Morty Muldoon's (a.k.a. Morty's Pub)
Bayfield, WI • 108 Rittenhouse Ave. • Sun.–Th. 'til 2 A.M. / F & Sat. 'til 2:30 A.M.

Recently renovated, Morty Muldoon's makes it into *True North* due to its history (the original Morty was one of the first to swim from Bayfield to Madeline Island and back). The linoleum has been removed to expose hardwood floors, which replaced the sawdust floors of 100 years ago. Morty's still features a beautiful stone fireplace, and the owners may bring back the Saturday night potluck dinners of days gone by. Behind the bar you'll find Leinie's and Summit on tap plus bottled imports and microbrews. Live music on weekends.

Patsy's Bar
Washburn, WI • 328 W. Bayfield • M 4 P.M. - 2 A.M. / T–Th. 9:30 A.M. - 2 A.M / Fri. & Sat. 'til 2:30 A.M. / Closed Sundays

Patsy's has been a South Shore staple for more than 30 years—much of it with the ever-fiesty Patsy herself behind the wood. The saloon is a wonderfully simple spot to enjoy a beer or a cocktail—no pretentions, no attitude (except Patsy's). The furnishings are classic: a long wooden bar and wooden coolers. A painting of the backs of naked ladies on bar stools adds a touch of whimsy to the men's room. Patsy's is the unofficial office of Warren Nelson and the gang from Big Top Chautauqua, so you might stumble across a free show.

South Shore Nightspots, continued

Club 13

Between Washburn & Ashland, WI • 35 Highway 13 • Sun–Th. 11 A.M. - 2 A.M. / F & Sat. 'til 2:30 A.M.

At the edge of Bayfield County (geographically the second largest county in Wisconsin and second smallest by population—there isn't a single traffic light within its borders) stands an example of Americana you rarely find in these parts: a roadhouse. Club 13 has everything you'd expect from a roadhouse short of chicken wire in front of the stage. You'll find Leinenkugel's and Miller Lite on tap along with lots of domestic beers, and you won't have to spend much to enjoy a few. Tap beer is a buck ($1.50 for a 16-ounce glass), canned beer and rail drinks two bucks, and call drinks just $2.50. They also sell off-sale beer to get you further on up the road. Anyone (yes, *any-one*) wearing lipstick on Monday night is entitled to two-for-one drinks. Thursday night has a dart league, and each and every Friday you'll find live music by local bands—that's what makes a roadhouse a roadhouse.

Tom's Burndown Café

La Pointe, WI • (on Madeline Island) • #1 Middle Road • (715) 747-6100 • Seasonal (call before you get on the ferry)

According to owner Tom Nelson, Tom's Burndown Café is "an open-air tent bar, slapped together from a deck, a semi trailer, a scrap of circus tent, a few beer coolers, and a lot of good patch work and rope." The bar also incorporates derelict cars, decks, and stages, each of which has its own tale to tell. Tom's brings in musicians on some weekends to entertain the crowd, ranging in styles from folk to jazz to reggae. And the café plays host to The Middle Road Literary/Arts Society, Inc., and the aptly named Nelson Phoenix Gallery. And just who was Madeline Island named for? Its Ojibwe name is Moningwunakauning or "home of the golden-breasted wood-pecker." It became Madeline Island after Equaysayway, daughter of Chief White Crane, married Michel Cadotte, a Frenchman who established a trading post in 1793. She was baptized a Christian and adopted the name Madeleine, after which her father renamed the island. (No one knows how Madeline lost that extra "e".)

Places to Eat

(or grab groceries or something to go)

True North Dining

When choosing which restaurants to include in *True North*, we decided to select from locally owned and operated establishments (no chains!), particularly those that offer a taste of the region, either in their menu, their décor, or their history. (Careful readers will note a lack of Bayfield eateries: while we found no restaurants there that met our criteria, many folks suggested our readers try Maggie's because of its excellent food.) Few of the restaurants would place high on a gourmet restaurant reviewer's "best of" list, but all make great examples of true north dining. Local residents might be surprised that some area eateries don't appear in this section, including the Anchor Bar, considered to have the best burgers around. We placed drinking establishments that serve food in the Nightlife chapter, so look there for the Anchor and others.

Unfortunately, many great spots that would have been at home among these pages no longer exist, but we haven't forgotten them. In Duluth, the Flame was once one of Duluth's best-known restaurants—the Great Lakes Aquarium now sits at one of its former locations. When Natchio's on 2nd Avenue West closed its doors, it also closed the book on authentic Greek cuisine in the Twin Ports. The Chinese Lantern/Brass Phoenix in the Duluth Athletic Club building never rose from the ashes after a fire in the early '90s (see page 127). Before Canal Park was permanently disfigured by a Burger King, the Canal Park Inn served up burgers and fries that fed local teens and seagulls. More recently one of the last great neighborhood grocers faded into history as Chester Park's Taran's Market closed its doors (see page 139), as did two favorite diners, 21st Delight in Lincoln Park and Ketola's Kafé, famous for its Finnish pancakes. The turn of the century was also tough on restaurants across the bay, as longtime local favorite The Library/Zona Rosa closed its doors. Bob's Chop Suey also shut down. Bob's served Asian food that few Asian folks would recognize served in a dining room decorated with neon lobsters and roast turkeys on the ceiling and divided into private rooms by pegboard walls like those in your dad's basement workshop. Bob's didn't serve alcohol, but if you brought your own, they'd supply the set-ups. Alas....

Key: Cheap = entrées less than $10 • Moderate = entrées $7– $15 • Spendy = entrées $12 and up

The Duluth Smoking Ban

On January 1, 2001, after a great deal of debate, the Duluth City Council passed an ordinance partially banning smoking in Duluth's restaurants. The ban was met with both praise and criticism. Anti-smoking groups considered it a victory for public health. Small restaurant owners worried it would be their financial ruin. Diners, for the most part, were confused—there were too many gray areas, and it was essentially unenforceable. It soon affected area restaurants. A few closed, others refused to comply, and five were given smoking ban exemptions (others cried foul). Duluth citizens decided the ban's fate in November 2001 elections, passing a stricter ban: you can't smoke in a Duluth restaurant, billiard hall, or bowling alley, period. Restaurants that allow smoking face fines up to $750.

A New Twist on Old Duluth

The Duluth Athletic Club

Downtown, Duluth • 21 N. 4th Ave. W. • (218) 720-4445 • S-Th 11 A.M. - 10 P.M. / F, Sat. 'til 10:30 P.M. / Lounge open until 1 A.M.

When first built to support local sports teams, the Duluth Athletic Club contained squash courts, a billiards room, a steam room, meeting space, and a kitchen and bar. The squash courts remained open as late as the 1980s, when the building housed the Chinese Lantern. Today the Athletic Club is back—the bar and the kitchen, anyhow—and it has become a great place to enjoy fine dining surrounded by images of old Duluth. Elegant without being stuffy, the club's tables are decked out with linen tablclothes and napkins and the walls adorned with wonderful black-and-white photos showing Duluth's past. The DAC serves a variety of fare, including Americana, Italian, Mexican, Thai, Jamaican, and locally influenced dishes (such as a Scandanavian appetizer plate featuring herring and a smoked salmon mousse), and has a solid wine list as well as a fine selection of microbrews. The bar, while loaded with TVs, avoids the "sports bar" feel with pockets of couches and comfy chairs under photos of the Duluth Eskimos and the Duluth Boat Club. Parking is tight, but it's worth the trouble. **MODERATE TO SPENDY**

Burger Joints*

A & Dubs

Lincoln Park, Duluth • 3131 W. 3rd St. • (218) 624-0198 • Open during the summer for lunch and dinner

Besides Gordy's Hi-Hat in Cloquet (see page 18), A & Dubs is the only drive-in restaurant left in the region. The menu teems with unbelievably underpriced burgers, coneys, shrimp, and steak and chicken sandwiches—all available solo or in a basket with fries and slaw. The crinkle-cut fries serve as another delicious reminder of days gone by. You won't find any vegetarian options at A & Dubs, but its deep fryer gets a workout, producing golden brown onion rings, potato wedges, cheese sticks, and chicken chunks. Besides the service, the real treat at A & Dubs is the homemade root beer, available by the mug, the quart, or the gallon. While Dukes baseball has left town, the Huskies have moved in, so you can still wash down a pregame meal at A & Dubs with a couple cold ones watching Duluth's boys of summer under the stars at Wade Stadium—a one-of-a-kind Duluth evening out.. **CHEAP!**

Big Daddy's

Piedmont Heights, Duluth • 2828 Piedmont Ave. • (218) 720-3181 • M–Sat. 6 A.M. - 7 P.M. / closed Sundays

Sadly, Ray's Place in Lakeside (home of the Big Ray Burger) closed its doors in October 2002. So we made an exception to our geographic bounderies to allow another "Big" burger man to fill the void. Big Daddy's may be located above Skyline, but it's locally owned and serves incredible burgers. The atmosphere is clean and sparse, with counter and booth seating, and Big Daddy has passed the decorating budget savings along to customers. Specialty burgers include a bacon-blue cheese burger and an olive burger—or test your limits with the Belly Buster: two half-pound patties with cheese, bacon, ham, and barbecue sauce. And the menu offers much more than just burgers, including golden brown, freshly made French fries and a meatloaf and mashed potato platter absolutely swimming in brown gravy—you'll think your momma is cooking in Big Daddy's kitchen. **CHEAP!**

*See also the Anchor Bar (page 109), Jim's Hamburgers (page 131), and T-Bonz (page 142).

Burger Joints, continued

My Buddy's Place
Downtown, Duluth • 220 W. Superior St. • (218) 722-5373 • M–Sat. 7 A.M. - 3 P.M. / closed Sundays

Home of the Charburger, Nick Petronas's Mr. Nick's was a staple of downtown Duluth. Then it closed, and a Burger King moved in (Petrona reportedly owns all the Burger Kings north of Hinkley). Then the Burger King closed, and so did the McDonald's across the street. Then, Mr. Nick's was back. Now it's gone again. In its place is My Buddy's Place, run by a member of the same family that operates Chef Yee's (see page 146). The new restaurant not only serves up a wide variety of burgers at reasonable prices for the lunch crowd (Buddy's closes the doors at 3 P.M.), but also offers quick and inexpensive breakfasts for the downtowner in a hurry. The decor isn't much to look at–kind of an incongruous rummage sale/sports bar hybrid–and the names of the "Buddies" the food is named after are so homogonized–Steve, Bob, Dave–that they don't exactly get you excited over your choices. Just ignore the half-baked marketing and enjoy the tasty food. **CHEAP!**

Ray's Grill
Irving (West Duluth), Duluth • 5610 Raleigh St. • (218) 628-1865 • T–Sat. 8 A.M. - 8 P.M. / M 8 A.M. - 1 P.M.

More than just another burger joint, Ray's Grill in West Duluth is sort of difficult to categorize. The menu reads like a diner's, but the interior looks like a neighborhood bar–and it was, up until the smoking ban. Even the biggest burger (the Big Boss Double) is less than half a sawbuck, but the menu doesn't stop with ground round. You can also get hot and cold sandwiches, coneys, and Polish and Italian sausage sandwiches. Daily specials include a roast beef dinner, and twice a week you can get all-you-can-eat spaghetti and meatballs (a family of four can stuff themselves silly for les than $20). The menu also has a few spendy items–including a 13-ounce steak–and some pretty atypical choices for a blue-collar eatery, such as mostaccioli and sausage topped with baked mozzarella cheese. A second dining room connects Ray's to the North Pole (see page 113). **CHEAP!**

Coneys!

Original Coney Island

Downtown, Duluth • 107 E. Superior St. • (218) 727-1077 • M–Sat. 6 A.M. - 11 P.M. / Sun. 8 A.M. - 9 P.M.

The Original Coney Island has been slinging chili sauce on top of skin-on, all-beef wieners in downtown Duluth since 1921, and they've gotten mighty good at it. Coneys are a bargain (99¢ on Wednesdays), and everything else on the menu is just as cheap (that goes for breakfasts, too, including biscuits & gravy). Besides coneys and breakfast, the Original offers bratwurst, Polish sausage, coney burgers, and chili. The Original's décor is a treat. Wood floors, tall wooden booths, and a bar-like counter complete with a brass footrail and bolted-down, high-back stools take diners back in time. (The oldies station on the radio and a 1959 wall menu advertising coneys for 25¢ and malts for 40¢ help, too.) Try your hand at the Bally's Skill-Roll game; if you score over 380 points, you win a free coney. **CHEAP!**

Coney Island Deluxe

Downtown, Duluth • 112 W. 1st St. • (218) 722-2772 • M–Sat. 6 A.M. - 9 P.M. / Sun. 8 A.M. - 8 P.M.

Part coney shop, part Greek grocery, the Coney Island Deluxe serves up good food at lunch counter prices that keep the downtown crowd happy. Besides coneys, burgers, and fries, Deluxe has a salad bar and also makes a mean gyros. Its Greek owners also stock feta cheese, kalamata olives, and other jarred and canned Greek delicacies for retail sale. Extremely clean and bright, Deluxe has plenty of booth, table, and counter seating. Its walls are adorned with large photos of Lake Superior ore boats and tugs, including a beauty of the *Edmund Fitzgerald*. And if the trophies are any indication, Deluxe once sponsored one heck of a bowling team. **CHEAP!**

So who makes the more authentic coney, Deluxe or Original? That's a matter of taste, but this may be telling to die-hard coney enthusiasts: Deluxe has another branch—in the Miller Hill Mall food court.

Downhome Diners

Jim's Hamburgers & Café

Central Hillside, Duluth • 502 E. 4th St. • (218) 727-9117 • M–Sat. 6 A.M. - 7 P.M. / Sun. 7 A.M. - 7 P.M.
Lincoln Park, Duluth • 2005 W. Superior St. • (218) 727-9400 • M–Sat. 6 A.M. - 7 P.M. / Sun. 7 A.M. - 7 P.M.

Jim's is a Duluth institution, and that has nothing to do with the brown-and-orange color scheme. With good ol' diner chow and no fuss made over the décor, Jim's passes the savings along to you (i.e., breakfasts–served any time–start at less than two bucks). Jim's has plenty of traditional diner options (even gravy for your fries), but the focus is hamburgers. You have your choice of quarter-, third-, or half-pound burgers, and if you take a seat at the counter, you can watch the cook fry them up. We do have one minor complaint about Jim's: even though its menu highlights burgers, you have to ask for the mustard, and they serve it to you in those little plastic packets. Few veggie options. **CHEAP!**

Joyce's Kitchen

Spirit Valley (West Duluth), Duluth • 5517 Grand Ave. • (218) 624-9798 • M–F 6 A.M. - 7 P.M. / Sat.–Sun. 8 A.M. - 3 P.M.

Joyce's has to be the epitome of old-fashioned home cookin' in Duluth. Let's put it this way: if you order the hot meatloaf sandwich with mashed potatoes, all you'll *see* when it arrives is a heaping plate full of gravy. Breakfast, lunch, or dinner, you won't pay much for a big meal, whether you order the baby beef liver, breaded veal, scalloped potatoes & ham, or the baked ribs with kraut. For around four bucks you can get a half-pound burger with fries or a grilled cheese sandwich with a full bowl of chili. The setting is also a classic–a sprawling lunch counter at its center completed by low stools with backs, jutting islands, and attached booths. More tables and booths surround the counter, providing additional seating. The only thing Joyce's Kitchen needs is new ceiling tiles. Very limited vegetarian options. **CHEAP!**

Downhome Diners, continued

Sunshine Café

Spirit Valley (West Duluth), Duluth • 5719 Grand Ave. • (218) 624-7013 • M–F 6 A.M. - 5 P.M. / Sat. 6 A.M. - 3 P.M. / Closed Sundays

A tiny diner in the heart of West Duluth, the Sunshine Café serves arguably the best breakfast in town. The diner itself claims to have the best omelettes in town, and everyone who's had one agrees. They start with up to three eggs and give diners a variety of options, including veggie, Denver, "everything," ham and cheese, and even corned beef hash. If eggs aren't your game, try the Swedish pancakes or come back at lunch time for a hot sandwich or burger with homemade fries or a complete dinner—roast beef, chicken, shrimp, etc. You'll find the Sunshine's décor clean but an odd mix, such as faux-brick wainscotting offset by wallpaper and a lamp near the counter that would look more at home in a 70s-era bachelor pad, but no one's complaining. The Sunshine proudly proclaims that it has been smoke free since before the ordinance. Some vegetarian choices. **CHEAP!**

Gallagher's Café d'Wheels

Lakeside, Duluth • 5231 E. Superior St. • (218) 729-7100 or 525-2282 • Daily 11 A.M. - 8 P.M.

Its location in the former Ray's Place makes Gallagher's Café d'Wheels your last chance for food before heading up the shore—the perfect spot to pick up picnic fare. In fact, Gallagher's is set up primarily for take out (hence the "d'Wheels"), offering home-cooked meals and boxed lunches for folks on the go, including entire families (they even offer holiday packages of roast turkey or baked ham with all the trimmings). You can also sit down and enjoy a meal in its clean, sunny dining area, but you'll have to wait on yourself—this here's a self-serve establishment (paper plates and plastic cutlery). The menu offers daily specials that rotate weekly, including everything from country fried steak to lasagna. Gallagher's also offers plenty of salad options and a variety of hot and cold sandwich choices, including beef burgers and a Mediterranian turkey burger. And you can satisfy your sweet tooth with their selection of desserts, from Jell-O with whipped cream to homemade pies. **CHEAP TO MODERATE**

Downhome Diners, continued

Billings Park Café
Billings Park, Superior • 1802 Iowa Ave. • (715) 394-6792 • M–F 11 A.M. - 7 P.M.

If you're looking for a real neighborhood café in a real neighborhood, get yourself over to Superior's Billings Park. The Billings serves good, simple food at simple prices—only the steak will cost you more than seven bucks. The menu features mostly burgers and hot sandwiches as well as some dinners, including a fish fry, barbecued ribs, and spaghetti. The café is home to the Big Izzy (a triple-patty cheeseburger) and the best patty melt in the Twin Ports, as far as we're concerned. The french fries are homemade, and you can even get a fried egg sandwich. Homey touches decorate the dining room, but the floral print curtains and paintings do little to off-set the browns and beiges of the tables, booths, and aged carpet. The friendly clientele and staff, however, more than make up for the earthy color scheme. Canned beer available. **CHEAP!**

East End Café
East End, Superior • 2209 E. 5th St. • (715) 398-3461 • Daily 6 A.M. - 8 P.M.

Located right next door to East End Hardware (a great neighborhood hardware store housed inside an old movie theater), the East End Café just about drips with local color. Its two large rooms are furnished with chairs and tables, and the plastic tablecloths are adorned with colorful prints in a variety of patterns. (The smoking section also has low counter dining.) Pretty much diner fare here, with hot and cold sandwiches, burgers, and basic breakfasts and dinners. For breakfast, you can order an egg, toast, and hash browns for less than two bucks or splurge and go for the three-egg ham-and-cheese omelette (about four bucks last time we checked). Dinners are equally inexpensive and range from burger baskets to an eight-ounce sirloin steak with soup and a salad or choice of potato. **CHEAP!**

Downhome Diners, continued

The Kitchen
North End, Superior • 803 N. 5th St. • (715) 392-4500 • M–Sat. 5:30 A.M. - 2 P.M.

The Kitchen is about as stripped down as a diner can be: simple tables and chairs, linoleum tile floors, paneled walls, and a ceiling with fans and fluorescent lighting. The only adornments come from a rather impressive collection of Marilyn Monroe memorabilia and the bleached skull of a long horn steer. But as far as diners go, simple equals good, and The Kitchen echoes that equation in its food. About the fanciest item on the menu is an omelette called the Nite Owl that includes ham, cheese, onions, peppers, tomatoes, and hash browns all wrapped inside three eggs. Breakfasts range from a simple eggs, toast, and hash browns combo to steak and eggs. For lunch and dinner (the Kitchen closes at 2 P.M.), you can order from a list of burgers, sandwiches, and baskets or complete dinners featuring roast beef, roast pork, pork cutlets, ham, or chicken. Have some pie for dessert, wear plaid flannel if you want to blend in, and expect to dine next to smokers. **CHEAP!**

Downhome Diners, continued

Louis' Café & Restaurant
Downtown, Superior • 1602 Tower Ave. • (715) 392-3058 • M–Sat. 24 hours / Sun. 12 A.M. - 9 P.M.

Although it has been operated by the same Greek family for three generations since either 1929 or 1946 (the menu gives conflicting stories), few local residents go to Louis' for its Greek cuisine. Most, in fact, go for the pancakes. Huge and tasty, there's something special about Louis' pancakes (nutmeg? cardamom?), and they offer lots of toppings. Louis' menu also serves up American and Greek fare, but you get the feeling they aren't exactly using old family recipes. Still, if you've got a hankering for moussaka, dolmades, or spanikopita, they're the only game in town. The café's décor follows the Greek theme, with white plastered walls and photos of Greece. Its doors remain open almost constantly, so add it to your mental list of late-night options. Good selection of veggie options. (There's another Louis' on London Road at 15th Avenue East in Duluth: same menu, but with all the atmosphere of a Perkins.) **MODERATE**

Uncle Louis' Café & Restaurant
Central Hillside, Duluth • 520 E. 4th St. • (218) 727-4518 • M–F 6 A.M. - 3:30 P.M. / Sat.–Sun. 7 A.M. - 3 P.M.

Over the past few years Uncle Louis' has become a favorite among Hillsiders and the weekend hangover crowd of hipsters and UMD students. Although it has no affiliation with Louis' in Superior (there was once a family connection), its pancakes are just as delicious—it has to be the same recipe—but less expensive. Same goes for the gyros/feta omelette and the rest of the breakfast menu. Lunch time at Louis' provides you with a variety of options, from burgers and sandwiches to dinner specials such as au gratin taters & ham, meat loaf, and roast turkey. Not many veggie options, but the grilled feta, raw onion, and tomato sandwich is tasty. The sign on the door may say Uncle Louis', but make no mistake: this is Penny's kitchen, where they say the food is so good "you'll think we stole your mom!" **CHEAP!**

Late Night Delights*

Frank's Fast 'n' Fresh Deli

North End, Superior • Inside the Hammond Spur at Hammond & 5th St. (base of the Blatnik Bridge) • M–Sun. 24 hours

Many folks discover Frank's after a night of drinking when, out of cigarettes, they pull into the Hammond Spur for cheap smokes before hopping on the Blatnik Bridge and heading back to Duluth. And that's just about perfect, because Frank's serves up an array of late-night gastronomic delights all deep-fried the same golden-brown hue and ready to help diners head off a hangover. Frank's late-night spread includes chicken breasts & wings, jalapeno poppers, mushrooms, cheese sticks, egg rolls, a vaguely Mexican treat called a tacito, mashed-potato balls, and chunky fried taters known as jojos. During the day you can get homemade unfried fare such as meatloaf and mac & cheese. Best of all, it's so cheap you can pay for it with change and crumpled one-dollar bills. **CHEAP!**

House of Donuts

Central Hillside, Duluth • 624 E. 4th St. • (218) 727-7421 • M–Th. 6 A.M. - 3 A.M. / F 6 A.M. 'til Sunday 3 A.M.

Affectionately known as the H.O.D., for years the Hillside's House of Donuts ("Open 24 hours, Sundays 'til 5") has been keeping smiles on the faces of college drinkers long after the bars have closed or the last keg has run dry. Despite its name, the H.O.D. is best known for its hot and cold subs, featuring mammoth amounts of meat stuffed into a hoagie roll and topped with big chunks of tomato, onion, and pickles–a sandwich served with a knife and fork. At $4.25, the 12-inch sub is the most expensive item on the menu. The H.O.D. also serves tacos, nachos, potato nuggets, and a burger & fries combo for just $3.25. And let's not forget the donuts: cake or raised, plain or glazed, they've got 'em all. Try a butter bar, named, we guess, because there must be an entire stick of butter in each one. **CHEAP!**

*See also Louis' Café & Restaurant (page 135) and Big Burrito (page 154).

Late Night Pizza*

Papa Don's Androy Restaurant

Downtown, Superior • 1213 Tower Ave. • (715) 392-8050 • 24 hours a day, 7 days a week

Papa Don's isn't set in the most family-friendly location. The Androy Hotel (and bar) has a reputation for serving those whose accomodation needs are sometimes monthly and (rumor has it) sometimes hourly. But that's not an issue if all you want is late night pizza. Papa Don's is open around the clock, so no matter when the bars close, it's open. The pizza is tasty, baked in brick ovens, and gimmick-free—no jalepeño-guacamole pizza here. The decor isn't much to look at—reddish-brown carpet, booths and tables, white walls adorned by a few antique photographs—but that hardly matters when you're hungry and need to refuel before crossing the bridge. Papa Don's menu also features diner fare such as breakfast, dinners, burgers, hot sandwiches, and appetizers. **CHEAP!**

Pizza Lucé

Downtown, Duluth • 11 E. Superior St. • (218) 727-7400 • M–F. 8 A.M. - 2 A.M. / SAT. & SUN 11 A.M. - 2 A.M.

Think Pizza Lucé is a Minneapolis transplant? Maybe so, but its roots are in Duluth. It was started by an Ely native who moved to Duluth in the mid-1980s and attended UMD before moving to Minneapolis and launching a restaurant. Located in the Tech Center (which some now call a "$20 million pizza place"), Pizza Lucé's interior is a visual treat, with a very large lift bridge anchoring a decidedly industrial look set off by local art and some murals by local artist Simon Gray. Oh, and the food's pretty good, too. Besides pizza (from tradtional to garlic mashed potato to spanish chicken), the "Looch" also serves other Italian fare and great hoagies—with many vegetarian and vegan selections. It also features a full bar and live music most nights. Try the bloody mary brunch with live music on Sunday mornings. **MODERATE**

*More pizza parlors on pages 142, 150–151

Soup, Sandwiches, & Coffee

Beaner's Central

Spirit Valley (West Duluth), Duluth • 324 N. Central Ave. • (218) 624-5957 • opens M–F 6:30 A.M., Sat. 8 A.M., Sun. 10 A.M. / closes between 9–11 P.M.

Much more than a coffee shop, Beaner's is a concert café that serves up gourmet coffees, chai, teas, a variety of unusual sodas, and even beer and wine along with great live music. They also offer tasty soups and panini and deli sandwiches (with veggie options) as well as muffins, scones, and cheesecake. Owners Jason and Anne Wussow have created an atmosphere unique to West Duluth, first by making their establishment more than an eatery—its stage and sound system are first rate, and the décor can't be beat—and then by inviting a variety of musicians who play anything from folk to reggae, rock to country, and just about everything in between. If you plan to see a show, come early so you can grab one of the comfy chairs near the windows. **CHEAP!**

Pepper McGregor's Coffeehouse & Café

Lakeside, Duluth • 4721 E. Superior St. • (218) 525-5016 • M–Th. 6 A.M. - 8 P.M. / F & Sat. 6 A.M. - 10 P.M. / Sun. 7 A.M. - 3 P.M.

A great little café in a great little neighborhood, Pepper McGregor's offers Lakeside residents (and visitors) a chance for more than pizza and burgers. Set in an old brick storefront, the café is clean and bright, with wooden tables and chairs surrounded by green, red, and yellow walls adorned with antique and reproduction signage (just a few—it is pleasantly uncluttered). McGregor's serves sweet treats, wraps, salads, soups, sandwiches, including a Rueben with raspberry mayonnaise and an incredible grilled cheese made with sharp cheddar, smoked gouda, and Swiss with grilled sun-dried tomatoes and chipotle mayo. Plenty of vegetarian choices, and specialty coffees that start with Alakef coffee, freshly roasted right in Duluth. An adjoining room features comfy couches and chairs surrounded by local art, and historic railroad trains roll by all day. They also have a great selection of antique, hand-carved coffee grinders for sale. **MODERATE**

Different Faces On Old Familiar Places

Mama Gets

North End, Superior • 525 Tower Ave. • (715) 395-6030 • M–Sat. 11 A.M. - 10 P.M. / Sun. 'til 9 P.M.

Berger Hardware (see page 253) was once a mecca for hardware enthusiasts, but has been vacant since closing its doors in the '90s. It has reopened as Mama Gets, and the new owners have done their best to preserve a bit of Twin Ports history. They've retained the worn wooden floors and turned offices into private dining rooms. Tables, booths, and a central bar dominate the interior, which is adorned by the original tin ceiling and old signage—including that of the old hardware store itself (even nail and screw bins have new life). Oh, and they serve darn good food, too. The fare is mostly appetizers and burgers, with some pasta and fish—including cajun prepared catfish and walleye tacos. Full bar and live music Wednesday through Saturday nights. It's simply a great place set in a not-so-great part of town. **MODERATE**

At Sara's Table / Chester Creek Café

Chester Park, Duluth • 1904 E. 8th St. • (218) 723-8569 • Daily 7 A.M. - 11 P.M. (M and T 'til 10 P.M.)

For years Chester Park residents relied on Taran's Market for groceries and Old World meats. Since closing, the market has been transformed into Taran's Marketplace, which houses At Sara's Table and the Chester Creek Café. While operating under two names, the new menu is the same for both establishments and is big on comfort food made with fresh, wholesome ingredients. It features sandwiches and soups and a few hot items—even organically raised beef burgers (there's still plenty of deli and vegetarian fare). Inside you'll find tin ceilings, comfortable seating in several sunny dining areas, a large stone fireplace to warm your bones over coffee in the winter, and an ample deck for enjoying the outdoors in summer. One of the dining rooms—the "reading room"—is decked out in comfy chairs surrounded by shelves and shelves of books—some for sale (both new and used). There's even a partial lake view. Who's Sara? She's a character in a novel by co-owner Barbara Naubert. **MODERATE**

Quick Lunches

Exchange Deli & Bakery

Downtown, Duluth • 301 W. 1st St. • (218) 727-8836 • M–F 6:45 A.M. - 4 P.M.

The Exchange plays on a little Duluth history as it serves the downtown crowd tasty morning treats and quick, inexpensive lunches. Located on the ground floor of the historic Board of Trade building (if for nothing else, stop by to admire the architecture), the Exchange's walls are adorned with photos of Duluth in days gone by and the stunning watercolors of famed Duluth painter Cheng Khee Chee. Even its menu reflects the town, with sandwiches named after neighborhoods, including the "East Ender" (veggies), the "Park Point" (95% fat-free ham), the "Morgan Park" (tender roast beef), and the "Gary-New Duluth" (hard salami and capicola). The sandwiches can be enjoyed with a cup of homemade soup or chili or a salad. The Exchange also offers a wide variety of bars, cookies, and muffins, and other baked sweets. **CHEAP!**

Holmes East End Bakery

East End, Superior • 2123 E. 5th St. • (715) 398-5523 • M–F 6 A.M. - 2 P.M. (lunch at 11 A.M.) / Sat. 6 A.M. - 12 A.M.

Essentially, Holmes is a tiny bakery that serves lunch—and it closes by two o'clock every afternoon, so it's not a place to grab a snack in the evening. Inside, a glass counter filled with bakery treats lines the left side of the store, and a lunch counter with low stool seating lines the right, creating a corridor to a few small tables in the rear. It's clean, bright, and simple. Simple, in fact, is a great way to describe the food. No frills here, just good eatin'. The lunch menu consists almost entirely of burgers and sandwiches on a plate with chips and pickles or in a basket with fries, onion rings, and a cookie. You can also enjoy homemade soup or chili, but we recommend saving room for some baked goodies. Holmes makes all sorts of bakery treats, from cookies and bars to turnovers and chocolate-iced cream puffs. **CHEAP!**

Gourmet to Go* (and catering)

Savories
Endion, Duluth • 5 S. 13th Ave. E. (Plaza Shopping Center) • (218) 625-5555 • M–Sat. 10 A.M. - 6 P.M.

Savories has served Duluth as a gourmet catering for some time, but it wasn't until the fall of 2001 that its owners opened a retail outlet near Leif Erickson Park. Besides catering for events of any size, Savories offers delicious sandwiches, salads, or complete dinners for individuals or entire families (dinners to go served from 4 P.M. to closing). Sandwiches include roast tenderloin, warm pastrami and Swiss, and a New York Reuben. Or try a field green salad or a caesar topped with lemon chicken. Dinners—which rotate weekly and offer a different meal every day—include chicken breast with roasted tomato and kalamata olive sauce served with crispy risotto cakes and a spinach soufflé. They also have lots of baked treats, including specialty desserts such as a triple-layer cheesecake. Pick up a movie at the video store next door for an indoor night out. **MODERATE**

Coco's to Geaux
Downtown, Duluth • 324 W. Superior St. • (218) 740-3039 • M–F 7 A.M. - 5 P.M. (lunch 11 A.M. - 1:30 P.M.)

Coco's to Geaux is the kitchen of chef Arlene Coco-Buscombe, a Louisiana native who derives her cooking style from Creole, Mediterranean, and Asian flavors. Coco-Buscombe's downtown shop in the former Miller's Cafeteria location serves lunch to the downtown business crowd cafeteria style, including soups, sandwiches, a variety of salads, and a random selection of hot meals. The rest of the day it sells premade items (spreads, pasta salads, etc.) from its deli case as well as desserts and specialty coffees. Coco's also offers lunch deliveries. Coco-Buscombe also owns Coco's Catering, which specializes in ethnic foods, and will travel to your home or cabin to help you throw a party. Occasional live music during the lunch hour. **MODERATE**

*See also Gallagher's Café d'Wheels, page 133.

Great Grub to Go

T-Bonz and Terry's Place (home of Pit Stop Pizza) are both neighborhood/sports bars located in Duluth's Lincoln Park neighborhood. They both make great bar grub, but since the smoking ban, they're no longer allowed to serve under their own roofs. Fortunately, their kitchens remain open, and you can order take-out and delivery. Both serve up pizza, burgers, and just about anything that will fit in a deep fryer. The food is good and the portions generous, but don't expect to find many vegetarian options at either location.

T-Bonz Grill & Pizza
Lincoln Park, Duluth • 2531 W. Superior St. • (218) 727-0020 • M–Sun. 11 A.M. - 11 P.M. (food)

T-Bonz specializes in big burgers and pizza. The burgers come in 1/3- and 2/3-pound sizes (except the T-Bonz Triple Cheese, which is a full pound) and are topped with everything from sour cream & onions to ham, mozzarella, and pineapple (The Hawaiian). The pizza is prepared in a traditional brick pizza oven and comes with your choices or in a variety of specials, such as the German Pizza (sausage, ham, kraut, and onions). T-Bonz also serves melts, sandwiches, wraps, and more appetizers than space allows us to list. **CHEAP!**

Pit Stop (located within Terry's Place)
Lincoln Park, Duluth • 2232 W. Superior St. • (218) 722-5900 • Sun.–M 11 A.M. - 11 P.M. / T–Th. 'til 12 A.M. / F & Sat. 'til 1 A.M.

Pit Stop serves everything from pizza to burgers and sandwiches to spaghetti and lasagna. The lunch specials change each week and range from sloppy joes (two of 'em with fries and slaw for under five bucks) to veal parmesan on a bed of pasta with garlic bread. The pizza is cheap and tasty, and Pit Stop delivers to anywhere in Duluth, including hotels. Is that PBS painter Bob "Happy Little Trees" Ross at the Terry's Place bar? Nope, Bob's dead—it's just his local look-alike. **CHEAP!**

Americana

Buena Vista

Top of the Hillside, Duluth • 1144 Mesaba Ave. • (218) 727-9047 • Every day 7 A.M. - 11 P.M.

It may look like an airport observation tower on the outside, but you'll forgive that as soon as you see the view the Buena Vista's dining room provides—after all, *buena vista* means "good view." Besides great scenery, the Buena offers full breakfast, lunch, and dinner menus. Dinners range from salads and burgers to pasta, steak, and seafood, including locally caught walleye and fish from Lake Superior. There's also a full children's menu, including their own "Sky High" pizza, and several vegetarian selections. You can enjoy a beer or a cocktail at the Buena or try something off their limited (but reasonably priced) wine list. Expect a wait on Sunday mornings—the brunch is quite popular. The Buena also has a lounge downstairs and an adjoining hotel. **MODERATE**

C.W. Chips

Central Hillside, Duluth • 610 E. 4th St. • (218) 727-9173 • M–Sun. 11 A.M. - 9 P.M.

C.W. Chips, at the site of the former Casa De Roma, is the latest in a string of bars and restaurants owned by Charlie Lemon. The restaurant's many small dining rooms, in fact, have been named for former Lemon establishments, such as the Bellows and Yellow Sub. The décor is a mix of Duluth history (old photos, newer paintings) patriotism (prints of the American flag through history) and Catholicism (photos of Pope John Paul II alongside a three-dimensional rendering of the Last Supper). The food is simple and modestly priced, and it must be good, because this is where a lot of Duluth's Finest take their dinner breaks. The menu offers lunch fare (burgers and sandwiches) and a wide range of dinners, including steaks, chicken, fish, and pasta. They even have some vegetarian options. Ask to be seated in a booth next to the back window—C.W. Chips provides a pair of binoculars for each window-side booth so diners can enjoy a closer view of the lake. **MODERATE**

Americana, continued

Eddie's

Itasca, Superior • 5221 E. 4th St. • (715) 398-0191 • T–Sat. 4 P.M. - 10 P.M. / Sun. 3 P.M. - 8 P.M.

Located next to the railroad yards in Superior's Itasca neighborhood, Eddie's restaurant may be the oldest eatery in Soup Town. When it changed hands a few years ago, the interior became a shrine to the automobile. Model cars line the backs of each booth, antique cans of motor oil weigh down shelves, and authentic auto advertisements cover the walls—so much memorabilia you'll be hard pressed to find a spot where your eyes can rest. The fare is very meat oriented: steak, chops, chicken, liver & onions, burgers, prime rib, and even a bacon-wrapped turkey tenderloin. They also serve fish and seafood, such as "walleyed" pike. But Eddie's specialty is barbecued ribs, at less than twenty bucks the most expensive item on the menu. Eddie's offers a simple wine list and serves liquor and beer (including brews from Duluth's Lake Superior Brewing Co.). Its smoking section boasts a full bar, which makes for a comfortable place to wait on busy nights. **MODERATE**

Hammond Steak House

North End, Superior • 1402 N. 5th St. • (715) 392-3269 • Sun.–Th. 5 P.M. - 9 P.M. / F & Sat. 5 P.M. - 10 P.M.

If you cross from Duluth to Superior on the High Bridge, the first place you encounter is the Hammond Steak House. An old-fashioned supper club like the kind your parents took you to when you were young, the Hammond is home to bread baskets, salad-dressing caddies, and cocktails served in high-ball glasses. The Hammond specializes in Angus beef, prime rib in particular. In fact, an entire menu page is made up of meat photos and a butcher's cow diagram showing various cuts. Besides prime rib and steaks, you'll find chicken, ribs and seafood, including lobster tail at market price. The décor is a mix of historic harbor photos and foliage—a birch tree dominates one of the dining rooms. The Hammond has a full bar and wine list, and there's a lounge downstairs adjoining a liquor store that claims to offer the cheapest off-sale in town. **MODERATE**

Americana, continued

Pickwick
Brewer's Creek, Duluth • 508 E. Superior St. • (218) 727-8901 • M–Sat. 11 A.M. - 1 A.M.

Duluth's oldest family-owned restaurant, Pickwick has been a Duluth staple since before it opened its doors in 1914. It actually first opened in 1888 as "The Saloon," and was part of the Fitger's Brewery. Employee Joseph S. Wisocki bought the place in 1918, when Prohibition made saloon ownership a losing proposition, and he turned it into the fine eatery it is today—in fact, his grandsons now run the place. Known for its meat and generous portions, the Pick's specialties include prime rib and a deep-fried pepper-cheeseburger. The Pick is also known for its atmosphere, including absolutely stunning woodwork. The dining rooms to the rear offer a view of Lake Superior, and its bar is also one of the nicest spots in town to enjoy a quiet drink. Prepare to spend some money: great food, service, and atmosphere add up. Vegetarians and vegans will be better served if they go next door and sup at Fitger's Brewhouse. **MODERATE TO SPENDY**

Shack Smokehouse & Grille
Billings Park, Superior • 3301 Belknap St. • (715) 392-9836 • M–Sun. 11 A.M. - 9 P.M.

If you're in the mood for big food, you're in the mood for the Shack. They serve up generous portions at reasonable prices in a supper club atmosphere, clean but not too fancy. The furnishings all look rather new and expensive, but look close and you'll see plywood and veneer here and there, and the gold-framed paintings look like they were purchased at Wal-Mart—but that hardly matters once you have a plate of food in front of you. At the Shack you'll find hearty sandwiches (er, Shackwiches), meal-sized salads, and lots of meat. Steak, ribs, liver, prime rib, chops, chicken, and plenty of fish and seafood (including surf-and-turf). The Shack has a full bar and wine by the glass or bottle. The only questionable item on the menu is the Cuban Chicken sandwich, which the menu says is made with Cajun chicken. **MODERATE TO SPENDY**

Asian

Cantonese House

Downtown, Duluth • 24 W. 1st St. • (218) 722-0778 • M–Th. 11 A.M. - 10 P.M. / F 'til 12 A.M. / Sat. 3 P.M. - 12 A.M.

Like most of Duluth's many Asian restaurants (the town has an abundance of them), the Cantonese House doesn't look like much on the outside, but walk through its doors and you'll find one of the cleanest, best-appointed eateries in town. The Yung family, which has operated the restaurant for more than 30 years, hails from Canton, so you can count on the recipes having authentic origins. The Cantonese House's menu lists both Cantonese and other popular Chinese dishes and wonderful family-sized combos that feed up to six people. No buffets here—everything is prepared fresh as it is ordered. And no "Chinese Zodiac" place mats either—even the plates are hand painted, a nice touch. Expect a wait on Friday nights. The Cantonese House serves some American fare but does not serve alcohol. **CHEAP! (LUNCH) TO MODERATE (DINNER)**

Chef Yee's

Downtown, Duluth • 319 W. 1st St. • (218) 722-3993 • M–Th. 11 A.M. - 9 P.M. / F 'til 10 P.M. / Sat. 12 P.M. - 10 P.M.

Known among the downtown lunch crowd as a great spot for a quick, inexpensive midday meal, Chef Yee's is home to one of the most popular lunch buffets in town. Between 11 A.M. and 2 P.M., diners plunk down about six bucks for as many trips through the line as their stomachs can handle (additional lunch specials available). At dinner time, Yee's offers diners a full array of Chinese cuisine, including specialties such as Imperial Beef in Mandarin sauce, Walnut Shrimp with lemon cream sauce, and Chow Champagne, a mix of lobster, barbecued pork, and chicken sautéed with mixed vegetables. There's also lots of vegetarian fare (like curry tofu or eggplant in garlic sauce), and beer and cocktails are available. Yee's dining room is rather small but very clean and comfy with large booths and tables and mural-covered walls. Limited delivery available. **CHEAP! (LUNCH) TO MODERATE (DINNER)**

Asian, continued

Chinese Dragon
Downtown, Duluth • 108 E. Superior St. • (218) 723-4036 • M–F 11 A.M. - 10 P.M. / Sat. 11:30 A.M. - 10 P.M.

For affordable Asian, the Dragon's prices can't be beat—but you'll have to get beyond the décor to enjoy the meal. Its tiny, all-but-windowless dining room off Superior Street is adorned with a mix of Asian clichés and country cabin chic. Paneled walls feature a rustic motif (game birds, deer, a farm house) dominated by large round dragon "welcome" medallions (no less than four of them). But if you came for good, inexpensive food, stop staring at the walls. The Dragon serves both Cantonese and Szechuan dishes and a wide variety of soups—egg drop, wonton, yecamin, hot & sour, etc.—at prices that can't be beat. The Dragon also has a better Asian spirits selection than other Duluth restaurants, serving everything from sake and plum wine to gekkeikan and wan-fu. It also serves beer. **CHEAP!**

Chinese Garden
Downtown, Duluth • 231 E. Superior St. • (218) 723-1866 • T–Sat. 11 A.M. - 10 P.M. / Sun. 11:30 A.M. - 10 P.M.

Located within the Hotel Duluth (Greysolon Plaza), the Chinese Garden provides an opportunity for modern diners to enjoy a meal in what was once a premiere hotel (see pages 82 and 246). It's also an opportunity to enjoy some pretty good Cantonese, Mandarin, and Szechuan dishes. The Garden's menu is absolutely vast, and you can choose from something as simple as chow mein to half a roast duck. The dinner combos make the Garden a great place for families, and lunch combos include an entrée, fried rice, soup, and your choice of appetizer. Placing a Chinese restaurant in a Classic-Revival hotel causes some clash in décor, none of which is helped by the blue-and-apricot plaid wallpaper. A dining room filled with beautiful, sturdy wooden tables and chairs and a fireplace decorated with Asian lanterns and wall dividers seems incongruent at first, but becomes charming by the time the meal arrives. Limited delivery available. **CHEAP! (LUNCH) TO MODERATE (DINNER)**

Asian, continued

Huie's Chopsticks Inn

Central Hillside, Duluth • 505 E. 4th St. • (218) 727-0820

M–Th. 11 A.M. - 9 P.M. / F 'til 10 P.M. / Sat. 2 P.M. - 10 P.M. / Sun. 4 P.M. - 9 P.M.

If you're still mourning the loss of the Chinese Lantern, it's time to stop your sobbin'. The restaurant may be gone, but its recipes are alive and well and come to life every day in the kitchen of Huie's Chopsticks Inn. Chef Ping Huie–nephew of Joe and cousin of Wing–was the head chef at the Lantern for 20 years until it burned down. He now serves the same great food on the Hillside in a stripped-down, cozier atmosphere than the Lantern's. Ping specializes in cuisine from four different regions: Canton, Mandarin, Shanghai, and Szechuan (Hunan) at reasonable prices. Ping has been talking about retiring, so if you miss the Lantern, you better get to Huie's before it's too late. Limited delivery available. **CHEAP! (LUNCH) TO MODERATE (DINNER)**

Jade Fountain

Spirit Valley (West Duluth), Duluth • 305 Central Ave. • (218) 624-4212

M–Th. 11 A.M. - 11 P.M. / F 'til 12 A.M. / Sat. 4 P.M. - 12 A.M. / Sun. 3 P.M. - 10 P.M.

Although Duluth is chock full of Asian eateries, the Jade Fountain alone serves the western side of town. The Fountain's huge menu covers all the Chinese basics and then some–all under $10 unless they involve shrimp or lobster–and includes American fare. Its two dining rooms are decorated with reds and golds typical of Chinese restaurants, but the back dining room's mix of red neon and dark paneling takes some getting used to. The Fountain takes great pride in its bar, featuring cocktails stirred up by its "master mixologists." They proudly pour ice-cream drinks, after-dinner liqueurs, and house specialties such as a Golden Cadillac, Cucumber Cocktail, Foxy Lady, and French Goddess. The Fountain's inexpensive lunch buffet is even cheaper for seniors and children. Limited delivery available. **CHEAP! (LUNCH) TO MODERATE (DINNER)**

Asian, continued

Lan-Chi's
Downtown, Superior • 1320 Belknap St. • (715) 394-4496 • M–Th. 11 A.M. - 10 P.M. / F & Sat. 11 A.M. - 11 P.M. / Sun. 12 P.M. - 10 P.M.

Lan-Chi's serves generous portions of tasty Vietnamese, Chinese (mostly Mandarin and Cantonese), and American food for prices easier to swallow than even the most delicate egg drop soup. Most lunch specials, which include an entrée, fried rice, and an egg roll, cost about five bucks, and most dinners are priced under ten. Another impressive aspect of Lan-Chi's is the décor. Its large, bright dining room is festooned with colorful garlands, window coverings, and Chinese lanterns—and silk flowers await diners at each booth and table. Oddly enough, the walls also display framed arrangements of Minnesota Twins and Milwaukee Brewers baseball cards from days long past. Limited delivery available. **CHEAP!**

Thai Krathong
Downtown, Duluth • 114 W. 1st St. • (218) 733-9774 • M–Th. 11:30 A.M. - 9 P.M. / F 'til 10 P.M. / Sat. 12 P.M. - 10 P.M.

The only Thai restaurant north of the Twin Cities, Thai Krathong has been a welcome change for Duluth diners since it opened its doors in 2000. The menu contains all you would hope for and expect from a Thai eatery—phad thai, chicken, beef, tofu, and seafood mixed with combinations of chilis, cilantro, mint, ginger, basil, coconut milk, peanut sauce, or red curry—and each entrée comes with steamed jasmine rice. Thai Krathong even offers Tom Yum and Tom Kha, soups so special the restaurant serves them as entrées (Beef Guiteo and Seafood Guiteo served on Saturdays during lunch only). Thai Krothong offers lunch time diners a fantastic buffet for about ten dollars. A variety of appetizers are available, as well as beer, wine, and jasmine tea. The dining room décor borders on elegant, as chandeliers, wall sconces, and candles provide soft light that reflects off the white linen table cloths to help create an intimate dining experience. **MODERATE TO SPENDY**

Indian / Italian (Pizza*)

India Palace

Downtown, Duluth • 319 W. Superior St. • (218) 727-8767 • Dinner: Sun.–Th. 5 P.M. - 9 P.M.; F & Sat. 5 P.M. - 10 P.M. Lunch Buffet: M–F 11:30 A.M. - 2 P.M.

You won't find another Indian restaurant north of the Twin Cities, and you'll find few eateries in Duluth as well appointed as the India Palace. The menu features a wide variety of lamb, chicken, beef, seafood, and vegetarian entrées including tandoori, rogan, tikka masala, and absolutely exquisite curries. The authentic cuisine is complemented by an elegant yet informal atmosphere created by Indian tapestries hung against brick walls. The wood trim and ceiling beams are painted a creamy pink, very appropriate for an Indian restaurant (pink in India is considered formal, like navy blue in the western world). India Palace also serves wine, imported beers, chai, and authentic Indian desserts. The lunch buffet is outstanding. **MODERATE TO SPENDY**

The Bulldog Pizza & Grill

Duluth • Mount Royal Shopping Center • (218) 728-3663 • M–Th. 9 A.M. - 10 P.M. / F & Sat. 9 A.M. - 11 P.M. / Sun. 10:30 A.M. - 10 P.M.

In 1986 Ken Wright dropped out of UMD to fill a need for his fellow Bulldogs—an eatery close to the campus with food they could enjoy and afford. Since that time, Ken and his wife Sue have grown The Bulldog into one of Duluth's favorite family restaurants. The Bulldog specializes in pizza and makes both a thick crust and its original, cracker-like thin crust—both cooked in traditional brick pizza ovens. You can order from a selection of traditional toppings or try one of their specialty pizzas, such as barbecued chicken, vegetarian alfredo, Mediterranean pesto pie, or taco. The Bulldog also serves burgers and other hot sandwiches, subs (another one of their specialties), and an assortment of pasta dishes. **MODERATE**

*See also T-Bonz and Pit Stop (both on page 130) and Pizza Lucé (page 137).

Italian (Pizza)

Sammy's Pizza

Downtown, Duluth • 103 W. 1st St. • (218) 727-8551 • call for hours
Lakeside, Duluth • 4631 E. Superior St. • (218) 525-6604 • call for hours
Spirit Valley (West Duluth), Duluth • 403 N. Central Ave. • (218) 628-2327 • call for hours
Woodland, Duluth • 4011 Woodland Ave. • (218) 724-1277 • call for hours
Downtown, Superior • 1309 Tower Ave. (back of the Elbo Room) • (715) 392-6292 • call for hours

The Perrella family started Sammy's as a small café in Keewatin, Minnesota, in the 1950s before opening as a pizzeria in Hibbing. They have since opened many more stores—most in Duluth—plus shops in Wisconsin and North Dakota. For this, we almost had to omit them from the book, citing our "no chains" criterion. But then we found out that a member of the Perrella family runs the show at every Sammy's location. And besides that, Sammy's Pizza is a tradition in these parts, and they pride themselves on home cooking, fair prices, and good service. A great place for the family and a variety of menu options in stores with seating. **CHEAP!**

Vintage Italian Pizza

Chester Park, Duluth • 1830 E. 8th St. • (218) 728-4411 • Sun.–Th. 'til 11:30 P.M. / F & Sat. 'til 12:30 A.M.
Downtown, Superior • 1222 Tower Ave. • (715) 392-5555 • Sun.–Th. 'til 11:30 P.M. / F & Sat. 'til 12:30 A.M.

No dining room at V.I.P., just pick-up or delivery. Still, many believe it to be about the best pie in the Twin Ports. Cooked in stone ovens, V.I.P.'s pies come in a variety of styles, so you can get gourmet toppings at pizzeria prices. You can order everything from a pepperoni with extra cheese to a "Pizza No. S-1302," which places spinach, ricotta, provolone, mozzeralla, and a touch of dill on a pizza shell brushed with olive oil pesto. Many, many other specialty pies are available, and they all come on traditional, deep dish, or whole wheat crust. Save a little money: order your pie uncooked and bake it at home. **CHEAP!**

Italian

The Elbo Room

Downtown, Superior • 1309 Tower Ave. • (715) 392-6292 • T–F 11 A.M. - 10 P.M. / Sat. 4 P.M. - 10 P.M.

If you have difficulty making up your mind, give yourself plenty of time to order at the Elbo Room. The menu is absolutely huge and includes *all* your Italian and American favorites, including prime rib. The Elbo Room also offers a fine selection of fish, including salmon, halibut, Lake Superior trout, and mahi mahi. The spaghetti sauce is made with meat, so vegetarians will want to ask for the marinara sauce (it costs more, but it is *much* tastier than the regular). The restaurant's main dining room is decorated with well-rendered fresco-like paintings in an Italian villa theme. Its lounge (a full bar, including a few microbrew selections) and smoking section have richly stained wood panels, deep, comfy booths, and low lighting. The Elbo Room also serves Sammy's Pizza (see page 151). **MODERATE**

The Italian Village

Spirit Valley (West Duluth), Duluth • 301 N. Central Ave. • (218) 624–2286 • T–F 10 A.M. - 5:30 P.M. / Sat. 9:30 A.M. - 3:30 P.M.

The Italian Village bills itself as "An Authentic Taste of Italy" and does not disappoint. This quaint little spot is a deli, cappuccino bar, and gourmet shop all in one, featuring homemade and imported goods that are the real thing. In the deli case you'll find homemade Italian sausage (regular and *hot!*), lasagna, and pizza along with a host of imported meats and cheeses like prosciutto, pancetta, parmesan reggiano, and fontanella. The shop's grocery shelves hold imported olive oils, pastas, roasted red peppers, polenta, and other delizioso items. If you stop by on a Saturday morning you can sample a variety of Italian treats that will tempt your palette and your pocketbook. You can also enhance your vocabulary by taking note of the Italian phrase of the week posted in the window. **MODERATE**

"Italian"

We've placed the word *Italian* between quotation marks above because although both eateries below call themselves Italian restaurants, we doubt true aficionados of Italian fare would agree. That's not to say the food isn't tasty, but its authenticity as Italian is questionable. We almost placed these two in the "Nightlife" chapters, since the restaurants of both are found within the walls of two great Duluth neighborhood bars.

The Gopher Lounge
Spirit Valley (West Duluth), Duluth • 402 N. Central Ave. • (218) 624-9793 • M–W 8 A.M. - 6 P.M. / Th.–Sat. 'til 8 P.M. / Sun. 'til 3 P.M.

The Gopher officially opens at 8:00 A.M., but according to the waitress, it's "whenever the cook gets here." You'll find the same casual attitude inside the Gopher, a West Duluth fixture. Primarily a bar, the Gopher offers a limited menu, specializing in spaghetti and other Italian fare, including lasagna, rigatoni, and even veal parmesan. A variety of American items, such as steak, shrimp, and liver & onions, is also available (steak and shrimp combo for $14). The Gopher also has burgers, appetizers, sandwiches, and serves breakfast. **CHEAP!**

Tappa Keg Inn
Norton Park, Duluth • 7036 Grand Ave. • (218) 624-9881 • M–F 11 A.M. - 11 P.M. / Sat.–Sun. 9 A.M. - 11 P.M.

The name may sound like something thought up by a bunch of drunken frat boys, but the Tappa Keg Inn is one of those little places that regulars don't mind keeping to themselves. Besides the usual bar fare of burgers, sandwiches, and appetizers, the Tappa serves American and Italian dinners (featuring homemade marinara sauce). Aside from steak, chicken, and chops, diners can choose jumbo beef ravioli, fettuccini alfredo, and "Spaghetti Dick's Way," topped with sautéed mushrooms, onions, and green peppers. Its location makes the Tappa Keg Inn the perfect place to fill up after a day of biking the Munger Trail. **CHEAP!**

Mexican

Hacienda Del Sol

Downtown, Duluth • 319 E. Superior St. • (218) 722-7296 • M–Sat. 11 A.M. - 11 P.M.

Since owner Kevin Deutsch opened its doors in 1982, this tiny café in Old Downtown has been serving up tasty Mexican-style food at rock-bottom prices, and it has long been a local favorite (the only complaint most folks have is that the Hac is closed Sundays). The menu features a variety of tacos, burritos, enchiladas, tostadas, killer nachos, and chile rellenos. The staff prepares all the food on site, including the chips and salsa. The mild salsa is mild (and, frankly, so is the medium), but the hot—a green sauce—is truly hot. During the summer, customers dine among murals featuring Mayan and Aztec themes in the restaurant's courtyard (but no view of the big lake). The theme continues inside, where you'll find wooden booths and a lunch counter. Currently the restaurant serves a wide variety of Mexican and domestic beers, sangria, and an assortment of soft drinks. A renovation (currently underway) will include upstairs dining and lounge with full bar, and an outdoor deck with a lake view. **CHEAP!**

Big Burrito

Downtown, Superior • 809 Tower Ave. • (715) 395-6033 • M–Th. 11 A.M. - 9 P.M. / F 'til midnight / closed weekends

If you can get past the fast-food feel of the tiny dining room and the paper plates and cups and plastic cutlery, you're in for a big treat at the Big Burrito. What happens after a Mexican-American from West St. Paul (and his East Side St. Paul bride) finishes his work painting the Blatnick Bridge? Why, he and his wife use family recipes to open a restaurant, of course. The burritos are mighty big and mighty tasty and range from green chile verde to red chile to steak and on to chorizo (no chicken until they get a bigger refrigeration unit). The menu also includes tacos (even deep fried), nachos, taquillos, tostadas, and enchiladas—and the rice and beans sides can't be beat. The owners plan to open another in restaurant in Cloquet with more formal service. **CHEAP!**

Bakery Goods to Go

European Bakery
Downtown, Duluth • 109 W. 1st St. • (218) 722–2120 • M–Th. 8 A.M. - 5:30 P.M. / F 7:30 A.M. - 5:30 P.M. / Sat. 8 A.M. - 3 P.M.

Besides European baked goods, the European Bakery features a mini grocery stocked with items from a variety of European countries. You'll find Hungarian stuffed red peppers, Croatian nougat wafer cookies, and canned mackerel salad along with plenty of good old fashioned American-style bakery fare.

Lakeside Bakery
Lakeside, Duluth • 4509 E. Superior St. • (218) 525-9988 • W–Sat. 6 A.M. - 5:30 P.M.

The Gustafson family operated Lakeside Bakery from the 1950s to 2003, serving a selection of Swedish baked goods, such as kringles flavored with plenty of cardamom. New owners plan to keep the tradition alive.

Positively 3rd Street Bakery
Hillside, Duluth • 1202 E. 3rd St. • (218) 724-8619 • M–F 8 A.M. - 5:30 P.M. / Sat. 10 A.M. - 4 P.M.

Home of the renowned Thunder Cookie, Positively 3rd Street is an employee-owned co-op that serves up the best organic baked treats around. From granola, bagels, and breads to blueberry bars, muffins, and the biggest and best cookies around, you can count on the folks at 3rd Street to bake with only the best ingredients.

Billings Park Bakery
Billings Park, Superior • 1827 Iowa Ave. • (715) 394-7213 • M–Sat. 6 A.M. - 6 P.M.

This tiny bakery makes all sorts of breads and baked treats, including a most delicious chocolate bavarian cream strudel. Yum.

Twin Ports Coffee Shops*

Browser's N'eTc. Cafe

Downtown, Duluth • 201 E. Superior St. • (218) 726-0530 • M–F 7:30 A.M. - 12 A.M. / Sat. 9 A.M. - 12 A.M. / Sun. 9 A.M. - 9 P.M.

A full-service coffee house with coffees, teas, chai, and sodas inside the Temple Opera Building, Browser's also has computers with high-speed internet connections and lots of big windows and comfy couches and chairs.

Coffee Zone

Downtown, Duluth • 31 W. Superior St. • (218) 720-4444 • M–F 7 A.M. - 5 P.M.

Located next to its sister company, the Comfort Zone, the Coffee Zone offers you a chance to get all hopped up on caffeine and then relax with a massage, or vice versa.

Jitters

Downtown, Duluth • 102 W. Superior St. • (218) 720-6015 • M–Sat. 7 A.M. - 7 P.M. / Sun. 8 A.M. - 5 P.M.

No gimmicks at Jitters, just quality coffee, teas, and chai and a bit to eat on weekdays, including soups, sandwich wraps, and lots of pastries. A great spot for hot cocoa during the Christmas City of the North Parade.

Northwoods Coffee & Guitars

Downtown, Superior • 1828 Tower Ave. • (715) 399-0979 • M–F 7 A.M. - 7 P.M. / Sat. 8 A.M. - 5 P.M.

Superior's gourmet coffee and sandwich shop also features guitar sales, repairs, and lessons. Local folk and blues musicians have made it a second home, and you can even join in their regular cribbage tournaments.

*See also At Sarah's Table (page 139), Beaner's (page 138), Lakeview Coffee (page 220), Pepper McGregor's (page 138).

Neighborhood Markets

Bay Side Market

Park Point, Duluth • 1901 Minnesota Ave. • (218) 727-7635 • Daily 7 A.M. - 8 P.M.

Living on Park Point has its trade-offs. The most expensive real estate in town is also about the most inconvenient location, as residents must contend with raised bridges and busy tourist traffic each time they leave the house. That's why the Bay Side Market is one of the best-loved places around. A complete grocery, with fresh produce, meat, dairy, and canned goods, Bay Side even sells gas and meets your other convenience needs.

Little John's 4th Street Market & Deli

Central Hillside, Duluth • 102 E. 4th St. • (218) 727-3811 • Daily 8 A.M. - 11 P.M.

The owner may have a diminutive nickname, but he does things in big style, serving the needs of local residents as the last neighborhood grocer on the Hillside. John's has produce, canned goods, fresh meat and dairy, and a deli with a surprising amount of selections. John's also fills all your convenience store needs, from smokes to movie rentals.

Romano's Grocery

Downtown, Duluth • 231 E. Superior St. • (218) 722-5256 • M–F 7 A.M. - 6 P.M. / Sat. 8 A.M. - 5 P.M.

Romano's Grocery, housed in the first-floor corner of Greysolon Plaza (the former Hotel Duluth), has served downtown residents for more than 20 years. The tiny store—more a convenience store with produce than a full-fledged grocery—was once a liquor store and, before that, a café. Today, many of its customers arrive via the elevator, as the hotel (now Greysolon Plaza) contains 150 senior apartments.

Specialty Grocers*

First Oriental Grocery (a.k.a. Duluth Oriental Grocery)
Downtown, Duluth • 323 E. Superior St. • (218) 726-0017 • M–Sat. 10 A.M. - 6 P.M.

If you need authentic ingredients for cooking up Asian meals, make your way to the First Oriental Grocery. Inside, you'll find items unavailable anywhere else in town (or the region, we wager). Its shelves are packed tight with everything from special varieties of rice to dried squid, and its selection of teas—especially green teas—is the best in town. Besides food, you can also find rice steamers, tea servers, and other kitchen needs.

Fichtner's Sausage & Meats
Downtown, Duluth • 134 W. 1st St. • (218) 722-2661 • M–F 8:30 A.M. - 5:30 P.M. / Sat. 8 A.M. - 3 P.M.

Fichtner's has been a downtown staple for four decades, three of them at its current location. A long glass case filled with all manner of meat products, including Fichtner's homemade sausages and hams, runs the length of the shop. They also offer a selection of grocery basics, such as dairy products, eggs, bagged chips, soda, barbecue sauces, and bread and buns from the European Bakery. Munch on a giant dill pickle from the big jar on the deli case while you browse the shop, finding everything you need for an impromptu picnic or barbecue.

Whole Foods Co-op
East Hillside, Duluth • 1332 E. 4th St. • (218) 728-0884 • M–F 7 A.M. - 9 P.M. / Sat. & Sun. 8 A.M. - 8 P.M.

Whether you're a vegan, a vegetarian, or just a health-concerned consumer, this complete organic grocery and deli has all sorts of produce and dry and frozen goods to meet your needs. The deli serves up tasty sandwiches, spreads, and homemade soups. The store planned to move before we went to press, so call ahead.

*See also the Italian Village (page 152).

Farmers' Markets

Duluth Farmers' Market

East Hillside, Duluth • Corner of 14th Ave. E. and 3rd St. • (218) 724-9955 • Wed. & Sat., 7 A.M. - Noon

Operated by the Duluth Market Gardeners' Association, the Duluth Farmers' Market gives local farmers of organic and traditionally grown produce a chance to bring their harvest directly to consumers looking for food that hasn't spent a month on a truck. You'll find every kind of vegetable that grows this far north plus plenty of local berries, especially blueberries and raspberries. And there's more than just good food. The market opens each spring the weekend before Mother's Day—when its stalls are filled with annual and perennial bedding plants—and sells produce through the end of October. It reopens for a few weeks in November and December to sell Christmas trees.

UMD Farmers' Market

UMD Campus, Duluth • Outside Kirby Plaza, Kirby Place, UMD • (218) 726-7258 • Wednesdays from 2 P.M. until sold out

Despite its location underneath the University of Minnesota Duluth's Resident Hall Dining Center, the food at the UMD Farmers' Market is fresh, locally produced, and won't add fifteen pounds to your frame during the first two months of your freshman year. And you don't have to be a UMD student to enjoy it, either—everyone is welcome. The market opens every Wednesday starting in mid-May and runs until the end of September. You'll find organic and traditionally grown vegetables and fruit produced by local farmers and gardeners, most of whom belong to the Sustainable Farmers' Association. Annual and perennial bedding plants and some house plants are also for sale. To find the market, take College Street or St. Marie Street to Kirby Place (formerly Oakland Avenue) and turn onto the UMD campus.

North Shore

New Scenic Café
Scenic 61 • 5461 North Shore Dr. (Scenic Highway 61) • (218) 525-6274 • M–F 11 A.M. - 9 P.M.

The New Scenic might just be the North Shore's worst kept secret. During the summer, expect to wait to be seated—even on a Sunday afternoon. The cost is a bit more than visitors to the area are used to, but the cuisine is upscale and many consider it the best around. The menu includes such nonregional delights as cilantro-pesto shrimp with couscous, pan-seared Chilean sea bass with saffron broth, and Indian masala vegetable curry with pineapple. The Scenic also serves a variety of salads and appetizers, including their incredible artichoke slather (mighty tasty, trust us). You'll find a good selection of beer (including Guinness in a nitro can) and a well-thought-out wine list. The Scenic also serves locally roasted Alakef Coffee. Many vegetarian choices. **MODERATE TO SPENDY**

Shorecrest Supper Club
Scenic 61 • 5593 North Shore Dr. (Scenic Highway 61) • (218) 525-2286 • 11:30 A.M. - 8 P.M. (Summer opens 8 a.m. Sat. & Sun.)

The Shorecrest Supper Club is like one of those country supper clubs you find about twenty miles from the family cabin—at once upscale and down-home—except it's on the shore of Lake Superior less than twenty miles from downtown Duluth. In the summer, the Crest opens for breakfast, lunch, and dinner (it closes for a time during the winter months), offering customers American fare that includes plenty of fish and seafood. Trout, broiled walleye, fried fillet of herring, fried shrimp, lobster, and Alaska king crab all grace the menu, but the Crest's specialty is its 16-ounce porterhouse steak. Simple décor—coffee motif tablecloths cover steel and formica tables—and a full bar. Very few vegetarian options. Opens at 8 A.M. on weekends during the summer to serve breakfast. **MODERATE**

North Shore, continued

Russ Kendall's Fish House
Knife River, MN • 149 North Shore Dr. (Scenic Highway 61) • (218) 834-5995 • M–Sun. 9 A.M. - 6 P.M.

Russ Kendall's father opened the fish house in 1924 after his truck broke down and he had to sell his smoked fish from the side of the road. Russ bought the place in 1952, and his fish has been a North Shore favorite ever since. Kendall's shop has evolved into a fish house/deli/thrift store/museum hybrid over the years, selling goods that range from picnic supplies (crackers, cheeses, drinks, etc.) to antique postcards from around the world. The back room is a treat for the eye, with paintings, old photos, and bric-a-brac everywhere (some for sale, some not). If the weather isn't cooperating for a picnic, Russ has seating available inside. But it's the fish that keeps people coming in, and Russ specializes in maple-smoked trout, ciscoes, salmon, whitefish, and bluefin. If Russ's place looks busy, his brother Smokey's is just up the road, as is Mel's Fish. Russ's may be the most popular, but folks still argue over whose is best. **MODERATE**

Emily's Inn, Deli, & General Store
Knife River, MN • 218 North Shore Dr. (Scenic Highway 61) • (218) 834-5922 • M–Sun. 8 A.M. - 9 P.M. (limited winter hours)

Emily Erickson opened her inn and eatery in 1929 in a building that was once a general store, serving traditional Scandinavian meals that reflected her heritage (Emily emigrated from Norway when she was 12). Her grand-daughter Carol now runs the store, which has become increasingly popular over the past few years. Perhaps it's the building's charming authenticity, but it probably has a lot to do with the food. Sandwiches, salads, soups, and desserts grace the menu at Emily's. Choices include wild rice cheese soup, Swedish pea soup, smoked fish appetizer, chili with Italian sausage, and grilled Lake Superior trout or salmon. The salads—including wild rice chicken and smoked trout—are especially good. You can even get a meat loaf sandwich, and every Friday from February to October Emily's hosts a fish boil. **MODERATE**

North Shore, continued

Judy's Café

Two Harbors, MN · 623 7th Ave. · (218) 834-4802 · Daily 5 A.M. - 8 P.M.

Like Bayfield across the lake, Two Harbors has become a tourist town. Driving down 7th Avenue in Two Harbors, it seems that every other storefront is now home to an antique store or a cleverly named restaurant. Judy's Café opens at five in the morning, so you know they don't cater solely to the tourist crowd. A simple, single-room diner, Judy's makes breakfast all day long, serving local residents and visitors alike. You'll find plenty of options on the menu, from typical diner burgers and sandwiches to complete dinners such as steak, veal, and walleye. Judy's also has something you wouldn't expect on a diner menu—Asian stir fry. Try a muffin or a piece of pie— they're homemade, and the selection changes daily. The décor, including industrial tables and chairs, lacks imagination compared to their great tin ceiling. **CHEAP!**

Northern Lights

Beaver Bay, MN · 1040 Main St. · (218) 226-3102 · M–Sat. 11 A.M. - 9 P.M. / Sun. 9 A.M. - 9 P.M.

If you're looking for a taste of the north woods, look no further than Northern Lights. The menu features regional fish (smoked salmon, pan-fried Lake Superior herring, and excellent fish cakes), big game (smoked elk, barbe-cued bison, caribou pot pie), and fantastic fowl (smoked breast of goose sandwich, smoked pheasant and duck). They also make some of the finest wild rice soup in the region and host a big buffet brunch on Sundays. Vegetarian options are increasing. The décor matches the menu—canoes and dog sleds hang from the ceilings, and walls are covered with pelts and mounts of a variety of animals. If you're thirsty, Northern Lights offers over 40 imported and domestic beers, including a fine selection of microbrews in bottles and on tap. During the sum-mer, diners can enjoy a meal from the screen porch/deck or the double-decker bus that is both a beer garden and an ice cream shop. **MODERATE TO PRICEY**

North Shore, continued

Beaver River Deli

Beaver River, MN • 1012 Main Street (Highway 61) • (218) 226-3373 • Hours unavailable, but open daily for lunch

This tiny deli is the perfect place to grab something to go and take it with you to a picnic spot along the shore or along a river bank. Located in downtown Beaver Bay, the Beaver Bay Deli is a bright little spot illuminated by skylights that serves wonderful sandwiches and homemade soups. Sandwiches are served hot or cold and include a muenster and homemade pesto, a grilled Reuben (or Rachel with smoked turkey instead of corned beef), and the Split Rock for the vegetarian: tomato, sprouts, and fresh basil grilled with two kinds of cheese. All sandwiches are served with french fries or soup (or chips with your choice of cole slaw or potato salad). They also serve grilled chicken, burgers, and appetizers such as cheese curds and tempura onion rings. If it's raining, eat inside at one of only four tables surrounded by iron "ice-cream-parlor" chairs. Many vegetarian options. **CHEAP!**

Northwoods Café

Silver Bay, MN • 6 Shopping Center • (218) 226-3699 • M–Sat. 6 A.M. - 7 P.M. / Sun. 6 A.M. - 6 P.M.

Although it is located within a shopping center, Northwoods Café is a true small town diner. Local residents young and old sporting seed caps and Twins hats (or camouflage in the fall) gather each morning to discuss events both local and worldwide—some even have their own tables. Northwoods is a big place, with two dining rooms that can seat up to 150 people, but its customers and décor—comfy booths and prints of outdoor scenes—give it a cozy feeling. Let's put it this way: it's the kind of place where the Tabasco never leaves the table. The food is all you would expect, including biscuits & gravy for breakfast. Northwoods serves breakfast (including the "Stacker": hash browns with bacon or sausage covered in cheese), lunch (burgers and such), and complete dinners (steak, fish, chops, chicken). They also serve beer and wine. Breakfast ends at 11 A.M. **CHEAP!**

North Shore, continued

Superior Outlook Grill & Saloon

Milepost 60 on Highway 61 • (218) 226-6492 • Daily 7:30 A.M. - 9:30 P.M. (kitchen closes at 7:30 P.M.)

Located at the intersection of Highway 61 and Highway 1, Superior Outlook is a clean (smoke free!), bright little restaurant with wooden furniture and knotty-pine walls covered in wildlife prints and mounted game birds. The menu features everything from appetizers to complete dinners, with lots of sandwiches and burgers in between. Dinners include breaded fish, chicken, lemon-pepper salmon, steak, and burgers. The Outlook also serves a good, cheap breakfast, including the Superior breakfast of two eggs, toast, hash browns, and sausage or bacon. Behind the beautiful polished-wood bar, you'll find a couple of domestic beers on tap plus a good selection of domestics, imports, and microbrews, including Red Hook, Newcastle, and selections from Duluth's Lake Superior Brewing Company. **CHEAP TO MODERATE**

Satellite's Country Inn

Schroeder, MN • Milepost 72 on Highway 61 • (218) 663-7574 • M–F 6 A.M. - 9 P.M. / weekend hours unavailable

The only problem with Satellite's Country Inn is the fact that you can easily drive by without noticing it. Satellite's sits on the landward side of the highway in the middle of a sprawling dirt parking lot and assorted outbuildings. The building itself looks more like someone's house; understandable, since it is someone's house, as the décor and layout inside attest. Many North Shore travelers say don't let the looks fool you—try the food before you make any assumptions. Besides a full breakfast menu (some say the best along the shore), Satellite's serves dinners you'd hope for so close to the big lake: Lake Superior herring, walleye, trout, and fish cakes—plus steak, chicken, and ribs. Oddly enough, Satellite's also sells oil, power steering fluid, brake fluid, and other items for your car. Closed during the winter. **CHEAP TO MODERATE**

North Shore, continued

The Pie Place
Grand Marais, MN • 2017 W. Highway 61 • (218) 387-1513 • T–Sat. 7:30 A.M. - 8:30 P.M. / Sun. 7:30 A.M. - 8 P.M.

The Pie Place takes pride in preparing everything from scratch—the meals, the pies, the breads, and even the ice cream—for a menu that features what they call "gourmet homecooking." In order to cook with the freshest ingredients, the menu changes weekly, catering to the North Shore's seasonal changes. Past menus have featured pecan waffles with banana syrup for breakfast and a roast beef, mushroom, and brie sandwich for lunch. For dinner you can choose from barbecued ribs, coconut chicken, and Thai pork chops. And of course, you don't call your restaurant The Pie Place without offering outstanding pies. Varieties include north woods apple, blackberry cherry walnut, lemon cream cheese, banana cream, sour cream raisin, and a slew of other fruit and cream flavors. Set in a remodeled house, The Pie Place has two dining rooms, one of which ("the porch") looks out over Lake Superior. **CHEAP TO MODERATE**

Angry Trout
Grand Marais, MN • 416 W. Highway 61 • (218) 387-1265 • Sun.–Th. 11 A.M. - 8:30 P.M. / F & Sat. 11 A.M. - 9 P.M.

Don't worry, we know: it doesn't get much more touristy than the Angry Trout. However, its location and cuisine caused us to make an exception. The restaurant is set *right on* Lake Superior, and it has both dockside and atrium dining, providing natural North Shore atmosphere. And the food is pretty good, too, especially if you're looking for some place fancy after roughing it in the rustic north woods. The Angry Trout serves up a grilled portabella mushroom sandwich, smoked trout salad, grilled Lake Superior catch of the day, grilled shitake mushroom fettuccini, and many other tasty treats. And for those concerned, they even use free-range chicken for their chicken nuggets. The name? Well, the design for the logo came to the owner in a dream; the name just describes it. **MODERATE TO SPENDY**

North Shore, continued

Leng's Soda Fountain & Grill

Grand Marais, MN • 5 W. Wisconsin • (218) 387-2648 • M, W, F 8:30 A.M. - 8 P.M. / T, Th, Sat. 11 A.M. - 8 P.M.

Leng's has been slinging burgers and twisting up malts since 1938, when a chocolate sundae cost 30 cents. The prices may have gone up, but not that much—nothing on the menu will run you over ten bucks. The menu is all you'd expect (burgers, fries, hot dogs, sandwiches, and all sorts of ice cream treats) with a few surprises, such as a grilled veggie sandwich, but the décor can't be beat. Stools wrap around two large horseshoe-shaped lunch counters, the tables are covered with checkerboard cloths, and black-and-white tiles cover the floor. Memorabilia and artifacts from a variety of eras decorate the place—Elvis, James Dean, Marilyn Monroe, a 1970s-era 7-Up sign, a full-size model of R2-D2 from *Star Wars*, and an old piano and wooden radio all compete for your attention. A great place to take the family. (Closed from 10:30 – 11 A.M. on Monday, Wednesday, and Friday.) **CHEAP!**

My Sister's Place

Grand Marais, MN • 410 E. Highway 61 • (218) 387-1915 • Sun–Th. 11 A.M. - 9 P.M. / F & Sat. 11 A.M. - 10 P.M.

If this was your sister's place, you'd have one pretty cool sister. This is a family joint, and they lay down the rules right on the menu: "No room for prejudice here; we won't allow it." And if you've had one too many beers, they'll toss ya. If you can handle those guidelines, you're in for a treat. My Sister's Place serves great food among a chaotic melange of decoration, including photos of every set of sisters that has ever dined there. They've covered the ceiling and walls in pelts, washboards, red flannel shirts, license plates, and hornets' nests. Even the barstools are a kitsch touch, hewn from logs. Oh, and they serve some good food as well: burgers, great chili, a fair amount of vegetarian items (like the black bean burger), and the biggest and best selection of hot dogs north of Chicago. The bar serves wine and a pretty good variety of beers, including Guinness and a mess of domestic and Canadian brands. **CHEAP!**

North Shore, continued

Cook County Whole Foods Co-op & Grand Marais Farmers' Market

Grand Marais, MN • Co-op: 20 E. 1st St. • (218) 387-2503 • M–F 10 A.M. - 6 P.M. / Sat. 10 A.M. - 4 P.M.
Farmers' Market: Senior Center Parking Lot • Saturday Mornings from May to September

We wanted to include the Cook County Whole Foods Co-op for those travelers who may be particular about where their food comes from, especially those taking their own food on a hiking, kayaking, or camping excursion. Besides a large variety of organic produce, customers will find organic juices and other beverages and some great trail food. The Farmers' Market opens every Saturday morning through the summer and offers organic and traditionally produced fruits and vegetables grown locally. **CHEAP TO MODERATE**

Ryden's Border Store & Café

Grand Portage, MN • Highway 61 • (218) 475-2330 • Summer: M–Sun. 5 A.M. - 10 P.M. / Winter: M–Sun. 7 A.M. - 8 P.M.

Ryden's has just about anything you might need. This hybrid café/gas station/general store/tourist mecca (complete with stuffed jackalopes for sale) is the last commercial enterprise before the Canadian border (it's also a duty-free shop for those traveling to Canada). The café has been operating since 1947 and has survived being burned to the ground and forced to relocate due to highway expansion. Great diner fare from a egg-and-toast breakfast special to complete dinners—and the hash browns are absolutely perfect. The café doesn't serve beer, but if you've got a hankerin', you can buy a brew at the store and drink it with your meal. The décor is pretty standard but includes a wonderful mural by artist Jim Korf showing nearby Minnesota Point (not to be confused with Duluth's Minnesota Point, a.k.a. Park Point), Wauswaugoning Bay, Pigeon Bay, the Susie Islands, and Isle Royale—the same view from the Mt. Josephine wayside two miles down the shore. **CHEAP!**

South Shore

Port Bar & Restaurant

Port Wing, WI • Highway 13 • (715) 774-3731 • M–F 5 A.M. - 8 P.M. / Sat. & Sun. 7 A.M. - 9 P.M.

Split into three rooms, the Port Bar is a combination small town bar and restaurant. The bar itself is all you'd expect from a roadside tavern: simple, utilitarian, and a comfy spot to enjoy a drink (and outside of Summit Porter on tap, a fairly basic choice of beers). The two dining rooms offer unique décor, with a stone fountain complete with goldfish in one and a fireplace made of petrified wood harvested from North Dakota in the other. The Port serves everything from burgers to walleye, but specializes in a pineapple-grilled Alaska salmon. The Sunday breakfast special is prime rib, three eggs, hash browns, and toast—and an optional bloody mary. During the Testicle Festival, held every Father's Day, deep fried Rocky Mountain oysters are the catch of the day. The Port holds a pig boil in August and hosts Wisconsin's largest fish boil on Labor Day. **CHEAP TO MODERATE**

Fishlipps Bar & Restaurant

Cornucopia, WI • (715) 742-3378 • M–Th. 8 A.M. - 9 P.M. / F & Sat. 'til 10 P.M. / Sat. & Sun. open at 7 A.M.

The first thing you'll notice walking inside Fishlipps is the darkness. Red and black furniture and dim lighting make it feel like perpetual night inside the bar/restaurant, but the food should be enough to brighten your day. Breakfasts include the Fishlipps omelette (with shrimp, crab, mushrooms, and onions) and the buttermilk pancakes are flavored with vanilla. Lunches offer burgers, sandwiches, and wraps, including a veggie-spinach (one of the few vegetarian options on the menu). The most tempting item is the Crabby Sandwich: Alaska king crab salad, garlic cheese spread, red onion, and tomato on sourdough bread. Dinners include whitefish with potato pancakes, steak, chicken parmesan, and prosciutto and gorgonzola on tomato basil pasta. Fishlipps also serves small pizzas and all sorts of appetizers. Great beer selection. **CHEAP TO MODERATE**

South Shore, continued

It's a Small World
Washburn, WI • 144 W. Bayfield • (715) 373-5177 • M–Th. 10 A.M. - 8 P.M. / Friday 'til 9 P.M. / Sat. & Sun. open at 8 A.M.

No Disney affiliation here—the name comes from the restaurant's ever-changing menu featuring cuisine from around the world. Whether the menu features French, Italian, Russian, Thai, Greek, Polish, Caribbean, or New Orleans fare, some of the café's favorites are always available, including fajitas, falafel, fish from Lake Superior, and gyros and burger baskets (including vegetarian and shrimp burgers). You can also get a bison burger or sixteen-ounce sirloin of bison. It's a Small World is also home to the locally famous Oddball Burger. The burger is named after Ray "Oddball" Divine, who originally sold burgers from a stand in downtown Washburn for twenty cents each. But if you could shoot pool and beat Ray in a game of nine ball—"oddball" in some circles—the burger was free. The restaurant's casual atmosphere is a reflection of its attitude—when your meal comes with a salad, they leave a bottle of their homemade dressing on the table. **CHEAP TO MODERATE**

Good Things A La Cart
Washburn, WI • 331 W. Bayfield • (715) 373-5272 • T–Sat. 11:30 A.M. - 8 P.M.

Good Things is a great thing for those looking for a quick and tasty meal they can take with them. The deli serves up food to go at prices that'll have you coming back. Located across the street from legendary Patsy's Bar in downtown Washburn, Good Things is a tiny deli with no seating available. Owner Jean Lonky serves a variety of hot and cold sandwiches as well as salads and barbecue. The sandwiches will please a variety of tastes and include a grilled brat, kosher beef hot dog, and barbecued beef. The salad selection is phenomenal: garden salads, oriental chicken, chicken caesar, chicken and wild rice, seafood, and tri-colored pasta. But the best value has to be the rib combo: ribs, roll, and choice of baked beans, cole slaw, or potato salad. Wash it all down with Blue Sky sodas, iced coffees (Coffee House Vanilla Mousse), or iced Arizona Teas. **CHEAP!**

South Shore, continued

Black Cat Coffeehouse

Ashland, WI • 211 Chapple Ave. • (715) 682-3680 • M–Sat. 7 A.M. - 10 P.M. / Sun. 9 A.M. - 5 P.M. • Smoke free

The Black Cat is unique among eateries along the South Shore. Caught somewhere between a tavern and a deli, it has the feel of a place that would be more at home in Portland, Oregon, or Burlington, Vermont. Long and narrow, *Le Chat Noir* comprises two rooms and an outdoor dining patio. Local art covers the walls, and each week the Black Cat brings in a variety of live music. The Black Cat's food sets it apart from the rest of the South Shore. Almost entirely vegetarian (smoked whitefish is available), the menu offers veggie sandwiches and specialty pizzas as well as Greek, taco, garden, and spinach salads. Fresh homemade soups, hummus, and a basil-parmesan spread also grace the chalkboard bill of fare. The café has a good selection of bottled beer, including Anchor Steam, Guinness, Bell Stout, and Gray's Oatmeal Stout, brewed in Janesville, Wisconsin. Non-beer drinkers can try a Buddy's orange or grape soda, Italian sodas, chai, and specialty coffees. **MODERATE**

Golden Glow Café

Ashland, WI • 519 Main St. W. • (715) 682-2838 • M–F 6:30 A.M. - 7 P.M. / Sat.–Sun. 6:30 A.M. - 2 P.M. • Smoke free

If you're looking for a good old-fashioned breakfast or dinner, look no further than the Golden Glow. This clean, spacious diner is home away from home to many local residents but welcomes folks from out of town just the same. You can get just about anything you want at the Glow. Full breakfast options (from oatmeal to steak & eggs) and great diner fare (burgers, sandwiches, walleye, lake trout, country fried steak, liver & onions, etc.). The house favorite at the Golden Glow is the Golden Burger, which is served on a toasted French round. The Glow serves Brown's Velvet Ice Cream, made locally since 1916 when dairyman Carl John Brown took advantage of nearby French Lake to start an ice business. When he mixed some of that ice with his dairy's own buttermilk and wild berries found nearby, he started making ice cream. **CHEAP!**

Places to Shop
(fun & curious shops & services)

True North Shopping

As any visitor to the region knows, popular destinations like Bayfield and Duluth's Canal Park are chock full of great places to spend money. There are shops selling gifts, souvenirs, outdoor gear, candy, and anything else you can stick a price tag on. They're a lot of fun to visit and you can't miss 'em. That's why we want to point out some out-of-the-way places that offer something special: they're locally owned, not part of a chain, and they offer wares and/or atmosphere that make them unique, at least to this area.

We also included listings of shops hobbyists might seek out wherever they go, since we understand what it's like to be passionate about a craft or creative endeavor. Thrift and used book stores were added for those who like to treat shopping as an adventure.

Of course, given our self-imposed geographic boundaries and our desire to focus on lesser-known business-es, we can't mention every last shop in the Twin Ports. But besides highlighting those on the following pages, we can also direct you to business districts where you might discover a gem on your own. You know about Canal Park, you probably know about Fitger's (an exceptional shopping mall east of Canal Park on Superior Street inside the former Fitger's Brewery Complex), but you may not know to check out Superior's East End, which still has an old neighborhood shopping area (on East Fifth Avenue at 22nd Street) featuring lots of clas-sic neon signs. You might not know that Duluth's Superior Street has shopping areas not just downtown, but also at 44th Avenue East and at 21st Avenue West. While you're out in the western side of town, cruise Grand Avenue from about 40th Avenue West through 60th Avenue West and beyond.

This region is fortunate to still have such a variety of locally owned shops. But they need visitors' business in order to thrive. We hope this chapter will encourage you to take some of your dollars out of the canal and away from the mall to where we here in the north truly shop. And if you feel you must buy a souvenir T-shirt, visit Bullseye Silkscreen at 34 East Superior Street; their designs stand head-and-shoulders above the rest.

Environmental Variety

Green Mercantile

Downtown, Duluth • 209 E. Superior St. • (218) 722-1771 • M–Sat. 10 A.M. - 6 P.M.

Green Mercantile isn't just a shop—it's a business with a mission. Its goal is to provide "healthy alternatives to everyday products"—products that are nontoxic, recycled, recyclable, sustainably produced, and that promote fair working conditions and wages. While this definition might sound limiting, Green Mercantile proves it's anything but. The shop offers a wide variety of products including hemp and organic cotton clothing for infants to adults, candles, art supplies, bath and body items, household cleaning supplies, diapers, office supplies, stationery, and much more. The shop also strives to educate consumers about its mission by providing information about how it chooses its wares and the importance of "voting" with your dollars. Visit its Web site (www.greenmercantile.com) to learn more.

Global Village

Downtown, Duluth • 25 W. Superior St. • (218) 723-1177 • M–F 10 A.M. - 8 P.M. / Sat. 'til 6 P.M. / Sun. 12 P.M. - 5 P.M.

Visitors from the Twin Cities area may be familiar with Global Village since there are two branches in Minneapolis. While the store is not unique to Duluth, it is unique to Minnesota and worth a mention here because it carries a range of items hard to find elsewhere in this region. Global Village comprises two floors of quality imported goods (and some made stateside) including clothing, scarves, hats, jewelry, incense, toys, greeting cards, and a wide selection of home décor items such as candles and candle holders, dishes, pottery, pillows, throws, and rugs. They also have an extensive selection of futons, futon frames, and futon covers. The sheer volume and variety of merchandise from around the world make Global Village a great place to browse, and its second floor is accessible from the Skywalk.

Tobacconists

Butts Smoke Shop

Spirit Valley (West Duluth), Duluth • 5610 Grand Ave. • (218) 628-1502 • M–Sat. 8 A.M. - 7 P.M. / Sun. 10 A.M. - 4 P.M.

Butts Smoke Shop is all about tobacco. The shop focuses on cigars and cigarettes, offering a wide selection of both, as well as chewing tobacco. The shop's large, walk-in humidor houses its imported cigar selection, including varieties from Honduras, Nicaragua, the Dominican Republic, Jamaica, and other warmer climes. Butts's cigarette selection encompasses all the usual domestic selections plus some imports from Canada, France, and other countries.

Duluth Tobacco & Gift

Downtown, Duluth • 11 N. 4th Ave. W. • (218) 722-2229 • M–F 9 A.M. - 5:30 P.M. / Sat. 10 A.M. - 4 P.M.

More than just a place to buy a good cigar, Duluth Tobacco & Gift offers a variety of tobaccos—from cigarettes and pipe tobacco to cigars and snuff—as well as premium coffee and espresso drinks. The Twin Ports' "traditional tobacconists" also carry a variety of snuffs and a wide assortment of smoking accessories, including pipes, lighters, and cigar clippers. A great spot to find gifts for the discerning smoker in your life.

Cheap or Imported Smokes

The Last Place on Earth (see page 176) has the least expensive cigarettes in Duluth that we are aware of (it's also a head shop that sells "adult" toys, so don't bring the kids). The Electric Fetus (see page 175) has a good selection of imported smokes from around the globe, including Cloves, but they're not necessarily cheap. The Hammond Spur just over the Blatnik Bridge has cheap smokes, but that's because Wisconsin has a lower tax on cigarettes than Minnesota.

Music, etc.

The Electric Fetus

Downtown, Duluth • 12 E. Superior St. • (218) 722-9970 • M–F 10 A.M. - 9 P.M. / Sat. 10 A.M. - 8 P.M. / Sun. 11 A.M. - 6 A.M.

Some out-of-town visitors may be acquainted with the Electric Fetus name. The first Electric Fetus opened in 1968 in Minneapolis, followed by locations in St. Cloud and Duluth in 1987. Since the Duluth branch opened, it has become *the* place for music enthusiasts to find whatever they need. Don't let the freaky name scare you— the Fetus (as local residents call it) is a great place to shop for music and a variety of gifts, clothing, and jewelry. The compact disc selection offers both new and used titles and is not to be beat in this area. From the wildly popular to the relatively obscure, the Fetus has it (or will order it on the off chance they don't), and someone on the staff is bound to know exactly what you're looking for. Besides the extensive music selection, the Fetus also offers a wide variety of jewelry, incense, candles, postcards, and novelty toys, as well as men's and women's apparel.

Great Northern Music

Downtown, Duluth • 132 E. Superior St. • (218) 722-5553 • M–F 9 A.M. - 6 P.M. / Sat. 9 A.M. - 5 P.M.

Great Northern Music is found in a great northern building—Duluth's old City Hall, built in 1878 (see page 82), and its downtown heritage stretches back decades (older residents might remember Great Northern when it was known as Brander's Music Shop). Inside its historic doors you'll find all sorts of musical instruments—for everything from rock groups to orchestras—and all the accessories you need to play them: bows, mouthpieces, guitar strings, slides, drum sticks and brushes, and even batons for conductors. And if you need to amplify your sound, Great Northern is the place to go: they have a full line of Peavey P.A. equipment, amplifiers, microphones, hardware, and even DJ equipment. Great Northern also features the region's largest selection of sheet music and can handle all of your instrument repairs and even provide lessons.

Curiosity Shops

The Last Place on Earth

Downtown, Duluth • 120 E. Superior St. • (218) 727-1244 • M–Sat. 10 A.M. - 9 P.M. / Sun. 12 P.M. - 6 P.M.

Whenever you walk into a store whose front window states it sells urine cleaner, you know you're in for something different. The Last Place on Earth may be so named because it has things you'll find nowhere else, but some joke that it's the last place on earth at which you'd want anyone to know you shop. Last Place deals in decorative items (posters and stickers celebrating musicians and illegal narcotics), nonfirearm weaponry (knives, martial arts weapons, stun guns, and self-defense gadgets), smoking devices (from simple pipes to elaborate bongs), and even a large assortment of adult movies and "marital aids" (anything you might imagine and some things you probably wouldn't have thought of in a lifetime). If you mention illegal narcotics, they won't sell you any smoking devices. Keep the kids outside: despite a separate section, the adult items are in plain sight.

Tony's Trading Post

Downtown, Duluth • 3 W. Superior St. • (218) 727-3872 • M–Sat. 10 A.M. - 5 P.M. / Sun. 12 P.M. - 4 P.M.

Walking into Tony's Trading Post, you're greeted by the unmistakable aroma of taxidermied critters and "Old Whitey," a huge polar bear who once lived at St. Paul's Como Park Zoo. A notecard explains that when a man trespassed in the bear's habitat, Whitey attacked him, and police were forced to shoot the bear. The man was fined $100. Besides this sad tale, Tony's offers a truly unique environment and selection of animal-related goods, including taxidermied animals of all sizes from North America and Africa, mounted animal heads, pelts, claws, leather, antler lamps and chandeliers, fur hats, and more. The shop also has a variety of American Indian arts and crafts, T-shirts, and military collectibles. A family-owned business for over 30 years, Tony's is a real trading post and will buy, sell, and trade goods with its customers.

Cool Toys for Good Girls & Boys

Explorations

Downtown, Duluth • 201 W. Superior St. • (218) 722-1651 • M–F 9 A.M. - 5:30 P.M. / Sat. 9 A.M. - 5 P.M.

Explorations is to toy stores what PBS is to television. There are no yapping mechanical dogs tethered to the entryway, no Pokemon anything anywhere. Instead, Explorations is filled with toys that will make kids think and have fun at the same time. The store offers developmental toys and games for kids of all ages, along with quality books, toys for infants, and fun stuff like stickers and rocks. Stow the kids in the children's play area while you look around for that perfect gift idea or new family game. If you're not sure what to get, the knowledgeable staff can help you find something appropriate for and popular with any age group. Educators, check out Explorations's selection of quality teaching materials. One more good thing about Explorations: it's directly accessible from the Skywalk.

Check our "The Beaten Path" section for two more great toy stores in Canal Park.

Better Homes & Gardens

Angela's Bella Flora
Downtown, Duluth • 138 W. 1st St. • (218) 279-3444 • M–F 8 A.M. - 6 P.M. / Sat. 9 A.M. - 5 P.M.

Open since 2000, Angela's Bella Flora has made its mark on downtown Duluth with its eye-catching signage and elegantly dressed windows. Just have a glance as you walk past and you'll see this is a place where even Martha would shop. Inside, the shop feels like a secret garden feel, its shelves filled with high-quality decorative items for the home, such as candles and candle holders, vases, dried flower arrangements, and wreaths. Angela's is also a full–service florist, offering everything from fresh cut flowers and delivery of bouquets to full wedding arrangements. Angela's Bella Flora encourages you to bring the outdoors in and provides everything you need to do it.

Grotto Home & Garden
East End, Duluth • 1434 E. Superior St. • (218) 728-7995 • M–Sat. 10 A.M. - 5 P.M.

Aptly named, Grotto Home & Garden is located in the basement of a quaint corner building many Duluthians and visitors will remember as the home of the Patty Cake Shop—a neighborhood bakery that occupied that spot for decades. While the shop is in a basement, the owners use the lack of natural light to great advantage, employing small lamps throughout to enhance the romantic atmosphere. Entering Grotto Home & Garden you get the feeling you've somehow been transported to a market in Provence. In fact, many of the shop's wares are French, and those that aren't would find themselves at home there. The shop offers dried flowers, cast iron garden items, candles, lamps, French soaps and tea towels, aromatherapeutic household cleaning supplies, and much more. Grotto Home & Garden also creates and delivers unique dried flower arrangements.

European Imports

Coppola Artistica

Brewer's Creek, Duluth • 728 E. Superior St. • (218) 722-0433 • Daily 11 A.M. - 6 P.M.

Artistic talent and fine craftsmanship are a family affair at Coppola Artistica. Owner Antonino Coppola, himself an Italian import from Sorrento, creates rich wood inlay decorative items and coasters while importing hand-painted porcelain and ceramic items from Italy, some designed by his mother. Coppola's brother and cousin also get in on the act, contributing their own woodworking skills. The end result is a lovely little shop overlooking Lake Superior (the view from the shop's windows is all water) full of skilled artisans' hand-crafted creations that will lend an air of Tuscany to even the most Northern home. Coppola offers all manner of tableware, from plates, bowls, and coffee mugs to serving bowls and platters, pitchers, and salt and pepper shakers, as well as candles, framed artwork, rosaries, and much more.

Reading Material & Much More

Fragments of History

Downtown, Duluth • 1 W. Superior St. • (218) 786-0707 • M 1 P.M. - 8 P.M. / T–Fri. 10 A.M. - 6 P.M. / Weekend hours vary

Fragments of History may at first glance seem like just another antique shop, but if you look closer you'll see it's much more. The shop offers an exceptional, well-organized, and neatly displayed selection of rare books (each hardcover is protected by a custom-fitted cellophane wrapper), as well as quality antiques, toys, photographs, prints, autographs, postcards, coins, estate jewelry, and much more. Collectors interested in a specific subject will appreciate owner Terry Roses's binders, organized by subject, filled with postcards and other documents on a variety of topics. If you don't see something you're looking for, be sure to ask—Roses's collection is too extensive to be displayed in the shop alone. Fragments of History also offers appraisal, book search, and estate liquidation services.

Globe News

Downtown, Superior • 1430 Tower Ave. • (715) 392-2090 • Daily 7:30 A.M. - 9 P.M.

Globe News has occupied the same corner space of a historic downtown Superior brick and brownstone building for decades. The building alone, along with the Globe's plentiful old signage, makes it worth a visit. But don't neglect to stop in to check out the variety of wares available inside. As the name suggests, the Globe offers a full selection of periodicals and newspapers for all interests. But the Globe is much more than just an indoor newsstand. You'll also find racks of used paperbacks, bins of used CDs and LPs, as well as a greeting card area and a separate shop-within-a-shop of sports trading cards and other collectible memorabilia. Behind the register you'll find a mini-drugstore offering basics like toothpaste, antacids, batteries and the like—items specially suited for the sailors who frequent the shop.

Used Book Stores*

Amazing Alonzo's Paperback Exchange
Endion, Duluth • 1831 E. Superior St. • (218) 724-3431 • M–F 10 A.M. - 5 P.M. / Sat. 10 A.M. - 4:30 P.M.

Alonzo's offers a wide variety of paperbacks in a variety of genres. Many young adult, romance, western, and mystery series. A few inexpensive hardcovers also available.

Books Bound
East End, Duluth • 2109 E. Superior St. • (218) 722-1419 • M–F 11 A.M. - 6 P.M. / Sat. 10 A.M. - 5 P.M.

Books Bound specializes in used and rare books, especially children's and regional titles. They buy, sell, and restore books and will search for out-of-print titles.

Gabriel's Bookstore
Lakeside, Duluth • 4915 E. Superior St. • (218) 525-7542 • M–F 12:30 P.M. - 4:30 P.M. / Sat. 10 A.M. - 3:30 P.M.

Housed in the basement of the former St. Michael's Church school, Gabriel's is a volunteer-run store specializing in rare and used books, from Oscar Wilde first editions to Stephen King, and *old* record albums and maps.

Old Town Antiques & Books
Downtown, Duluth • 102 E. Superior St. • (218) 722-5426 • M–Sat. 10 A.M. - 5 P.M. / Sun. 11 A.M. - 4 P.M.

Old Town Antiques & Books offers used books from several antique and used-book dealers, including North Woods Books. They'll buy your used books, whether you have one rare book or an entire library.

*See also Fragments of History and Globe News (both on page 180).

Used Book Stores, continued

Second Look Books

Lincoln Park, Duluth • 1925 W. Superior St. • (218) 723-1366 • T–Sat. 9 A.M. - 5 P.M.

A huge collection of used paperbacks (Second Look is also a paperback exchange), including many romance and series titles and a few hardcover and children's titles. Second Look also has tons of used jigsaw puzzles.

Sunhillow Books

Central Hillside, Duluth • 510 E. 4th St. • (218) 786-9624 • M, W, F 9 A.M. - 7:30 P.M. / T, Th, Sat. 9 A.M. - 5:30 P.M.

Sunhillow is fairly new to the Duluth used book game, but they already have an extensive collection, plus the largest selection of new magazines in town.

Windever Books

Lakeside, Duluth • (218) 525-1594 • By appointment and on the web at www.abebooks.com/home/WNDVRBKS/

Windever specializes in children's and young adult titles but carries a wide variety of genres. Once located above Lizzard's on Superior Street and First Avenue West, they no longer needed brick-and-mortar space after Internet sales took off.

Carlson Used Books & Records

Downtown, Duluth • 206 E. Superior St.

Once billed as Duluth's best tourist attraction, Carlson Used Books & Records was shut down by the Feds in summer 2003 (apparently the IRS likes folks to pay their taxes). When this edition went to press, the local rumor mill claimed the store would reopen under the same management as The Last Place on Earth (see page 176).

Crafts & Hobbies

Creations Unlimited

Spirit Valley (West Duluth), Duluth • 319 N. Central Ave. • (218) 628-2900 • M–F 10 A.M. - 5 P.M. / Sat. 10 A.M. - 4 P.M.

Quilting supplies: fabric, notions, tools, books, etc. Classes run every four months from beginner to advanced (triangles, mitering) and a rotary bonanza (free). Call for a newsletter.

Fabric Works

Downtown, Superior • 1320 Tower Ave. • (715) 392-7060 • M, T, W, F 9:30 A.M. - 5 P.M. / Th. 'til 8 P.M. / Sat. 10 A.M. - 4 P.M.

Quilting supplies: fabric, notions, tools, books, etc. Seasonal classes (four times a year) range from beginner to advanced. Call for newsletter.

Superior Beads

Lakeside, Duluth • 4521 E. Superior St. • (218) 525-7434 • M–F 9:30 A.M. - 5:30 P.M. / Sat. 9:30 A.M. - 5 P.M.

Beading and jewelry-making supplies: Seed beads, delicas, findings, castings, semi-precious stones, etc.

The Bead Palette

Chester Park, Duluth • 1826 E. 8th St. • (218) 728-9332 • M–Th. 12 P.M. - 7 P.M. / Fri. 12 P.M. - 5 P.M. / Sat. 10 A.M. - 5 P.M.

Beading and jewelry-making supplies: Seed beads, charms, vintage beads & buttons, stones, closures, etc. Classes available, call to sign up.

Crafts & Hobbies, continued

The Stamping Post

Spirit Valley (West Duluth), Duluth • 5705 Grand Ave. • (218) 624-4722 • M–F 10 A.M. - 5:30 P.M. / T 'til 8 P.M. / Sat. 10 A.M. - 5 P.M.

Stamping, scrap-booking, and paper-making supplies along with stickers, wrapping paper, stationery, pens, and a lot more fun stuff.

Cogwheel

Lakeside, Duluth • 4328 E. Superior St. • (218) 525-6474 • M, T & Th.–Sat. 9 A.M. - 5 P.M. / W 9 A.M. - 9 P.M.

Stained glass supplies and classes as well as other crafting supplies such as styrofoam forms, wood items, and paints.

Glass Menagerie

Brewer's Creek, Duluth • 736 E. Superior St. • (218) 727-1789 • M, T, Th., F 10 A.M. - 7 P.M. / Sat. 9 A.M. - 5 P.M.

All you need for working with stained glass—from supplies to patterns to classes—in a beautiful studio overlooking the Lakewalk and Lake Superior. And, oddly enough, they also sell hand-raised baby exotic birds.

Duluth Leather & Craft

Lincoln Park, Duluth • 2007 W. Superior St. • (218) 722-9074 • M–F 9:30 A.M. - 5:30 P.M. / Sat. 9 A.M. - 3 P.M.

Leather-working supplies: tools, kits, belts, buckles, bead supplies, etc.

Crafts & Hobbies, continued

Carrs Hobbies

Lincoln Park, Duluth • 2009 W. Superior St. • (218) 722-7129 • M–Sat. 9 A.M. - 5 P.M.

Planes, trains, or automobiles, Carrs is a model-builder's paradise, and the store is full of railroad antiques. Even if you're not into models, you really must have a look around.

Robin Goodfellow

Downtown, Duluth • 23 N. Lake Ave. • (218) 279-3443 • M - Th. 10 A.M. - 10 P.M. / F & Sat. 'til 1 A.M. / Sun. 12 P.M. - 10 P.M.

A gaming store with all you need: role playing games, collectible card games, and classic board games, plus dice, miniatures for gaming and collecting, and other gaming supplies. Also features comic books, an in-store gaming room, and new and used (contemporary and vintage) sci-fi, fantasy, and horror books.

Lester River Fly Shop

Downtown, Duluth • 308 E. Superior St. • (218) 727-1789 • M, T, Th., F 10 A.M. - 7 P.M. / Sat. 9 A.M. - 5 P.M.

One-stop fly fishing paradise, whether you buy 'em or tie 'em yourself. Full fishing outfits and classes available. (Call for classes and times—they fill up fast!)

The Superior Fly Angler

Downtown, Superior • 310 Belknap St. • (715) 395-9520 • M - F 12 P.M. - 8 P.M. / Sat. 9 A.M. - 5 P.M.

All the fly fisherperson needs for a day hip-deep in icy waters, including flies, tying supplies and equipment, and classes. They also supply guides. Call for a newsletter.

Laundromats with a Spin

Chester Park Laundromat: Birds & the Great Outdoors
Chester Park/Endion, Duluth • 1328 E. 4th St. • (218) 724-5025 • M–Sun. 6 A.M. - 11 P.M.

Serving Hillside residents and UMD and St. Scholastica students for years, the Chester Park Laundromat might be one of the more unique clothes washing facilities anywhere. Besides your choice of double- and top-loading washers, you can enjoy the sounds of parakeets singing and parrots chatting from within an enclosed aviary. If you get bored with the birds, enjoy Chester Creek, right across the street.

Lincoln Park Wash 'n' Web Laundry: Internet Surfing & Laundry Roulette
Lincoln Park, Duluth • 10 N. 20th Ave. W. • (218) 722-3220 • M–Sun. 8 A.M. - 8 P.M.

If you have a pile of dirty clothes and want to explore the internet, then Lincoln Park Wash 'n' Web has everything you need. The laundromat makes available to its customers five computers with high-speed internet access—for free! The only catch is that you have to do your laundry at Lincoln Park. You can also play "Laundry Roulette" (the machines are set to randomly allow free loads).

Spirit Valley Laundry: Washing in a Greenhouse
Spirit Valley (West Duluth), Duluth • 232 Central Ave. • (218) 628-3147 • M–F 8 A.M. - 9 P.M. / Sat.–Sun. 8 A.M. - 8 P.M.

The Spirit Valley Laundry facility is impressive. It boasts over 120 washing machines in six different styles (top loaders, side loaders, double loaders) plus extractors and plenty of dryers. The thing is, you hardly notice all the machinery because the place is filled with plants—over 200 the last time anyone bothered to count. The plants help dilute the chemical smells of detergents and fabric softeners, making laundry day a bit more pleasant.

Saunas

Duluth Family Sauna

Downtown, Duluth • 18 N. 1st Ave. E. • (218) 726-1388 • Sun.–Th. 12 P.M. - 10 p.m. / F–Sat. 12 P.M. - 10:30 P.M.

Family-owned since 1922, Duluth Family Sauna is a slice of Minnesota history—one of the state's last vestiges of the days-gone-by tradition of public saunas. The high-ceilinged, ceramic-tiled lobby hints at grander times, but still retains some of its original charm. The establishment's main floor features six individual, private saunas (some constructed of cedar, some tiled), each adjoining a sitting room of sorts. The sitting rooms contain a bed, table, and chair, as well as a TV/VCR and stereo. A stint in a private sauna costs $11 per person, $15 per couple. Duluth Family Sauna's lower floor contains its "men's club," a private club featuring both smoking and non-smoking lounges and a large sauna for patrons to share. You'd be hard pressed to find a more unique way to warm your feet on a chilly winter day in Duluth.

Yoshiko Sauna

Lincoln Park, Duluth • 18 N. 21st Ave. W. • (218) 722-5225 • Open 24 hours a day, seven days a week

Note that there is no "family" in the name of this one. We can't tell you much about this place because even though it's open around the clock each and every day of the year, we never made it through the door. We found the Yoshiko Sauna's locked door in a small, dark entryway and pushed a grimy buzzer. Shortly thereafter, a young woman slid open a small window and told us that "all the saunas [were] down." However, she told us, we could still get an "erotic massage." We passed. Enter at your own risk.

Tattoo Parlors

As any Great Lakes sailor will tell you, there's nothing like a permanent ink stain under your skin to commemorate a weekend in the Twin Ports. How about a begging seagull on your shoulder? A "state bird" mosquito? Perhaps the Aerial Lift Bridge across your chest. Whatever you want, the shops below will be happy to ink you up. But remember, whatever you choose will be with you for *the rest of your life* (unless you undergo laser surgery).

Everlasting Tattoo Studio
Downtown, Duluth • 207 E. Superior St. • (218) 722-6745 • M–Sat. 12 P.M. - 9 P.M.

Featuring the award-winning work of artists Jay and Ritt Graham. Body piercing available.

Superior Tattoo Studio
North End, Superior • 818 Tower Ave. • (715) 392-9004 • T–Sat. 5 P.M. - 12 A.M.

Tattoo artist Zono claims to have the largest selection and lowest prices in the Twin Ports. No piercings.

Tatts by Zapp
Downtown, Duluth • 122 W. 1st St. • (218) 733-9019 • M–Sat. 12 P.M. - 9 P.M. (W closes at 5 P.M.)

Zapp was voted Artist of the Year at the 7th World Tattoo Convention and guarantees all his work.

True Colors Tattoo Studio
East End, Superior • 2301 E. 5th St. • (715) 398-6331 • M–Sun. 6 P.M. - 11 P.M.

Jim, the tattoo artist with no last name, won first place at Lakeview Castle's annual tattoo convention.

Gifts Galore

Mainstreet Gifts
Lakeside, Duluth • 4433 E. Superior St. • (218) 525-3755 • M–F 9:30 A.M. - 5:30 P.M. / Sat. 9:30 A.M. - 5 P.M.

Mainstreet Gifts, located in a quaint corner building of the Lakeside neighborhood, offers a variety of gift items from quality makers. Throughout its two tastefully decorated rooms you'll find Ty Beanie Babies, Burt's Bees bath and body products, Mary Engelbreit decorative items, Department 56 figurines, seasonal décor items, candles, dinnerware, and more.

Rocking Horse Gift Shoppe
Downtown, Superior • 310 Belknap St. • (715) 392-5141 • M–Sat. 10 A.M. - 5 P.M.

Throughout its over ten years in business, Rocking Horse Gift Shoppe has gradually expanded from one room to five rooms full of quality craft and gift items, so come with plenty of time to browse. You'll find framed works, braided rugs, potpourri, wreaths, candles, tea towels, cloth napkins, table runners, Lang calendars, lots of seasonal décor items, and much more.

Lots of Fun
Spirit Valley (West Duluth), Duluth • 5626 Grand Ave. • (218) 624-0977 • M, Sat. 10 A.M. - 4 P.M. / T–F 10 A.M. - 5 P.M.

Lots of Fun features a large selection of craft and gift items covering a variety of styles. Among its offering of decorative items are stained glass window ornaments, framed artwork, handmade doilies, wreaths, swags, candles and candle holders, holiday and seasonal items, and collectibles such as Precious Moments figurines. Lots of Fun also offers useable items such as dinnerware, old-fashioned mixing bowls, coffee mugs, bulk potpourri, kitchen towels, hand-knitted dishcloths, and embellished sweatshirts.

Twin Ports Thrift Stores and Pawn Shops

Duluth

Almost New Thrift & Consignment
28 W. 1st St.
(218) 726-5959

2nd Chance Furniture Outlet
2105 W. Superior St.
(218) 723-1785

2wice But Nice
614 E. 4th St.
(218) 727-4030

Dannie-Duluth Consignment
932 E. 4th St.
(218) 724-8507

Green Jean's Duluth Thrift
Proceeds go to a variety of local charities.
320 E. Superior St.
(218) 724-3335

Goodwill
700 Garfield Ave.
(218) 722-3050

St. Michael's Used-A-Bit
16 N. 1st Ave. W.
(218) 722-2171

St. Vincent DePaul
321 N. Central Ave.
(218) 624-7379

St. Vincent DePaul
109 W. 4th St.
(218) 727-9145

Salvation Army
2101 W. Superior St.
(218) 722-7723

First Street Exchange
126 E. 1st St.
(218) 727-5338

Al's Duluth Pawn & Variety
118 W. 4th St.
(218) 727-3563

The Pawnbroker
701 E. 4th St.
(218) 722-8788

Twin Ports Pawn
18 W. 2nd St.
(218) 726-1716

Superior

Frank's New & Used Furniture
1402 Tower Ave.
(715) 392-6075

Goodwill
1717 Belknap St.
(715) 392-1726

Salvation Army
1621 Broadway St.
(715) 394-5331

Twin Ports Antique Stores (outside of Canal Park)

Duluth

Antiques On Superior Street
11 W. Superior St.
(218) 722-7962

Clean Lines
2005 W. Superior St.
Phone number not available

Early Bird Antiques
17 N. Lake Ave.
(218) 727-1298

Memory Lane Antiques
4721 E. Superior St.
(218) 525-7493

Moen's Miscellaneous Salvage
8 N. 2nd Ave. E.
(218) 727-8174 | call ahead

Old Town Antiques & Books
102 E. Superior St.
(218) 722-5426

The Rooster's Nest
101 W. 4th St.
(218) 279-2929

Seaman's Yesterday's Treasures
5617 Grand Ave.
(218) 628-1969

Sunset Antiques
2705 E. 5th St.
(218) 724-8215

A Vintage Attitude
406 W. Superior St.
(218) 279-2839

Woodland Antiques
1535 Woodland Ave.
(218) 728-1996

Superior

Allouez Antiques
4101 E. 2nd St.
(715) 398-0529

Bayside Warehouse
1515 N. 1st St.
(715) 395-9110

Billings Park Antiques
1822 Iowa Ave.
Phone number not available

Curious Goods
1717 Winter St.
(715) 392-7550

Northwind Antiques
2902 Belknap St.
(715) 394-7225

Superior Antique & Art Depot
933 Oakes Ave.
(715) 394-4611

North Shore Antique & Thrift Stores

Two Harbors

Adventure Mall Antiques
Highway 61
(218) 834-9330

Home Sweet Home Antiques
716 7th St.
(218) 834-4017

North Woods Antiques
2777 Highway 61
(218) 834-6456

Second Chance Antiques
127 7th St.
(218) 834-3334

Beaver Bay

Bay Antique Emporium
1008 Main St.
(218) 226-4626

Second Hand Rose
4898 Highway 61
(218) 226-4844

Grand Marais

Lake Superior Collectibles
Highway 61
(218) 387-2200

Rosebush Antiques And Gifts
101 Highway 61 W.
(218) 387-1315

South Shore Antique & Thrift Stores

Cornucopia

The Hedgehog Shop
Huron Ave.
(715) 742-3284

Bayfield

Antiques at Twenty North First
20 N. 1st
(715) 779-3909

Bayfield Antique Jewelry
207 Rittenhouse Ave.
(715) 779-5904

Blue Water Antiques
104 Rittenhouse Ave.
(715) 779-2381

Washburn

Washburn Antiques
136 W. Bayfield St.
(715) 373-0926

Wooden Sailor Antiques
18 W. Bayfield St.
(715) 373-2680

Ashland

AP Cameras & Collectibles
Highway 2 (look for signs)
(715) 682-9132

Myott Antique Inn
2016 Lake Shore Dr. E.
(715) 682-5452

Senior Center Bargain Hut
420 Chapple Ave.
(715) 682-8522

Other Notable Shops Along the Shores

Towns along the North and South Shores are filled with all sorts of shops, but as tourism grows, many of them are turning into antique dealers and souvenir stands. We thought we'd mention a few places that remain unique.

Joyne's Department Store

Grand Marais, MN • 205 Wisconsin • (218) 387-2233 • M–Th., Sat. 8 A.M. - 6 P.M. / F 8 A.M. - 7 P.M.

Joyne's has been serving Grand Marais since the 1930s. A few souvenirs, but mostly lots of stuff you need and won't find in all of Grand Marais's ye olde touriste shoppes. Clothes, boots, gear, toiletries—Joyne's has it all.

Cornucopia's "Mini Mall"

Cornucopia, WI • Cornucopia Marina • Hours: According to one shopkeeper, "Some time in the morning 'til around 5 P.M."

Five gift/antique/used book shops in actual former fish processing shacks, worn and weathered with age: Good Earth Shop, What Goes 'Round, River's End, Art & Sol, and Sea Hag Antiques & Gifts.

Ehlers General Store

Cornucopia, WI • (715) 742-3232 • M–Sat. 8 A.M. - 6 P.M. / Sun. 8 A.M. - 1 P.M.

Since 1915 they've had a saying at Ehler's: "If we don't have it, you don't need it." Locals say if Ehler's doesn't have it, they'll get it for you within a week. A *real* general store with everything from fresh produce to motor oil.

Chequamegon Book & Coffee

Washburn, WI • 2 E. Bayfield • (715) 373-2899 • M– Sat. 10 A.M. - 6 P.M. / Sun. 10 A.M. - 5 P.M.

A wonderful used bookstore inside a classic old brownstone, specializing in regional and American Indian titles.

Places to Stay

(locally owned bed & breakfasts, motels, & campgrounds)

Places to Stay

We held fast to one simple rule in this section: no chain hotels or motels or overgrown tourist resorts. Instead, we've tried to include all the locally owned establishments we could identify. We've only stayed at a few of those listed, but we've called or stopped by all of them in order to provide information on features and cost. All costs reflect summer rates for two people. Keep in mind that by listing these places to stay, we aren't recommending any of them in particular—we just want you to have an alternative to the nationwide franchises, as they tend to fill up before the smaller, local establishments do. Besides, our goal is to get you to venture away from the typical tourist spots, and that's where most chain motels are found.

We do know a few things about some of the hotels. The Voyageur on Superior Street in Duluth was modeled after a prison and once had secret passages and peepholes (which new owners have remodeled and removed). If you like dogs, stay at the Casa Motel in Duluth, where a black lab spends his days on the motel's front lawn. Duluth's Buena Vista on Skyline Parkway offers guests the best view of any inn in the city. The Androy in Superior and the Seaway in Duluth are for the adventurous—they're not exactly family friendly places (many guests are month-to-month residents). If you're a bicycle enthusiast, stay at the Willard Munger Inn, which has direct access to the Munger trail and bikes to rent. Finally, musicians in town for a gig and looking for a place to crash can call Mark Lindquist at Shaky Ray Records (see page 200).

You'll also want to check the "Events" chapter before planning a visit because some weekends are booked up to a year in advance. For instance, you have to be thinking well ahead of time if you want to stay in Duluth the weekend of Grandma's Marathon or the Bayfront Blues Festival. Bayfield is full on Apple Festival weekend, so you'll want to look to the other towns along the South Shore for somewhere to stay.

Key: Cheap up to $65 • Moderate $65 – $150 • Spendy $150 and up

Grand Hotels of Yesteryear

Back in its boomtown days, downtown Duluth was full of grand hotels. Before the Kitchi Gammi Club was created, the St. Louis Hotel (not pictured) served as a gathering place for financiers and politicians (and was the unofficial home of the Duluth Snowhoe and Toboggan Association). The Hotel Holland (far left) was the first "fireproof" hotel in the area. The Hotel Lincoln (second from left), located behind Duluth City Hall and the St. Louis County Courthose, still stands but has been abandoned and may well meet the wrecking ball by the time this book is in print. The Spalding (second from right) was located across from the Lyceum Theatre at 5th Avenue West and Superior Street. The last of those hotels, The Hotel Duluth (far right), was built in 1929 for $2.4 million. Among its famous guests was President John F. Kennedy, who visited Duluth just months before his his death in 1963. It still stands as Greysolon Plaza, serving housing needs of area seniors and providing a wonderful ballroom for wedding receptions and proms. Its sidewalk-embedded compass graces our cover and inspired the title "True North." (See page 82 for more information).

Hotel Holland   Hotel Lincoln   The Spalding Hotel   Hotel Duluth

Places to Stay in Duluth

Bed & Breakfasts

A. Charles Weiss Inn
1895 Victorian | Moderate
1615 E. SUPERIOR ST.
(218) 724-7016 | 800-525-5243

A.G. Thomson House B&B
1909 Dutch Colonial | Spendy
2617 E. 3RD ST.
(218) 724-3464 | 877-807-8077

Cotton Mansion B&B
1906 Renaissance Revival | Spendy
2309 E. 1ST ST.
(218) 724-6405

The Ellery House
1890 Queen Anne Victorian | Moderate
28 S. 21ST AVE. E.
(218) 724-7639

The Mansion
1930 English Tudor | Spendy
3600 LONDON RD.
(218) 724-0739

Mathew S. Burrows 1890 Inn
1890 Victorian | Moderate to Spendy
1632 E. 1ST ST.
(218) 724-4991

Firelight Inn On Oregon Creek
1910 Traditional Mansion | Spendy
2211 E. 3RD ST.
(218) 724-0272

Immigrant House
1890 Queen Anne/Neo-Classical
Moderate
2104 E. SUPERIOR ST.
(218) 724-3090

Lord Frazer House
1903 Four-square | Moderate
2426 E. SUPERIOR ST.
(218) 728-1889

Manor on the Creek Inn
1907 Arts & Crafts/Neo-classical
Moderate to Spendy
2215 E. 2ND ST.
(218) 728-3189

Olcott House B&B
1904 Georgian Colonial | Moderate to
Spendy
2316 E. 1ST ST.
(218) 728-1339 | 800-715-1339

Stanford Inn
1888 Brick Victorian | Moderate
1415 E. SUPERIOR ST.
(218) 724-3044

Places to Stay in Duluth, continued

Hotels & Motels

Allyndale Motel
No frills, free a.m. coffee | Cheap
66TH AVE. W. & CODY ST.
(218) 628-1061

Buena Vista Motel
Great views, bar/restaraunt | Moderate
1144 MESABA AVE.
(218) 722-7796

Casa Motel
Cable TV, microwave | Cheap
923 E. CENTRAL ENTRANCE
(218) 727-9229

Chalet Motel
Continental breakfast | Cheap
1801 LONDON RD.
(218) 728-4238

Duluth Motel
No frills | Cheap
4415 GRAND AVE.
(218) 628-1008

Gardenwood Motel & Cabins
No frills | Cheap
5107 NORTH SHORE DR.
(218) 525-1738

Grand Motel
No frills | Cheap
4312 GRAND AVE.
(218) 624-4821

The Inn on Gitche Gumee
Lake views, fireplaces, etc. | Moderate
8517 CONGDON BLVD.
(218) 525-4979

Lake Breeze Motel Resort
Pool, sauna, lodge | Cheap to Moderate
9000 CONGDON BLVD.
(218) 525-6808

Mountain Villas
Fireplace, deck, grill | Moderate
9525 W. SKYLINE PKWY.
(218) 624-5784 | 800-642-6377

Seaway Hotel
No frills (not a "family" motel) | Cheap
2001 W. SUPERIOR ST.
(218) 722-7476

Skyline Court Motel
No frills | Cheap
4880 MILLER TRUNK HIGHWAY
(218) 727-1563

South Pier Inn
Built in 2001, next to Lift Bridge
Moderate to Spendy
701 LAKE AVENUE SOUTH
(800) 430-7437

Sundown Motel
No frills | Cheap
5310 THOMPSON HILL RD.
(218) 628-3613

Voyageur Lakewalk Inn
Continental breakfast, some "lodge"
rooms w/whirlpool & fireplace
Moderate
333 E. SUPERIOR ST.
(218) 722-3911

Willard Munger Inn
Perfect for biking the Munger Trail;
continental breakfast, bikes | Cheap
7408 GRAND AVE.
(218) 624-4814

Places to Stay in Duluth, continued

Camping

Buffalo Valley Camping
Tent and RV | Cheap
Showers, bathrooms, bar/restaurant
on grounds
2586 GUSS RD.
(218) 624-9901

Indian Point Campground
Tent & RV | Cheap
902 S. 69TH AVE. W.
(218) 628-4977

Island Beach Resort & Campground
Tent & RV (w/showers & baths) | Cheap
Cabins with kitchen, decks, grills
Moderate
6640 FREDENBERG LAKE RD.
(218) 721-3292

Knife Island Campground
Tent & RV | Cheap
Historic property
234 HIGHWAY 61 W.
(218) 879-6063

Spirit Mountain Camp Ground
Hike-in tent sites, drive-in tent sites, &
RVs | Cheap
9500 SPIRIT MOUNTAIN PL.
(218) 628-2891

Musicians' Crash Pad

If you or your band are in the Twin
Ports for a gig and need a place to
crash, call Mark Lindquist at Shaky
Ray Records. Lindquist, a local writer,
musician, producer, and all-around
ne'er-do-well, will be happy to put you
up:

The Shaky Ray
No frills | Damn cheap (free, but be
prepared to buy drinks)
923 N. 12TH AVE. E.
(218) 728-1795
SHAKYRAY@AOL.COM

Places to Stay in Superior

Hotels & Motels

Androy Hotel
No frills (not a "family" motel) | Cheap
1213 TOWER AVE.
(715) 394-7731

Barker's Island Inn
Restaurant, pool, sauna, whirlpool, lake
views, deluxe suites, lounge | Moderate
300 MARINA DR.
(715) 392-7152

Bay Motel
No frills, free a.m. coffee | Cheap
306 E. 3RD ST.
(715) 392-5166

Budget Uptown Motel
No frills | Moderate
104 E. 5TH ST.
(715) 394-4449

Driftwood Motel
Coffee, fridge, cable TV | Cheap
2200 E. 2ND ST.
(715) 398-6661

Manning Motel
Continental breakfast, cable | Cheap
3209 BELKNAP ST.
(715) 392-2281

Park Motel
No frills | Cheap
3411 BELKNAP ST.
(715) 392-6226

Stockade Motel
No frills (coffee in room) | Cheap
1616 E. 2ND ST.
(715) 398-3585

Sunshine Motel
Cable, fridge, some kitchenettes |
Cheap
1807 N. 58TH ST.
(715) 394-7055

Superior Inn
Pool, sauna, whirlpool
Continental breakfast | Moderate
525 HAMMOND AVE.
(715) 394-7706

Bed & Breakfasts

Raspberry Inn
1901 Dutch Colonial | Moderate
1616 JOHN AVE.
(715) 394-7277

Campgrounds

Amnicon Acres Campground
Tent & RV | Cheap
Bathrooms and showers
4505 E. TRI LAKES
(715) 399-8443

Places to Stay Along the North Shore

Bed & Breakfasts

Scenic Highway 61

Spinnaker Inn B&B
Modern home w/nautical theme
Moderate
5427 NORTH SHORE DR.
(218) 525-9292

J. Pepper Inn
1892, oldest home in Knife River
Moderate
243 RIVERVIEW ST.
(218) 590-3839

Two Harbors

J. Gregers Inn
Former dance hall & saloon | Moderate
3320 HIGHWAY 61
(218) 226-4614 | 888-226-4614

Lighthouse B&B
Lighthouse keeper's home | Moderate
1 LIGHTHOUSE ROAD
(218) 834-4814

Little Marais

The Stone Hearth Inn B&B
Renovated 1920s inn | Moderate
6598 LAKESIDE ESTATES RD.
(218) 226-3020

Grand Marais

Bally's B&B & Boarding House
1910, close to lake | Moderate
121 E. 3RD ST.
(218) 387-1817 | 888-383-1817

Dream Catcher B&B
Modern lodge | Moderate
2614 COUNTY ROAD 7
(218) 387-2876

MacArthur House B&B
Modern house | Moderate
520 W. 2ND ST.
(218) 387-1840

Old Shore Beach B&B
Modern lodge | Moderate
1434 OLD SHORE RD.
888-387-9707

Pincushion Mountain B&B
Modern lodge | Moderate
968 GUNFLINT TRAIL
(218) 387-1276

Snuggle Inn B&B
1913 Arts & Crafts | Moderate
8 7TH AVE. W.
(218) 387-2847

Superior Overlook B&B
Modern home | Moderate
1620 E. HIGHWAY 61
(218) 387-1571 | 800-855-7622

Places to Stay Along the North Shore, continued

Motels, Inns, & Cabins

Scenic Highway 61

Emily's Inn & Deli
One room in quaint old bldg with restaurant/deli on site | Moderate
218 NORTH SHORE DR.
(218) 834-5922

Heinz's Beachway Motel & Cabins
Lake views, cabins with kitchenettes | Cheap
5119 NORTH SHORE DR.
(218) 525-5191

Lakeview Castle Motel
Lake view, restaurant | Cheap
5135 NORTH SHORE DR.
(218) 525-1014

North Shore Cottages
1950's cabins, fireplaces | Cheap
7717 NORTH SHORE DR.
(218) 525-2812

Shorecrest Motel
Restaurant, some kitchenettes | Cheap
5593 NORTH SHORE DR.
(218) 525-2286

Two Harbors

Flood Bay Motel
No frills | Cheap
1511 HIGHWAY 61
(218) 834-4076

Gooseberry Park Motel & Lake Cabins
Lake view | Cheap
Cabins w/kitch. on lake | Moderate
2778 E. HIGHWAY 61
(218) 834-3751 | (218) 834-6087

Grand Superior Lodge
Restaurant, pool, spas | Moderate
Log homes | Spendy
2826 E. HIGHWAY 61
(218) 834-3796 | 800-627-9565

Northern Rail TrainCar Suites
Rooms in renovated train cars | Cheap to Moderate
1730 HWY 3
(218) 834-6084

Radosevich's Earthwood Inn
Restaurant/bar, cable | Cheap
933 STANLEY RD.
(218) 834-3847

Silver Cliff Motel
No frills | Cheap
436 A E. HIGHWAY 61
(218) 834-4695

Stone Gate Resort
Cabins, some on lake w/frplc | Moderate
P.O. BOX 72 | E. HIGHWAY 61
(218) 834-3355

Viking Motel
Cable TV | Cheap
1429 7TH AVE.
(218) 834-2645

Voyageur Motel
Cable TV, coffee | Cheap
1227 7TH AVE.
(218) 834-3644

Beaver Bay

Beaver Bay Inn
Historic inn, restaurant | Cheap to Moderate
HIGHWAY 61
(218) 226-4351

Places to Stay Along the North Shore, continued

Beaver Bay Motels, continued

Cove Point Lodge on Lake Superior
Guest rooms and cottages | Spendy
HIGHWAY 61
(218) 226-3221

Silver Bay

Mariner Motel
Cable TV | Cheap
46 OUTER DR.
(218) 226-4488

Northland Trails Guest House
Log homes with lake views | Spendy
36 SHOPPING CENTER
(218) 226-4199

Whispering Pines Motel
Some kitchenettes | Cheap to
Moderate
5763 HIGHWAY 61
(218) 226-4712

Schroeder

Superior Ridge Resort & Motel
Rooms and condos, some with lake
view, satellite TV | Cheap to Moderate
HIGHWAY 61
(218) 663-7189

Tofte

Bluefin Bay
Restaurant, bar, bakery, pool | Moderate
to Spendy
7192 W. HIGHWAY 61
800-258-3346

Chateau Leveaux on Lake Superior
Rooms and condos with kitchens,
fireplaces; pool, sauna | Moderate
6626 W. HIGHWAY 61
(218) 663-7223

Lutsen

Caribou Highlands Lodge
Rooms and condos, pools, saunas,
restaurant | Moderate
371 SKI HILL RD.
(218) 663-7241 | 800-642-6036

Cascade Lodge
Rooms & cabins, whirlpools & fireplaces,
restaurant | Moderate to Spendy
3719 W. HIGHWAY 61
(218) 387-1112 | 800-322-9543

Eagle Ridge
Studios and condos, some with
whirlpools, kitchens; common pool,
whirlpool, sauna | Moderate to Spendy
565 SKI HILL RD.
800-360-7666

Lutsen's Mountain Inn
A variety of options, from rooms to
condos | Moderate to Spendy
(218) 663-7244 | mtn-inn.com

Lutsen Resort & Sea Villas
Lodge rooms, log homes, condos,
some lake views, restaurant | Moderate
to Spendy
(218) 663-7212

Solbakken Resort
Cabins, motel rooms, lodge rooms, all
w/kitchens, some fireplaces | Moderate
4874 W. HIGHWAY 61
(218) 663-7566

Places to Stay Along the North Shore, continued

Grand Marais

Devil Track Lodge & Vacation Homes
Lodge rooms, condos, vacation homes, some lake views | Moderate to Spendy
205 FIREWEED LN.
(218) 387-9414

Gunflint Motel
All suites, some with kitchens, some with lake views | Cheap
101 W. 5TH
(218) 387-1454

Harbor Inn
Cable TV, some lake views; continental breakfast, restaurant | Moderate
DOWNTOWN GRAND MARAIS
(218) 387-1191 | 800-595-4566

Lund's Motel & Cottages
Rooms with fridge, coffee maker; Cabins with kitchens, some fireplaces, all have cable TV | Moderate
919 W. HIGHWAY 61
(218) 387-2155

Naniboujou Lodge
Larger rooms have fireplaces | Moderate
HIGHWAY 61
(218) 387-2688

Traveler's Rest Motel & Cabins
Cabins with kitchenettes | Cheap to Moderate
(218) 387-1464 | 800-249-1285

Opel's Lakeside Cabins
Kitchenettes, lake views | Moderate
800-950-4361

Outpost Motel
Rooms & suites w/kitchenettes; some lake views | Cheap
2935 E. HIGHWAY 61
(218) 387-1833 | 888-380-1833

Seawall Motel & Cottages
Rooms: fridge, lake views | Moderate
Cabins: no view, kitchenettes | Moderate
301 W. HIGHWAY 61
(218) 387-2095

Trailside Cabins & Motel
Rooms: microwave, fridge | Cheap
Cabins: kitchen | Moderate
1100 W. HIGHWAY 61
(218) 387-1550

Wedgewood Motel
No frills, free a.m. coffee | Cheap
1663 E. HIGHWAY 61
(218) 387-2944

Grand Portage

Ryden's Border Store, Cafe & Motel
Full-service cafe on site | Cheap
HIGHWAY 61
(218) 475-2330

Places to Stay Along the North Shore, continued

Campgrounds

Scenic Highway 61

Duluth Tent & Trailer Camp
Tent & RV | Cheap
8411 CONGDON BLVD. (SCENIC HWY. 61)
(218) 525-1350

Knife River Campground
Families & fishermen, cost unavailable
196 SCENIC HIGHWAY 61
(218) 834-5044

Penmarallter Campground
Tent & RV | Cheap
725 SCENIC HIGHWAY 61
(218) 834-4603

Two Harbors

Big Blaze Camp & Cabins
Tent & RV: Cheap
Cabins: Moderate (some facilities on lake, some wooded)
560 BIG BLAZE CIR.
(218) 834-2512

Burlington Bay Campgrounds
Tent & RV | Cheap
626 PARK RD.
(218) 834-2021

Wagon Wheel Campsite
Tent & RV | Cheap
on Lake Superior
(218) 834-4901

Schroeder

Lamb's Resort & Campground
Tent & RV | Cheap
Log Cabins, no TV or phone | Moderate
HIGHWAY 61
(218) 663-7292

Silver Bay

Northern Exposure Campground
Tent & RV | Cheap
On Lake Superior
5346 HIGHWAY 61
(218) 226-3324

Grand Marais

Go-Fer Campground
Tent & RV (water & shower) | Cheap
1201 E. 5TH ST.
(218) 387-1252

Grand Marais Campground
Tent & RV | Cheap
(218) 387-1712 | 800-998-0959

Gunflint Pines
Tent & RV | Cheap
Cabins | Cheap
GUNFLINT TRAIL
(218) 388-4454

Okontoe Family Campsites
Tent & RV | Cheap
Horse camping | Cheap
110 BOW LAKE RD.
(218) 388-2285

Recreation Resource Management
Seven campgrounds in Superior National Forest, all primitive | Cheap
22 PINE MOUNTAIN CT.
(218) 387-2609

Places to Stay Along the South Shore

B & Bs and Cottages

Port Wing

Garden House B & B
Modern house with gardens | Moderate
9255 Sunnyside Ln.
(715) 774-3705

Holiday Pines Resort
Pine cabins | Moderate
9130 Beach Rd.
(715) 774-3555

Cornucopia

The Fo'c'sle Inn on Siskiwit Bay
Historic fish processing barn | Moderate
Highway 13
(715) 742-3337

Lazy Susan's Bed & Brunch
Modern lodge | Moderate to Spendy
89405 Jack Pine Dr.
(715) 742-3443

Swenson's Cottages
Housekeeping cottages | Cheap to
Moderate
88700 Siskiwit Falls Rd.
(715) 742-3282

Bayfield

Artesian House
Modern Lodge | Moderate
Route 1, Box 218K
(715) 779-3338

At Ship's Quarters
1898 Shipbuilder's home | Moderate
20 N. Broad Street
(715) 779-5123

Cooper Hill House
1888 "Bayfield"-style house | Moderate
33 S. 6th St.
(715) 779-5060

Grey Oak Guest House
1888 Victorian | Moderate
105 S. 7th St.
(715) 779-3690

Old Rittenhouse Inn
1890 Queen Anne | Moderate to
Spendy
301 Rittenhouse Ave.
(715) 779-3264

Pinehurst Inn at Pikes Creek
1885 Queen Anne/Victorian | Moderate
R.R. 1, Box 222
(715) 779-3676 | www.pinehurstinn.com

Thimbleberry Inn B & B
Modern Lodge on Lake | Moderate
15021 Pageant Rd.
(715) 779-5757

Washburn & Ashland

Pilgrim's Rest (Washburn)
Modern Lodge | Moderate
Route 1, Box 39-K
(715) 373-2964 | www.ncis.net/pilgrimr/

The Residenz B & B (Ashland)
1889 Victorian | Moderate
723 Chapple Ave.
(715) 682-2425

Places to Stay Along the South Shore, continued

Hotels & Motels

Port Wing

The Village Inn
Bar & restaurant | Cheap
HIGHWAY 13 & COUNTY TRUNK C
(715) 742-3941

Cornucopia

South Shore Motel
No frills | Cheap
SUPERIOR AVE. & HIGHWAY 13
(715) 742-3244

Bayfield

Bay Front Inn
Restaurant and lounge | Moderate to Spendy
15 FRONT ST.
(715) 779-3880

Bayfield Inn
Continental breakfast | Moderate
17 S. 1ST ST.
(715) 779-5905

Chapman House
Kitchen, no TV/phone | Moderate
100 RITTENHOUSE AVE.
(715) 779-9576

Greunke's First Street Inn
Rooms in a historic Inn | Moderate
17 RITTENHOUSE AVE.
(715) 779-5480

Harbor's Edge Motel
No frills, on Lake Superior | Moderate
33 N. FRONT ST.
(715) 779-3962

Isaac Wing House
Historic 1854 home | Moderate
17 S. 1ST ST.
(715) 779-3907

Seagull Bay Motel
No frills | Cheap to Moderate
325 S. 7TH ST.
(715) 779-5558

Silvernail Guest House
1889 Victorian home
Continental breakfast | Moderate
249 RITTENHOUSE AVE.
(715) 779-5575

Washburn

Redwood Motel & Chalets
No frills | Cheap
26 W. BAYFIELD ST.
(715) 373-5512

Washburn Motel
Cabins w/kitchenettes | Cheap
800 W. BAYFIELD ST.
(715) 373-5580

Ashland

Anderson's Chequamegon Motel
Continental breakfast | Moderate
2200 LAKE SHORE DR. W.
(715) 682-4658 | 800-727-2776

Ashland Motel
Restaurant | Cheap
2300 LAKE SHORE DR. W.
(715) 682-5503

Bayview Motel
No frills, on Lake Superior | Cheap
2419 LAKE SHORE DR. E.
(715) 682-5253

Places to Stay Along the South Shore, continued

Hotels & Motels, continued

Bell Motel
No frills | Cheap
407 LAKE SHORE DR. E.
(715) 682-4109

Crest Motel
No frills | Cheap
115 SANBORN AVE.
(715) 682-6603

Farm House
Converted farm house | Cheap
R.R. 4, BOX 79
(715) 685-9778

Harbor Motel
No frills | Cheap
1206 LAKE SHORE DR. W.
(715) 682-5211

Hotel Chequamegon
Classic Victorian hotel with restaurant,
lounge, etc. | Moderate to Spendy
101 LAKE SHORE DR. W.
(715) 682-9095

Lake Aire Inn
Spa, sauna, cont. breakfast | Moderate
101 LAKE SHORE DR. E.
(715) 682-4551 | 888-666-2088

Lakeside Motel
No frills | Cheap
1706 LAKE SHORE DR. W.
(715) 682-4575

Mission Springs Resort
Cottages | Cheap
30175 MISSION SPRINGS RD.
(715) 682-5014

Town Motel
No frills | Cheap
920 LAKE SHORE DR. W.
(715) 682-5555

Places to Stay Along the South Shore, continued

Camping & Cabins

Port Wing

Anchor Inn Campground
Tent & RV | Cheap
HIGHWAY 13
(715) 774-3658

Deering Tourist Homes
Cottages on Lake Superior | Moderate
22545 HIGHWAY 13
(715) 742-3994

Bayfield

Buffalo Bay Campground
On Lake Superior | Tent & RV | Cheap
19550 CAMPGROUND RD.
(715) 779-3743

Dalrymple Campground
Overlooking Lake Superior | Tent & RV |
Cheap
N. HIGHWAY 13
(715) 779-5712

Point Detour Campground
On Lake Superior shore | Tent | Cheap
3 MILES NORTH OF BAYFIELD ON HIGHWAY 13
(715) 779-3743

Washburn

Big Rock Park Campground
No frills • Cheap
3 MILES NORTH OF WASHBURN ON COUNTY C
NO PHONE NUMBER AVAILABLE

Memorial Park
On Lake Superior | Tent | Cheap
EAST END OF WASHBURN
(715) 373-6174

West End Park
On Lake Superior | Tent & RV | Cheap
WEST END OF WASHBURN
(715) 373-6174

Apostle Islands

Big Bay State Park
Tent | Cheap
MADELINE ISLAND
(715) 747-6425

Big Bay Town Park
Close to beach | Tent & RV | Cheap
MADELINE ISLAND
(715) 747-6913

Apostle Islands National Lakeshore
Tent | Cheap (great group rates)
(715) 779-3397
WWW.NPS.GOV/APIS/CAMPING.HTM

Ashland

Kreher Park
On Lake Superior | RV only | Cheap
2020 6TH ST.
(715) 682-7061

Prentice Park
Tent & RV | Cheap (no water/shower)
TURERN ROAD
(715) 682-7061

Shady Oaks Lodge
No frills | Cheap
RTE. 4, BOX 18
(715) 372-4657

The Beaten Path
(Canal Park & the
Fitger's Brewery Complex)

The Beaten Path

Before it became a tourist mecca in the late 1980s and early 1990s, Duluth's Canal Park was the heart of its waterfront. It has been home to Finnish immigrants, various commercial enterprises, vast warehouses, and saloons and brothels. Before the I-35 highway expansion and revitalization of Canal Park, there were few reasons to visit the strip of land if you didn't work there—the Canal Park Inn (now a Burger King) for burgers (and fries to throw at seagulls), the Warehouse for college drinking, Club Saratoga for "exotic dancers," and Grandma's Saloon & Deli.

The "cleaning up" of Canal Park and the development of the Lakewalk have been vital to Duluth's growth in tourism. It hasn't only improved the city financially, but aesthetically as well. Many great old buildings have been given facelifts to recreate the feel of early Duluth. The sidewalks are now dotted with free-standing sculptures, fountains, and even sculpted reliefs on the low walls surrounding parking lots. Visitors are greeted by a large clock tower in the middle of Lake Avenue that resembles a lighthouse (some of the more cynical local residents say it resembles something quite different).

Likewise, Fitger's Brewery has received new life. The brewery started in 1857 and later grew under the guidance of master brewer August Fitger. The brewery made soda pop during prohibition and boasted the first ice machine in the state of Minnesota. It closed as a brewery in 1972 and reopened in 1984 as a shopping complex with restaurants, a nightclub, and a hotel. Fitger's also features a brewery museum (see page 99) and is once again making beer, this time under the guidance of master brewer Dave Hoops at Fitger's Brewhouse (see page 112).

Many local residents actually avoid Canal Park and—less often—Fitger's in the summer because of high tourist traffic. Others steer clear of the Canal because they feel not enough of Canal Park's establishments are locally owned (*e.g.,* Park Inn and South Pier are the only locally owned Canal Park hotels that we are aware of), and they would like to support their neighbors rather than out-of-town investors. It is in that spirit that we include the following lists of locally owned establishments in Canal Park and the Fitger's Brewery Complex.

Canal Park: Locally Owned Restaurants

Amazing Grace Bakery & Café
DeWitt-Seitz Marketplace • (218) 723-0075 • every day 7 A.M. - 11 P.M.

Located in the basement, Amazing Grace offers specialty coffees, sweets, and sandwiches. The Grace also features live music (folk, singer/songwriter) and hosts an annual jug band contest. **MODERATE**

Blue Note Café
357 Canal Park Drive • (218) 727-6549 • M–F 9:30 A.M. - 9 P.M. / Sat. 'til 10 P.M. / Sun. 'til 8 P.M.

Specialty coffees and sandwiches with a jazz theme. Live music on Friday and Saturday nights. **MODERATE**

Lake Avenue Café
DeWitt-Seitz Marketplace • (218) 722-2355 • Sun.–Th. 11 A.M. - 9 P.M. / F & Sat. 11 A.M. - 10 P.M.

Duluth nouvelle cuisine in a sunny corner of a great old building featuring excellent food you might not expect to find this far north. From the Thai chili to the black bean and shrimp burrito to the create-your-own pasta options, "Lake Ave's" menu always pleases and surprises—and offers plenty of vegeterian options. **MODERATE TO SPENDY**

Taste of Saigon
DeWitt-Seitz Marketplace • (218) 727-1598 • Sun.–Th. 11 A.M. - 8:30 P.M. / F & Sat. 11 A.M. - 9:30 P.M.

Owned and operated by Vietnamese immigrants the Nguyen family, most local residents consider Taste of Saigon's offerings the best Asian food in town (and we have *a lot* of Asian eateries). A bright dining room and the fastest service in town make for a great dining experience. Lots of vegetarian options. **MODERATE**

Canal Park: Grandma's, Inc.

Local residents have a love/hate relationship with Grandma's: they either love it, hate it, love to hate it, or hate that they love it. Some folks think the food is great (especially the Saloon & Deli's onion rings) while others think the huge portions hardly begin to make up for (some say) a lack of flavor. Not everyone in Duluth has warm feelings about Grandma's patriarch Jeno Paulucci or one or two other members of his family who run the restaurant businesses, yet Grandma's Marathon has been vital to Canal Park's renaissance and the Paulucci's have donated generously to such local projects as Bayfront Festival Park. Not only do the Pauluccis own several Canal Park restaurants, but also Grandma's Marketplace and several of the buildings other establishments are housed in—and the central parking lot. The Grandma's empire has grown to include the Canal Park eateries listed below as well as a Grandma's spinoffs near Miller Hill Mall, in West Duluth, in Cloquet, in downtown Minneapolis, in Bloomington, Minnesota, and even in South Carolina—in other words, Grandma's may be famous in Minnesota as a Duluth restaurant, but today it is essentially a chain. By the way, "Grandma" herself was reputed to be a local madam back when Canal Park was a red-light district.

Grandma's Saloon & Deli
The original. Big servings of heavy stuff—Duluth's comfort food in a memorabilia-cluttered setting (great outdoor deck with a close-up view of the lift bridge). **(218) 727-4192** | **MODERATE**

Grandma's Sportsgarden
A huge sports bar and college dance club. Pizza and bar chow. **(218) 722-4724** | **MODERATE**

Bellisio's
Upscale Italian with a good wine bar and limited outdoor seating. **(218) 727-4921** | **SPENDY**

Angie's Cantina and Grill
Southwestern cuisine served by folks who say "You betcha." Some outdoor dining. (Another Angie's is located in Miller Hill Mall). **(218) 727-4192** | **MODERATE**.

Canal Park: DeWitt-Seitz Marketplace

394 Lake Ave. S.
May 1 – January 1: M–F 10 A.M. - 9 P.M. / Sat. 10 A.M. - 8 P.M. / Sun. 11 A.M. - 5 P.M.
January 1 – May 1: M–W 10 A.M. - 6 P.M. / Th. & F 10 A.M. - 9 P.M. / Sat. 10 A.M. - 8 P.M. / Sun. 11 A.M. - 5 P.M.

The DeWitt-Seitz Marketplace is housed inside a great old building that has been home to a mattress manufacturer and a Christmas tree outlet, among other enterprises. Today it is the home of shops, restaurants, and offices—all locally owned. Restaurants (see page 213) and offices keep their own hours, but shop hours follow those of the marketplace, listed above.

Northern Waters Smokehaus (218) 724-7307
Premium smoked fish, fine cheeses, smoked salmon paté, and other goodies.

Hepzibah's Sweet Shoppe (218) 722-5049
Chocolates and candies, including solid chocolate ore boats and lift bridges, "lake Superior rocks," and milk and dark chocolate-covered cappucino coffee beans. Yum.

Cruisin' by Sandra Dee (phone unlisted)
Souvenirs galore—t-shirts, mugs, postcards.

The Blue Heron Trading Company (218) 722-8799
Upscale kitchen gadgets and accessories, glasses, crockery, flatwear, as well as canned and jarred delicacies and fine coffees and teas.

Canal Park: DeWitt-Seitz Marketplace, continued

Art Dock (218) 722-1451
A consignment shop selling art by only local artists and artisans ranging from painting to photographs to sculpture to folk art.

Minnesota Gifts (phone unlisted)
Upscale, "gifty" souvenirs of Duluth, the North Shore, and greater Minnesota operated by the same owner as Cruisin' by Sandra Dee (also a store in Miller Hill Mall).

J. Skylark (218) 722-3794
Just about the coolest toy store around, featuring plenty of "nostalgia" toys (you know: wheel-o, gyroscopes, that bowling game with the top and the little wooden pins). Plus rubber stamp accessories, books, and more.

Two & Co. (218) 727-2414
An eclectic mix of clothing, home décor items, and bath accessories. Really nice stuff uniquely displayed (a claw-foot bathtub and antique sink sit in the middle of the store).

Waterfront Art Works (218) 722-1399
Art supplies for artists and graphic artists and anyone else who feels creative. Paints, pens, canvas, easels, framing materials and equipment, and plenty of gadgets.

Canal Park: Locally Owned Shops

Northern Lights Book & Gift

307 Canal Park Dr. • (218) 722-5267 • 9 A.M. – 6 P.M. daily

New books in a great old building, including a vast selection of regional titles.

Harbor House

329 Canal Park Dr. • (218) 727-5201 • 10 A.M. – 6 P.M. daily (extended hours in summer)

Attic/bowery style antiques and vintage garden décor housed in the last remaining original house on Park Point (see page 86).

Blue Lake Gallery

331 Canal Park Dr. • (218) 725-0034 • 10 A.M. – 6 P.M. daily (extended hours in summer)

Regional art by regional artists in what once was a boarding house of questionable reputation....

Antique Center

335 Canal Park Dr. • (218) 726-1994 • Open daily

A variety of wares from local antique dealers.

Spirit of the Lake

335 Canal Park Dr. • (218) 727-7553 • Open daily

A regional art gallery and gift shop and the home of Superior Wreath.

Canal Park: Locally Owned Shops, continued

Teeny Weeny Miniature Cottage
339 Canal Park Drive (upstairs) • (218) 722-1229 • Open daily

Doll houses and supplies, laser holograms, and Victorian books.

Tiki's
339 Canal Park Drive • (218) 279-4054 •)pen daily

Regionally inspired gifts, clothing, and art.

Sivertson's Gallery
361 Canal Park Drive • (218) 723-7877 • Open daily

Local and regional art from local and regional artists—painting, photography (including Jim Brandenberg), sculpture—as well as Inuit art from Alaska and Canada. There's another Sivertson's Gallery in Grand Marais.

The Duluth Pack Store
365 Canal Park Drive • (218) 722-1701 • Open daily

While Duluth Pack was recently bought out by a group of investors from out of state, the Duluth Pack gear they sell is still manufactured by Duluthians in Duluth's West End (Lincoln Park). Besides the wonderful Duluth Pack packs and bags (now including briefcases), the Duluth Pack Store offers a variety of other gear, clothing, and a wonderful selection of regional books.

Canal Park: Locally Owned Shops, continued

Waters of Superior
395 S. Lake Ave. • (218) 727-8204 • Open daily

Waters of Superior features the photography of Craig Blacklock, son of famed outdoor photographer Les Blacklock and famous himself for his nature shots of Lake Superior. Waters of Superior also offers jewelry, home furnishings, clothing, and art. (Blacklock also has galleries in Moose Lake and Grand Marais).

Father Time Antiques
395 S. Lake Ave. • (218) 625-2379 • Open daily

Over 75 dealers compete for space in this 12,000-square-foot antique megaplex.

Canal Park Antique Mall
310 S. Lake Ave. • (218) 722-1229 • Open daily

Housed in a building built in 1885, the Antique Mall claims to be northern Minnesota's largest antique and collectible complex.

Toys for Keeps
306 S. Lake Ave. (upstairs) • (218) 720-3568 • Open daily

Innovative and engaging toys that challenge the child, Toys for Keeps offers toys for children of all ages as well as a variety of puzzles, craft kits, games, and train sets. One of the shop's most notable features is its gallery of dolls (both playable and collectible) that hosts a selection surely unrivaled anywhere else in the region.

Fitger's: Locally Owned Restaurants

Bennett's

Fitger's Brewery Complex • (218) 722-2829 • Daily 6 A.M. - 11 P.M.

Chef Bob Bennett's work is known throughout the Lake Superior region, where he is considered its top chef. He and his wife Kathy operate Bennett's in the lower level of the Fitger's Brewery Complex, where the restaurant's main dining room offers a look at Lake Superior. The menu features local delicacies from Lake Superior (salmon, whitefish, trout, etc.) plus other delights such as sage roasted kosher chicken and cinnamon smoked breast of Peking duck—in Duluth! Breakfast from 6 to 10:30 A.M., lunch until 3 P.M., a limited lounge menu from 3 to 5 P.M., and a full dinner menu for the rest of the night (seating until 9:45 P.M.). **Spendy**

Lakeview Coffee Emporium

Fitger's Brewery Complex • 600 E. Superior St. • (218) 720-4464 • M–Sat. 7 A.M. - 8 P.M. / Sundays 8 A.M. - 6 P.M.

No other coffee shop in Duluth has a view of Lake Superior, and few other establishments have as good a view as Lakeview. Big windows and comfortable seating make this a great spot to enjoy a conversation, play a game of cards or chess, or catch up on your work away from the office or school. All you'd expect from a coffee shop, including sandwiches and sweets, plus the work of local artists adorns the walls.

Fitger's Brewhouse

Fitger's Brewery Complex • (218) 723-0075 • Food served daily from 7 A.M. - 11 P.M., open until 1 A.M.

Duluth's only brewpub. See the write-up on page 112.

Fitger's: Locally Owned Shops

Fitger's Brewery Complex Hours: M–Sat. 10 A.M. - 9 P.M. / Sun. 11 A.M. - 5 P.M.

The Bookstore at Fitger's
Fitger's Brewery Complex • (218) 727-9077 • Open daily

A great selection of new regional and children's books and magazines (and where we first launched *True North*!).

Catherine Imports
Fitger's Brewery Complex • (218) 722-7514 • Open daily

A wonderful collection of clothing, bath accessories, cards, books, jewelry, and much more.

Collection of the Spirit
Fitger's Brewery Complex • (218) 279-9995 • Open daily

Native American antiques and jewelry.

Fitger's Wine Cellars
Fitger's Brewery Complex • (218) 733-0792 • Open daily

Perhaps Duluth's finest wine shop, featuring hard-to-find vintages.

Gabby's
Fitger's Brewery Complex • (218) 740-3353 • Open daily

Women's and children's clothing featuring Fresh Produce.

Fitger's: Locally Owned Shops, continued

Goose Next Door
Fitger's Brewery Complex • (218) 722-2283 • open daily

Gifts, home décor, and hand-crafted decorations.

Sandpiper of Duluth
Fitger's Brewery Complex • (218) 726-0706 • open daily

A fine women's clothier. Fitger's also houses Sandpiper Too (726-1141) featuring Vera Bradley designs.

Snow Goose
Fitger's Brewery Complex • (218) 726-0927 • open daily

A variety of gifts.

Spirit Bay Trading Post
Fitger's Brewery Complex • (218) 722-1839 • open daily

Native American artwork.

Torke Weihnachten
Fitger's Brewery Complex • (218) 723-1225 • open daily

Christmas decorations and fine chocolates.

Annual Events
(festivals, parades, & other
yearly get-togethers)

Annual Events

When you're planning a weekend along the shores of Lake Superior, take events into consideration. There may be some you won't want to miss and some you might want to avoid. For example, a trip to Duluth on the same weekend as the Bayfront Blues Fest or Grandma's Marathon requires some planning, as area hotels are booked a year in advance. You'll find similar difficulties finding accommodations in Bayfield during the Apple Festival. Since many events are held on weekends and costs change from year to year, call for specific dates and prices.

January

Warmer by the Lake
Duluth, MN · January 1 · (218) 723-3337 · FREE

Hayrides, sledding, skating, bonfire, fireworks, free hot chocolate and cookies at Bayfront Festival Park.

Sleigh & Cutter Parade
Duluth, MN · mid-January · (715) 378-2392 · FREE

Parade of horse-drawn antique & restored sleighs and bobsleds at Lester Park Golf Course; rides available.

Annual Memorial Winter Carnival
Duluth, MN · late January · (218) 723-3567 · FREE

Three days of luge rides, lutefisk eating contests, and many other activities in West Duluth.

February

Annual Art Show at M & I Bank
Ashland, WI · early February · (715) 682-3422 · FREE

Local art from local artists.

John Beargrease Sled Dog Marathon
Duluth, MN · early February · (218) 722-7631 · FREE

Watching the sled dog teams take off makes for a fun family outing.

Asaph Whittlesey Showshoe Race
Bayfield, WI · early February · (715) 779-3335 · FREE

All things snowshoe to celebrate the 1870s-era legislator who snowshoed 250 miles to prove a point; races, volleyball, obstacle course, fireworks, caberet, Asaph Whittlesey look-alike contest, and more.

February, continued

Run on Water
Bayfield, WI • early February • (715) 779-3335 • FREE

A five-mile foot race over frozen Lake Superior on the "ice road" from Bayfield to Madeline Island and back.

Undergroundhog Day
Duluth, MN • first Saturday • (218) 727-7585

Several local bands play two stages at the historic NorShor Theatre. (Small cover charge.)

Winter Frolic & Showshoe Challenge
Two Harbors, MN • early February • 800-777-7384 • FREE

Pancake breakfast, showshoe race, sliding, snow sculptures, kids' games, and the "Smoosh" race.

Winter Lakefest
Ashland, WI • mid-February • 800-284-9484 • FREE

Broomball tournaments, flying kites on the ice, sled dog rides, and more.

Book Across the Bay
Ashland, WI • mid-February • 800-284-9484 • FREE

Cross-country skis and snowshoes move the Winter Lakefest (above) from Ashland to Washburn.

March

Annual Spring Carnival
Bayfield, WI • early March • (715) 779-3227 • FREE

Ski and snowboard competition, food, and fun at Mount Ashwaby.

Fun Fair
Duluth, MN • mid-March • (218) 726-8564 • small fee

A three-day indoor expo geared to kids, with rides, food, and music at the DECC auditorium.

Fitger's Bock Fest
Duluth, MN • mid-March • (218) 722-8826 • FREE

Four days celebrating spring: music, contests, and bock beer caramelized with a red-hot poker.

April

Gitchee Gumee Brewfest
Superior, WI · early April · phone number unavailable

More than 125 beers from 30 Upper Great Lakes breweries; Wessman Arena. (Cost unavailable.)

Earth Day Art Crawl
Duluth, MN · April 20 · Phone number unavailable

Celebrate your mother by visiting Duluth's art galleries (see "Arts & Culture" for a list of galleries).

Geek Prom
Duluth, MN · mid-April · (218) 727-7585

If you're through being cool, this prom's for you! Folks dress in their geekiest finery, dine at local eateries, and dance the night away at the NorShor Theatre. (Sorry, no post-party at the head cheerleader's house.)

Northland Folk Festival
Ashland, WI · mid-April · (715) 682-1289 · FREE

Folk music, food, and crafts at Northland College.

Smelt Fry
Herbster, WI · late April · (715) 774-3427

Music and deep-fried fishies. (Cost unavailable.)

May

Homegrown Music Festival
Duluth, MN · first weekend · (218) 727-7585 · $10–$15

Many, many local and regional acts play for several days and nights at various venues all over town.

Scandinavian Heritage Day
Ashland, WI · mid-May · 800-284-9484 · FREE

Cultural displays, food, music, and dancing at the Bay Area Civic Center.

Big Top Chautauqua Tent Raising Social
Bayfield, WI · mid-May · 888-244-8368 · FREE

A social gathering to help hoist the huge canvas. (The Big Top hosts world-class folk and bluegrass music from June to September; cost varies with acts.)

Mayflower Festival at Chester Park
Duluth, MN · mid-May · (218) 724-9832 · FREE

Music, flower market, kids' activities, craft village, etc.

Horse Extravaganza
Superior, WI · mid-May · (715) 399-2928 · small fee

Expanded all-breed show, pony club tack sale, demos, equipment vendors, and model horse show at the Head of the Lakes Fairground.

May, continued

Battle of the Jug Bands
Duluth, MN • late May • (218) 723-0075

Get ready to stomp your feet to five hours of northern hillbilly music that kicks like a rutting moose. Sponsored by the Amazing Grace Bakery & Café.

June

Gatsby Night
Duluth, MN • mid-June • (218) 727-0947 • charge to see bands

Dining, dancing, and an auction to raise funds for the Duluth-Superior Symphony Association.

Grandma's Marathon
Duluth, MN • mid-June • (218) 727-0947 • charge to see bands

Watch the race and enjoy live music, food, beer, and merchandise at Canal Park.

Testicle Festival
Port Wing, WI (Port Bar) • Father's Day • (715) 774-3731

Deep-fried Rocky Mountain oysters are the catch of the day. (Cost unavailable.)

June, continued

Park Point Rummage Sale
Duluth, MN • June • 800-438-5884 • FREE

The entire neighborhood fills its lawns and driveways with things they no longer want so you can buy them.

Voyageur Art Show
Two Harbors, MN • mid-June • (218) 834-2366 • FREE

Local art by local artists in a variety of media (no crafts) at the Two Harbors Art Center.

Blessing of the Fleet
Bayfield, WI • mid-June • (715) 779-3335 • FREE

The annual tradition of blessing the fishing fleet dates back to Bayfield's early history.

Summer Solstice Celebration
Two Harbors, MN • mid-June • (218) 834-4898 • fundraiser

Bonfire, food, and music on the lawn at the lighthouse in Two Harbors; donations go toward the upkeep and maintenance of the lighthouse.

Ice Cream Social
Ashland, WI • late June • 800-284-9484 • cost unavailable

Gather on Ashland's courthouse lawn for music, hot dogs, brats, and ice cream, ice cream, ice cream.

June, continued

Park Point Music Festival
Duluth, MN • late June • (218) 722-5883 • moderate entry fee

Mostly local music and food at the Park Point Recreation Facility; children six and under free.

Park Point Art Fair
Duluth, MN • late June • www.parkpoint.org • FREE

Sort of like the Park Point Rummage Sale, but instead of cast-offs, you can buy local art from local artists.

July

Annual Tour of Homes
Duluth, MN • mid-July • (218) 724-3168 • $20 per person

Self-guided tours of Duluth's premier homes and gardens, followed by lunch.

Lake Superior Shakespeare Festival
Duluth, MN • July • (218) 590-5773 • call for ticket prices

Shakespeare plays and parodies performed outdoors at Leif Erickson Park.

July, continued

Head of the Lakes Fair
Superior, WI • last week of July • (715) 394-7848 • small fee

Carnival rides, races, and headliner entertainment at the Head of the Lakes Fairground. Admission gets you into all the grandstand events.

Patriotic Parade
Ashland, WI • July 4 • 800-284-9484 • FREE

Fifty entries, from high school bands to VFW vets and Shriners—a quintessential Fourth of July parade.

Fourth Fest
Duluth, MN • July 4 • (218) 723-3337 • FREE

Music, food, rides, and what is often the largest fireworks display in the midwest at Bayfront Festival Park.

Cornucopia Community Club Fish Fry
Cornucopia, WI • first Sunday • (715) 742-3942

A feast of Lake Superior whitefish at Town Hall. (Cost unavailable.)

Heritage Days
Two Harbors, MN • early July • 800-554-2116 • FREE

Ethnic festival with art fair, rides, parade, merchants, sidewalk sales, and water ski show.

Bay Days
Ashland, WI • late July • 800-284-9484 • FREE

Off-road bike race, 10k run, sailboat races, arts & crafts, etc.

Festival of Arts
Bayfield, WI • late July • (715) 779-3335 • FREE

Food, art, and musical variety shows.

Woodies on the Water
Superior, WI • late July • (218) 722-7884 • FREE

Over 50 hand-built or restored wooden boats: canoes, sailboats, kayaks, mahogany runabouts, and power boats at Barker's Island.

Annual Festival of Music & Dance
Duluth, MN • mid-July • (218) 727-0570 • FREE

The Ressl Dance company turns the Lakewalk into a long, narrow winding dance floor.

Grand Marais Arts Fair & Festival
Grand Marais, MN • mid-July • (218) 387-1284 • FREE

A two-day festival featuring work by two- and three-dimensional artists, strolling musicians, and dancers.

Two Harbors Folk Fest
Two Harbors, MN • mid-July • (218) 834-2600 • small fee

Concerts, workshops, dances, storytelling, artisans, food, and kids' tent at Van Hoven Park and Agate Bay; no alcohol or pets.

Brownstone Days
Washburn, WI • late July • (715) 373-5017 • FREE

A celebration centered on Washburn's many wonderful buildings made of brown Lake Superior sandstone (see page 90).

August

Bayfront Blues Festival
Duluth, MN • August • www.bayfrontblues.com

It's not all blues, but it's a fest: music, crafts, food, beer, and about 20 renditions of "Mustang Sally." (Prices go up yearly; $25 a day in 2002.)

August, continued

Spirit Valley Days
Duluth, MN • early August • (218) 624-7737 • FREE

Five days of fun in West Duluth: parade, street dance, food, beer garden, etc.

Lion's Club Fisherman's Picnic
Grand Marais, MN • early August • 888-922-5000

Four days of tournaments, fireworks, parade, street dances, raffle, kids' tractor pull, log-sawing contest, etc.

Cornucopia Day
Cornucopia, WI • 2nd Saturday • (715) 742-3211 • FREE

Flea market, food, raffle, parade, fire trucks, kids' activities, and more.

Duluth International Folk Festival
Duluth, MN • August • (715) 398-5970 • small fee

Ethnic singers, dancers, musicians, exhibits, demonstrations, and food at Leif Erickson Park.

Green Man Festival
Mont du Lac, WI • August • (218) 279-5253 • moderate fee

Dozens of local, regional, and national bands gather at Spirit Mountain for three days music, food, drink, and random, spontaneous acts of weirdness.

August, continued

Dragon Boat Festival
Superior, WI • August • (218) 722-5642 ext. 2057

Teams of 20 paddlers, a steerperson, and a drummer compete in beautiful boats. Held at Superior's Barker's Island.

Corn Feed Fund Raiser
Herbster, WI • early August • (715) 774-3411

Music, games, crafts, and lots of food—including plenty of corn on the cob. (Donations accepted.)

Steam Train Days
Two Harbors, MN • mid-August • (218) 834-5631 • FREE

Merchants, sidewalk sale, flea market, food, and trains, trains, trains.

Annual Midsummer Organic Food Fest
Duluth, MN • mid-August • (218) 728-0884 • FREE

A celebration of organically grown foods and sustainable farming hosted by the Whole Foods Co-op.

Cook County Fair
Grand Marais, MN • mid-August • (218) 387-3000

Exhibits, rides, animals, contests, and more.

August, continued

Lake Superior Fish Boil
Bayfield, WI • late August • (715) 373-0495 • cost unavailable

Come for the fireball of fat, stay for the fish.

Lake County Fair
Two Harbors, MN • late August • (218) 834-8300

Exhibits, rides, horse show, animal barn, pie contest, and refreshments. (Cost unavailable.)

September

Duluth Preservation Alliance House Tour
Duluth, MN • early September • (218) 728-4903
moderate fee

Tour of five historic Duluth homes. (For a self-guided tour any time of the year, see pages 66–72.)

Harvest Festival
Duluth, MN • early September • (218) 727-1414

Youth and family activities, live music, crafters, exhibits, etc. (Cost unavailable.)

September, continued

Fish Boil & Craft Show
Port Wing, WI • early September • (715) 774-3624

At Port Wing's Port Bar; the regulars claim this is the largest fish boil in Wisconsin. (Cost unavailable.)

Lion's Club Fall Festival & Craft Show
Port Wing, WI • early September • (715) 774-3624

Crafts, food, music, and more. (Cost unavailable.)

Barker's Island Sailing Regatta
Superior, WI • early September • 800-826-7010 • FREE

More than 40 boats race in this Lake Superior classic. Picnic follows the race.

Fall Color Car Show
Bayfield, WI • early September • (715) 779-3335

Beautiful fall colors and vintage cars in mint condition. (Cost unavailable.)

Annual Fallfest
Duluth, MN • early-mid-September • (218) 724-9832 • $1

Food, crafts, games, music, and more at Chester Park.

September, continued

Tour of Historic Buildings
Superior, WI • mid-September • (715) 392-8449 • small fee

Open houses at four historic sites in Superior, starting at the old Post Office.

Hawk Ridge Weekend
Duluth, MN • mid-September • (218) 722-4011 • FREE

Watch the hawks come in—and help count them—on their annual migration to Hawk Ridge.

North Shore Inline Skating Marathon
Duluth, MN • mid-September • (218) 723-1503

With over 4,000 skaters, this is North America's largest inline skating race; spaghetti feed, expo.

Fall Colorama
Superior, WI • mid-September • (715) 399-3111 • FREE

Apple cider pressing, leaf printing, tree identification hike, Smokey the Bear, and more. (Pattison Park, 10 miles south of Superior on WI Highway 35.)

Spirit of the Lake Fall Fest
Superior, WI • mid-September • 800-942-5313 • FREE

One-hundred-unit parade with dignitaries, marching groups, bands, floats, horses, classic cars, etc.

September, continued

Fisherfolk Art Show
Tofte, MN • mid-September • (218) 663-7804 • small fee

Juried art show with entries in all forms of artistic media portraying fishing in the lives of North Shore people.

Grandma's Oktoberfest
Duluth, MN • late September • (218) 438-5884

German food, drink, and entertainment, including polka and beer-drinking contests, held at the original Grandma's Saloon & Deli in Canal Park.

Lester River Rendezvous
Duluth, MN • late September • (218) 525-0838

A reenactment of a 1780 voyageur village at Lester Park, with appropriately styled wares and food for sale. Live music, and kids' games. (Cost unavailable.)

October

Art Show & Fall Flea Market
Cornucopia, WI • early October • (715) 742-3211 • FREE

Local artists and vendors show and sell their works and wares at the beach. (Usually the same weekend as Bayfield's Apple Festival.)

Marketfest
Ashland, WI • early October • 800-284-9484 • FREE

A celebration of Ashland's shops.

Bayfield Apple Festival
Bayfield, WI • early October • (715) 779-3335 • FREE

Art & craft booths, food vendors, carnival, parade, live music, and—you guessed it—apples, apples, apples.

Duluth Art Fair
Duluth, MN • early October • (218) 724-4205 • FREE

Forty regional artists display their work at The Depot.

Scandinavian Festival
Superior, WI • early October • (218) 624-5158 • $2

Rosemaling, arts & crafts fair, demonstrations, and food and refreshments celebrating Scandinavian heritage at the Head of the Lakes Fairground.

October, continued

Whistlestop Festival
Ashland, WI • mid-October • 800-284-9484

Marathon, 1/2 marathon, 5k race, 10k race, toddler's race, fish boil & pasta feed, rock 'n' roll and blues fests.

Grand Marais Birding Festival
Grand Marais, MN • late October • 888-922-5000

Migratory birding field excursions, speakers, presenters, vendors, birding game show, and more. (Cost unavailable.)

Moose Madness
Grand Marais, MN • late October • 888-922-5000

Guided moose-calling excursions, moose T-shirts, desserts, gifts, and general community-wide "mooseness." (Cost unavailable.)

Jack O'Lantern Jamboree
Superior, WI • late October • (715) 996-2261

Pumpkin-carving contest, Halloween folklore, apple cider making, games, chili sampling, etc. (Pattison Park, 10 miles south of Superior on WI Highway 35; cost unavailable.)

October, continued

Ship of Ghouls
Duluth, MN • mid-late October • (218) 722-5573

The *S.S. William A. Irvin* in Canal Park transforms from an ore boat to a ghost ship, complete with live ghouls and special effects. (Costs change annually.)

Boo at the Zoo
Duluth, MN • October 31 • 723-3748 • small fee

Trick-or-treating among the animals at the Lake Superior Zoo. (Just $1 for non-trick-or-treating kids.)

The Boogieman Project (a.k.a. "Old Ghosts")
Duluth, MN • Saturday closest to Halloween • (218) 727-7585

Several local bands play two stages at the historic NorShor Theatre. Everyone wears a costume, and the contest has become very competitive. (Small cover charge.)

November

Gales of November
Duluth, MN • early November • (218) 727-2497 • $15 - $60

Speakers on shipwrecks, lighthouses, diving, research, and other Lake Superior topics.

Edmund Fitzgerald Memorial Beacon Lighting
Split Rock Lighthouse • November 10 • (218) 226-6372

A film about the *Fitzgerald* is screened; lighthouse tours close temporarily at 4:30 P.M. for the ceremony. (a small fee goes to help preserve the lighthouse)

Christmas Bazaar
Port Wing, WI • late November • (715) 774-3624

Celebrate Christmas in November in the oldest active fishing village in Wisconsin. (Cost unavailable.)

Volunteer Fire Department's Annual Turkey Feed
Cornucopia, WI • late November • (715) 742-3211

A Thanksgiving dinner preview to help raise funds for Corny's Bravest held the Sunday before Turkey Day. (Cost unavailable.)

November, continued

Christmas City of the North Parade
Duluth, MN • late November • (218) 723-3337 • FREE

Evening holiday parade on Superior Street featuring bands, lighted floats, reindeer, elves, and tons of dance groups; held the Friday before Thanksgiving.

Washburn's Merry Ol' Christmas
Washburn, WI • late November • (715) 373-5017

An early Christmas among Washburn's historic brownstones. (Cost unavailable.)

December

Garland City of the North Parade
Ashland, WI • early December • 800-284-9484 • FREE

Holiday parade featuring more than 30 bands, floats, reindeer, elves, and more.

Holiday Craft Show
Bayfield, WI • early December • (715) 779-3335 • FREE

A celebration of locally made holiday crafts.

Santa Lucia Festival
Two Harbors, MN • early December • (218) 834-2969 • FREE

Scandinavians celebrate the life of an Italian saint from the third century A.D. who could not be killed by fire.

Christmas Dinner Concert
Bayfield, WI • mid-December • 800-447-4094 • cost unavailable

Dinner and music at the Lakeside Pavilion.

Old Fashioned Christmas Tea
Bayfield, WI • mid-December • (715) 373-0495

A holiday tea the way it used to be. (Cost unavailable.)

December, continued

Holiday Sing Along
Duluth, MN • mid-December • (218) 723-3337 • FREE

Christmas carols and hot chocolate at Bayfront Festival Park.

Handel's *Messiah* Sing Along
Duluth, MN • mid-December • (218) 723-6000

Performed by St. Scholastica students at St. Scholastica's Mitchell Auditorium. (Cost unavailable.)

Winter Solstice at Lighthouse Point
Two Harbors, MN • mid-December • (218) 834-4898

Bonfire, food, and music on the lawn of the lighthouse in Two Harbors; donations go toward the upkeep and maintenance of the lighthouse.

Zoo Year's Eve
Duluth, MN • December 31 • (218) 723-3748 • FREE

Sliding, skating, zoo visits, and fireworks from 2 P.M. to 5 P.M. at the Lake Superior Zoo.

New Year's Eve Gala
Bayfield, WI • December 31 • (715) 779-3335

Ring in the New Year at the Lakeside Pavilion. (Cost unavailable.)

December, continued

New Year's Eve at the NorShor
Duluth, MN • December 31 • (218) 727-7585

Several local bands play two stages at the historic NorShor Theatre. Small cover charge.

Local Lore
& Places of Yore
(Twin Ports tales of days gone by)

Local Lore & Places of Yore

The city of Duluth takes its name from French explorer Daniel Greysolon Sieur du Lhut, Gendarme de la Garde du Roi, who grew up outside Lyon, France, and moved to Montreal before exploring the Great Lakes region. (A statue of Sieur du Lhut by sculptor Jacques Lipschitz stands in UMD's Ordean Court.) The explorer met with Ojibwe natives in 1679 at Fond du Lac (French for "bottom of the lake") and tried to persuade them to trade with the French instead of the British. But no Europeans visited the area again until the late 18th century, and it wasn't until 1817 that Englishman John Jacob Astor set up the American Fur Trading Company in Fond du Lac. Different villages and towns developed in the area over the next 100 years—Fond du Lac, Gary, Oneota, Endion, etc.—eventually combining to form the city as it is today.

Duluth has a rich history and has seen more than its share of colorful characters. It has gone from boom to bust to boom again (and again). It was once thought that the city would eclipse Chicago in size and prominence, and at one point it had more millionaires per capita than anywhere else in the U.S. More recently, its economy has struggled but has been bolstered in part by tourism.

We thought we'd use this part of the book to present to readers some of the interesting people and moments in the town's history, along with some notorious events typical visitor guides find inappropriate to discuss. Some of it isn't very pretty, but we think you'll find all of it interesting—it's all part of the story of Duluth.

Part of any city's history is tied to its houses and buildings—monuments to days gone by and examples of the tastes of different times. Unfortunately, many of Duluth's great structures have been lost. And so we have filled the latter pages of this chapter with photos of some of the more remarkable buildings that are no longer standing. We hope reminding the community of what the city has lost will help to save what remains. For, as the *New York Times* stated when Penn Station was levelled in 1963, "We want and deserve tin-can architecture in a tinhorn culture. And we will probably be judged not by the monuments we build but by those we have destroyed."

Dylan Does Duluth

Folk and rock music legend Bob Dylan came into this world at St. Mary's Hospital in Duluth on May 24, 1941, as Robert Zimmerman. He lived with his parents, Abe (a supervisor for Standard Oil Company) and Beatrice, on the second floor of the duplex pictured below and attended Nettleton School. When young Bob was six years old his family moved north to Hibbing, his mother's hometown. (The Duluth house was auctioned off on eBay in the summer of 2001 for $94,600.)

On January 31, 1959, high school senior Zimmerman hitched a ride to Duluth to see Buddy Holly and the Crickets, J.P. "The Big Bopper" Richardson, Ritchie Valens, and Dion & the Belmonts play at the National Guard Armory on London Road (see page 84). He had a third-row seat. Two nights later, Holly, the Big Bopper, and Valens gave their final show in Clear Lake, Iowa, and died in a plane crash—the day the music died, according to Don McClean's "American Pie." In his 1998 Grammy award acceptance speech, Dylan recalled the concert and claimed to have made eye contact with Holly. The Armory, once on the Preservation Alliance of Minnesota's list of Ten Most Endangered Historic Properties, may be renovated by a local arts group.

Dylan has played in Duluth twice. His first appearance was at the DECC Arena in the fall of 1998, and he did not acknowledge his hometown in words. During his second appearance, outdoors on July 3, 1999, at Bayfront Park, he pointed up toward his childhood home on the Hillside and joked about an old girlfriend.

Dylan's first digs, 519 North Third Avenue East, Duluth.

The Infamous Lynchings

Like any city, Duluth has had some ugly moments in its past, but none more horrible than June 15, 1920. The John Robinson Show Circus was in town the previous day for two performances in West Duluth. Later that night, 18-year-old Duluthian James Sullivan claimed that a black man from the circus held a pistol to his head and forced him to watch five other black circus workers rape Irene Tusken, 19, also from Duluth. It was a lie. A doctor who examined Tusken found no signs of sexual assault, yet he did not report his findings to authorities. Police rounded up a group of black circus workers and eventually held several of them, including Elmer Jackson, Elias Clayton, and material witness Isaac McGhie; all were between 19 and 21 years old.

Though not reported in the newspapers, news of the alleged rape spread through West Duluth, where outraged businessman Louis Dondino began rounding up a mob, causing a chain reaction throughout the community. By 8:40 P.M. a riotous group of an estimated 10,000 people stormed the downtown jail on Superior Street. By 9:30 they had broken through. After beating and harassing the prisoners, the mob took Jackson and Clayton—and later, McGhie—a block away to the corner of First Street and Second Avenue East. Some tried to stop the mob, including Reverend W. J. Powers, who climbed a light pole to address the crowd. The mob pulled him down and used the same light pole and some rope to kill Jackson, Clayton, and McGhie. The killers then posed for photographs next to their victims before a militia arrived and dispersed the crowd. Later, the photos were sold as postcards. The only punishments given to members of the lynch mob were convictions of rioting, but not murder.

In the 1940s, a St. Louis County Historical Society employee discarded records of the incident, deeming it too unseemly for study by students at the Duluth Normal School (now UMD). Like many towns, Duluth is still not free of racial tension, and many local African Americans and American Indians feel they are unfairly treated by police. One group is trying to set things on the right course. The Clayton Jackson McGhie Memorial Committee has successfully lobbied to establish a memorial to the lynching victims on the very street corner where they were killed. If you'd like to donate, write them at P.O. Box 7352, Duluth MN 55807-7352 or visit claytonjacksonmcghie.org

The Forgotten Lynching

Before lies and racial prejudice caused the death of three innocent black men, a group of Duluth vigilantes displayed their ignorance by hanging another man for his political beliefs. Actually, they tarred and feathered him first, then they hanged him.

Olli Kinkkonen was an immigrant from Finland and, like many Finns, a Socialist. He refused to join the American army to fight in World War I and renounced his U.S. citizenship. Some say Kinkkonen considered the war an imperialist conflict, a struggle for economic power, an unjust war. Others say he was simply a peaceful man, a dockworker and logger who wanted no part of war and was mistaken for a more outspoken antiwar Finn. Whatever the case, Kinkkonen had made plans to return to Finland, but he never made it. Historians say it may not matter whether Kinkkonen was against the war, as anti-Finnish sentiment flourished in the area in 1918. What happened to him may have been as much inspired by ethnic bias as by politics.

In September 1918, Kinkkonen was abducted from his boarding house bed by a group calling themselves the Knights of Liberty, vigilantes who labeled those who did not join the army "slackers." The group first phoned then sent a letter to a local newspaper, claiming that they tarred and feathered Kinkkonen as a warning to all slackers. Two weeks after the abduction, Kinkkonen was found hanging by his neck from a tree north of Lester Park, covered in tar and feathers; $410 was found in his shoes. Duluth authorities ruled that Kinkkonen must have committed suicide because he was embarrassed about what had happened to him. His abductors—and probable murderers—were never charged. One local paper, *The Truth*, called the chief of police "unfit for office" and suggested that the *Duluth Tribune* knew the truth behind Kinkkonen's hanging.

Kinkkonen was buried in an unmarked grave in the poor section of Duluth's Park Hill Cemetery (two years later, Duluth's three other lynching victims would be buried just a few rows away). In 1993 a Finnish cultural group placed a marker on Kinkkonen's grave. It reads, "Olli Kinkkonen, 1881 to 1918, Victim of Warmongers."

Getting Away with Murder

Many a tourist has walked the halls of Glensheen, the Duluth mansion built by Chester Congdon and his wife, Clara. But the tour guides won't discuss the night of June 27, 1977, when Elisabeth Congdon and her night nurse, Velma Pietila, were murdered by Roger Caldwell, husband of Elisabeth's adopted daughter Marjorie.

The Caldwells had big problems with finances, and Roger had a bigger problem with alcohol—and Marjorie. Caldwell asked the Congdon estate for $750,000 so he and his wife could buy a ranch. After the trustees denied his request, Caldwell claims he hatched a plan to steal a few valuables from the house and sell them. Prosecutors, however, argued he planned to kill Elisabeth Congdon and make it look like she had died in her sleep, then collect an inheritance worth millions. They also believe Marjorie masterminded the plot.

Caldwell was convicted of two counts of murder and sent to prison, but Marjorie was acquitted and her trial opened the door for an appeal by Caldwell. Instead, he made a deal: a confession for freedom. In his confession, Caldwell claims he flew to Minneapolis from Colorado, took a bus to Duluth, drank in a bar for several hours, then took a cab to Glensheen. He broke into the house through the billiard room and made his way upstairs. He was surprised by Pietila near the stairwell leading to the second floor, struggled with her, and beat her to death with a candlestick. He then entered 83-year-old Elisabeth Congdon's bedroom and smothered her with a satin pillow. He took a few pieces of Congdon's jewelry and Pietila's car, which he drove to Minneapolis to catch a plane home to Colorado. He claims to have been drunk the entire time he was in Minnesota. Caldwell's confession did not implicate Marjorie or a third party as prosecutors had hoped, and they regret the deal with Caldwell.

When convicted, Roger Caldwell told the jury "you're wrong." He maintained his innocence while in prison, then confessed to the crimes, and then once again claimed his innocence. A few years later, he committed suicide. He protected Marjorie to the end. She in turn never spoke to him after his conviction, married again, was convicted of arson in Minnesota, is suspected of killing her third husband (and his first wife before that), and served time in an Arizona prison for arson. Now Marjorie Hagen, she will be released from prison in January 2004.

The Pirates of Park Point

Back in 1889, Minnesota Point—at the time, the village of Park Point—was not nearly as heavily populated as it is today. Few houses stood along the world's largest sand bar, and no roads had been built. It was mostly sand dunes and scrub pine, the perfect place to hide pirate booty.

Park Point's pirates weren't your typical, cutlass-wielding-aaargh-exclaiming-peglegged-hook-handed-eye-patch-wearin'-parrot-totin' buccaneers of the Caribbean, and they hardly plundered ships for gold doubloons and pieces of eight. Duluth's pirates were a band of about six young men who apparently had an aversion to labor and turned to crime on the not-so-high seas to earn their keep.

They dug themselves a cave on Park Point at a site close to 39th Street, near what in 1906 would become the Duluth Boat Club's Oatka Boat Club Branch. With open water on both sides, this was a strategic spot for their operation. While they hardly fit the stereotype, their style was not much different than traditional pirates. They plundered various vessels, sawmills, and warehouses.

Apparently, the cave was a temporary lair, and the pirates' goal was to set up permanent housing on the point, as the lumber they stole was used to build a house. Much of that lumber was stolen from the mill of Duluthian R. A. Gray, and Gray had had enough.

When Duluth's buccaneers tried to make off with more of his lumber one night, Gray decided to do something about it. He watched, then pursued the thieves. But the band of ne'er-do-wells had a large sailboat and managed to escape in the Lake Superior darkness.

The patient Mr. Gray eventually found their cave—and his lumber, in use in the unfinished house—and captured the gang after a struggle that history books called a "fierce battle." The half-dozen or so thieves all ended up in the penitentiary.

The Ghost Fleet of Lake Superior

Many a Great Lakes seaman believes Lake Superior is home to a "Ghost Fleet" made up of ships that have disappeared without a trace somewhere between Duluth and Sault Ste. Marie (The Soo). The Ghost Fleet's roster includes, among others, the *Adella Shores*, the *Bannockburn*, and the *Hudson*.

For those who believe in superstitions, the fate of the lumber hooker *Adella Shores* was sealed as she was launched. Built in Gibraltar, Michigan, and towed to Ashland, Wisconsin, before she was finished, the *Adella Shores* was constructed for Ashland mill owner Walter Shores, a leading supporter of the temperance movement in Wisconsin. Rather than have a ship named after his daughter christened with champagne, a bottle of lake water was used to launch the vessel. Mariners considered this very bad luck and an act that doomed the ship. In April 1909, the *Adella Shores* left her home dock in Ashland with a load of lumber. She was never seen again.

The *Bannockburn* also disappeared from Lake Superior, but she has been seen again—in spectral form. The steamer vanished November 21, 1902, while on her way from Port Arthur to The Soo with a load of wheat and 21 men on board. Only a life preserver and an oar were ever found. Still, several sailors claimed to have seen the *Bannockburn* on stormy nights. This has caused many to call the *Bannockburn* the "*Flying Dutchman* of Lake Superior," after the legendary phantom ship that disappeared off the coast of Good Hope.

The *Hudson* was lost near Michigan's Keweenaw Point on September 16, 1901, and like the *Bannockburn,* she has been seen since. Even boarded. As the story goes, a tugboat captain and his mate were near Keweenaw Point on a September 16 in the late 1940s when they spotted a rusty ship covered in brown slime. The tug captain claims to have boarded the vessel to see if it was in distress. In the pilot house he encountered the ragged apparitions of the *Hudson's* helmsman and captain, who explained to him that the ship and its crew were damned to relive the sinking each September 16 and warned him to get off. He leaped from the boat and swam in icy waters to the tug, refusing to explain to his mate what happened to him on board. (And yet somehow we hear the story....)

Haunted Twin Ports

The NorShor Theatre

Built as the Orpheum vaudeville house and once host to Ethyl Barrymore, Groucho Marx, and Charlie Chaplin, the NorShor Theatre still contains the spirit of those days—or at least one spirit. According to witnesses (bartenders closing up late in the night) the ghost is a man in his mid-20s or 30s and decked out in black evening attire common in the 1920s. He appears disheveled and sinister and has been seen climbing the south staircase that leads to the mezzanine. One night an employee, alone after closing, looked up into the mirror behind the bar and saw the ghost standing behind him. Patrons seated at the bar have also felt someone behind them, and drinks have reportedly disappeared. Some employees have even heard laughter when they thought the building empty.

Fairlawn Mansion

Built in 1891 by lumber baron Martin Pattison, Fairlawn is a sprawling Victorian mansion that later served as an orphanage. The house is thought to be haunted by a former servent girl, allegedly killed by her husband. The ghost supposedly helps visitors find specific displays and then she simply vanishes, her presence noted by a chill in the air. It is believed that she has returned to Fairlawn Mansion because it was one of the only places that she knew happiness in her short life. It is also said that the ghosts of two children are seen and heard near the basement's old swimming pool. While nothing indicates any children died in the house, some believe that they may have accidentally drowned while living at the orphanage. County records from that period have been sealed.

Glensheen Mansion

Some believe the ghosts of Elisabeth Congdon and Velma Pietila—brutally murdered in the mansion (see page 242)—now haunt the house. There have allegedly been reports of shadowy figures walking about the basement (though the murders occured on the second floor), lights turning on and off, a report of a piece of candy rolling back and forth across a dresser, and an incident in which a bathtub, disconnected form the house's plumbing, filled with rusty water. There is very little support for the validity of these incidents.

Bear and Drunk Square Off

Early on a Sunday morning in August of 1929, Arvid Peterson was driving down London Road with a truckload of fish fresh from the North Shore. At 26th Avenue East he noticed a large black bear following his truck. The bear followed him all the way to the corner of Superior Street and Third Avenue East—to the Hotel Duluth (home of the sidewalk compass that inspired this book's name). The bear apparently lost its taste for fish when it smelled the food from the hotel's coffee shop. The bear stood on its hind legs, swung a paw, and smashed through a 15-foot- tall plate glass window. It then entered the hotel through the window and ran straight to the coffee shop.

A man described by newspapers as a "local drunk" grabbed a hammer and followed the bear through the broken window. He yelled and waved the hammer, facing the bear in a standoff. All the commotion woke night watchman Albert Nelson. When Nelson saw the bear, he ran to alert the assistant manager, who called police.

Nelson and the drunk occupied the bear, who had been attacking the mezzanine stairway, the inebriated man waving his hammer as the night watchman threw tables and chairs at the bruin. As the battle went on, guests began gathering in the lobby, and the faces of curious passersby filled windows. Soon a crowd had gathered.

Duluth police officers Sergeant Eli Le Beau and Patrolman John Hagen answered the assistant manager's call. Along with others, the officers tried to lasso the bear. After avoiding capture, the bear appeared to be bearing down on Nelson. Sergeant Le Beau raised his rifle and fired once, striking the bear in the head. The bear stood on its hind legs, wobbled for a moment, then fell down the stairs.

The bear's carcass was stuffed, mounted, and displayed in the front window of the hotel for years. Later, the coffee shop became the Black Bear Lounge, which has since closed.

The stuffed bear is on now display at Grandma's Saloon & Grill in Canal Park.

Duluth: Home of the Washington Redskins

Most folks around here know about the Duluth-Superior Dukes, the semi-pro baseball team whose intermittent history began in the 1950s and continued in the Northern League until 2002. But not many are aware that Duluth was once the home of the Washington Redskins, back when they were known as the Duluth Eskimos.

The Eskimos actually started in 1923 as the Duluth Kelleys (named for their sponsor, Kelley-Duluth Hardware), later playing as the Eskimos from 1926 to 1928. They were a traveling team featuring future NFL hall-of-famers Ernie Nevers, Walter Kiesling, and Johnny "Blood" McNally (McNally also played for Green Bay). The Eskimos played against teams such as the Potsville Maroons, the Milwaukee Badgers, and the Canton Bulldogs (as well as the Chicago Bears and the Green Bay Packers).

The 1926 Eskimos, featuring all-American fullback Nevers (a ticket attraction that rivaled Red Grange), were called "The Iron Men of the North." The team played 29 exhibition and league games—28 of them on the road—and Nevers played almost every minute of every game. The team earned a 6-5-3 record that season and played from September until February. Nevers had a good year in 1927. He played professional football, baseball, and basketball that year—the only man ever to do so—scrimmaging with Red Grange and pitching against Babe Ruth.

The Eskimos folded in 1928, and in 1929 the franchise was sold to New Jersey's Orange Athletic Club. They were renamed the Tornadoes, played one season in East Orange, and moved to Newark in 1930. The NFL then reclaimed the franchise and sold it to a Boston group who renamed it the Braves and, later, the Redskins. The Redskins moved to Washington in 1932. (Eskimos, Braves, Redskins—not the most ethnically sensitive names.)

The Duluth team has not been forgotten by all. You can buy Eskimo hats and sweatshirts from Internet retailers, and *Sports Illustrated* writer Rick Reilly coauthored a screenplay centered on the 1927 Eskimos, a romantic comedy entitled *Leatherheads* (the Eskimos played to a 1-8-0 record that season).

Duluth's Famous Old Soldier

Duluth's Central Hillside was home to Albert Woolsen, the last surviving Union Army soldier of the Civil War. Woolsen lived to be 109 years old. He was born in Watertown, New York, on February 11, 1847, and arrived in Duluth in 1862. At 17, Woolsen joined the Union Army as a "volunteer private." He was assigned to Company C of the First Minnesota Heavy Artillery Regiment, detailed to the drum corps—Albert Woolsen was a drummer boy. He saw no action, but witnessed Sherman's March.

A lifelong Republican, Woolsen cast his first vote for Abraham Lincoln. He was just 17 at the time and voted under a special war clause for members of the armed forces. As the last Union survivor, he was named commander-in-chief of the Grand Army of the Republic.

Woolsen lived most of his life in Duluth at 215 East 5th Street. As he aged—and as other Union veterans died, making him the last—Duluth newspapers annually featured accounts of Woolsen celebrating his birthday; he was often photographed shoveling snow. When he was 105, he recommended the following for a long life: 1. exercise, used judiciously, 2. not worrying over trifles, and 3. due respect for the laws of nature, such as not overeating. "Moderation in all things; that goes for whiskey, women, and food," Woolsen said.

On July 12, 1954—when he was 107 years old—Woolsen wrote a letter that now hangs in an alcove close to City Hall's entrance alongside a plaque, an American flag, and a bust of Woolsen. It reads as follows:

To My Fellow Americans,

On April 9, 1865, the terrible war of rebellion ended; the differences between the Union and the Confederacy were forgotten and the North and South were once again united.

As the last survivor of the Union army, I have seen these United States grow into the greatest nation in the history of mankind.

Our sacrifices were not in vain.

Woolsen died August 2, 1956, at the age of 109 years. A statue of him stands near the end of Canal Park.

Duluth's Not-So-Famous Old Soldier

Colonel Hubert V. Eva, though not as celebrated as Albert Woolsen, was also a last survivor of one of America's wars—one of the war's last battles, to be precise. Unfortunately, it was not a war Eva was exactly proud of. He was the last surviving veteran of the Indian Campaigns.

Often called an "Ex-Indian Fighter" by the press, Eva did not care for the term. In his 29 years in the military, Eva spent about a month involved in conflicts with American Indians. "It was rather foolish," Eva said of the battles. "You don't hunt people like you hunt deer."

Eva was born August 8, 1869, in Penzance, Cornwall (England), and came to Duluth as a lad of 16. In 1889 he enlisted in the Minnesota National Guard. By 1898 he had become a captain and volunteered for service in the Spanish-American war. After that conflict, he fought as part of the 3rd U.S. Regiment during the Leech Lake Indian uprising led by Chippewa Chief Bu-A-May-Geh-Shig, the last Indian conflict in Minnesota in which shots were exchanged. Seven soldiers died and nine were wounded; two Chippewa were wounded. Two years later Eva helped quell an uprising of 500 to 600 Sioux and Chippewa along the Canadian Border. Eva convinced Indian leaders to end the conflict. No shots were fired.

In 1910 Eva found himself in Baudette, Minnesota, leading a detachment to clean up after a major forest fire; he was also involved in helping with the aftermath of other forest fires in the early years of the century. In 1916 Eva served with General Pershing along the Mexican border protecting U.S. citizens against attacks by Pancho Villa and his bandits. During World War I he was stationed in New Mexico, training American troops for combat in Europe. He retired from the military in 1918.

In 1971, at 102 years old, Eva was killed when he and his nurse were struck by a car driven by a UMD student as they crossed Superior Street near 17th Avenue East after attending a dinner at St. Paul's Episcopal Church.

Bridge Boys

Many Twin Ports residents and visitors cross between Duluth and Superior on the Bong and Blatnick bridges each day, but who were they named for?

Richard Ira Bong (1920–1945)

According to the Richard I. Bong World War II Heritage Center Web site, Dick Bong was born in Superior and grew up on the family farm in Poplar, one of nine children of Swedish immigrants. His downing of forty enemy planes while flying P-38 fighter planes in the Pacific during World War II made him America's all-time Ace of Aces. He was awarded many decorations for outstanding skills and extraordinary courage, including the Congressional Medal of Honor. He was ordered home for his safety before the war ended and married his sweetheart, Marge, in Superior. Six months later, in August 1945, Dick was killed test piloting the first Lockheed jet fighter plane. He died the same day that the atomic bomb was dropped on Hiroshima. The Bong Heritage Center opened in September 2002 near Superior's Barker's Island. The Center features a great deal of World War II history as well as "Marge," Bong's famed P-38, named for his future wife, which has been caringly restored. Visit www.bongheritagecenter.org to find out more about the heritage center.

John Anton Blatnick (1911–1991)

Born in Chisolm on Minnesota's Iron Range, Blatnick was a politician, serving in the U.S. Army Air Force in World War II, as a member of Minnesota State Senate 60th District from 1940 to 1944, as U.S. Representative from Minnesota's 8th District from 1947 to 1975, and was a Minnesota delegate to the Democratic National Convention in 1960 and a member of Democratic National Committee from Minnesota in 1963. When the bridge was rededicated in Blatnick's name in 1971, Secretary of Transportation John Volpe said that Blatnick "played a key role in establishing and fostering the foundation for this magnificent [Interstate Highway] program back during the Eisenhower Administration." The 7,975-foot bridge and its 2,800-foot approaches were built in 1961. It was originally called the "Duluth-Superior Bridge (Minnesota-Wisconsin)." Local folks often refer to it as the High Bridge.

Helter Smelter

During the 1970s and '80s, late April to early May found the shores of Lake Superior lined with drunken revelers waist deep in frigid waters, toting nets, buckets, and even plastic bags in the hope of filling them—and later, their bellies—with smelt. But the smelt no longer run as thick as they once did, and all-night smelting parties at the mouths of the big lake's tributary rivers have ceased.

Smelt (pronounced "shmelt" by many local residents) are small, silver-colored fish native to salt water. People argue over how they got to Lake Superior. Some say that in 1912, live smelt native to the Atlantic Ocean were transported from Green Lake, Maine, to Crystal Lake in Northern Michigan, where they followed drainage systems into Lake Michigan and, eventually, Lake Superior. Others claim smelt are a Pacific Ocean transplant that arrived in Lake Superior after being accidentally introduced to Lake Michigan.

In the 1950s, the sea lamprey (another exotic import from the Atlantic) nearly wiped out Lake Superior's populations of lake herring and trout. In the wake of the lamprey's appetite for their predators, smelt flourished.

By the 1970s, people were hauling away pick-up truck loads of the little fish caught as they gathered at the mouths of rivers to spawn. Folks from out of town arrived in motor homes, set up camp, and netted smelt until they had more than they could possibly handle. Local pizzeria's cashed in by delivering pizza to hungry, inebriated crowds gathered at river mouths. A local Vietnam veterans group even staged an annual Smelt Fry, where hundreds would gather for a weekend, eat buckets of deep-fried smelt, drink beer, and enjoy a variety of live bands. The last, dubbed "Helter Smelter," was held at the Douglas County Fairgrounds in Superior in 1984.

Since the sea lamprey population has been controlled and the smelt's predator's populations have risen, the smelt population has declined dramatically, resulting in the decline of the human population's drunken revelry (at least outdoors at night for a few weeks in April and May). Since smelt is an exotic species, there is a debate over what, if anything, should be done to revive its population.

Spirit Little Cedar Tree

The Spirit Little Cedar Tree ("Minido Geezhi-Gans" in Ojibwe, also known disrespectfully as the "Witch Tree" or "Witch's Tree") is a cedar monarch that sprouted from seemingly barren rock on the Hat Point prominence some 400 years ago. For generations the Ojibwe left offerings of tobacco at the tree for safe passage on the big lake. When they encountered Grand Portage, French voyageurs respected the tradition and left offerings of their own.

Now gnarled with age and exposure to the elements, the Spirit Little Cedar Tree has been the subject of countless books and works of art. Reports conflict as to how it came to be called the "Witch Tree." Some say it was dubbed by the voyageurs and other early European explorers; others give credit to Dewey Albinson, one of many artists drawn to draw the tree (the drawing of the tree on the left was drawn by Kent Aldrich of the Nomadic Press).

Unfortunately, vandals have caused the local band of Grand Portage Ojibwe, who now own the land near Grand Portage where the tree is found, to close off public access to the tree. Over the years, ignorant visitors had carved their initials in the tree or cut away portions of it as souvenirs. If you want to see the Spirit Little Cedar Tree yourself, you have to arrange a tour with a member of the band. For a distant view, you can take the *MV Wenonah* from Grand Portage to Michigan's Isle Royale; it passes by Hat Point to give passengers a view of the tree.

Superior's Berger Hardware

When Berger Hardware opened its doors at 525 Tower Avenue in Superior in 1915, owner Morris Berger's goal was to turn it into the best-stocked general goods store around. By the time it closed 70 years down the road, it was not only a hardware store extraordinaire, but an antique store and tourist attraction—a hardware museum.

Berger filled every nook, cranny, and corner of his store with stock purchased from other stores or factories that had gone out of business. The merchandise was stocked haphazardly on high, packed shelves and even hung from the ceiling. Customers who tried to find items on their own were quickly frustrated—only Berger and his son Sam knew where everything was kept.

At Berger customers could find brand new buggy whips, axe handles unloaded by the WPA in the 1930s, and unused milk bottles along with tons of nuts, bolts, and nails. Cases of soldering irons sat adjacent to blacksmith tongs. A home restorer's dream, Berger stocked hinges and doorknobs from days gone by. If you couldn't find something anywhere else, there was a good chance Berger's had it—no matter how old or odd.

Morris Berger ran the hardware store until he died in the late 1970s. Sam took over the helm and kept the doors open another dozen years—until he died at his desk.

In 1994 Jim Kremer bought the store and soon found himself overwhelmed trying to locate merchandise. But that didn't stop people from coming in. According to Kremer, many visitors didn't come to buy anything but just to have a look around. He said that some interested parties had even called ahead to arrange group tours.

In March, 1999, the Berger Hardware inventory was auctioned off. People came from hundreds of miles away to bid on obscurities. Even a group of Amish gentlemen attended to stock up on items, such as buggy parts, they have trouble finding anywhere else. In the spring of 2002, the building reopened as a restaurant, Mama Gets, which has retained much of the Berger Hardware charm (see page 139).

Duluth's Young at Heart Records

For 41 years beginning in 1956, Richard Wozniak operated the Young at Heart record store ("for the young and the young at heart") at 22 1st Avenue West in downtown Duluth. From the basement to the third floor, Wozniak filled the building with thousands and thousands of 45-, 33-, and 78-rpm vinyl disks—as well as an impressive number of books—creating a mecca for music collectors.

The store takes its name from a 1950s-era Frank Sinatra hit, appropriate enough since the store itself seemed anchored in time. Wozniak decorated with pinks and reds to maintain the "heart" motif. All of the signs were handpainted, as were many of the boxes in which the 45s were kept. Wosniak stocked everything from rock 'n' roll to country and western to jazz to show tunes to classical—just about anything, as long as the lyrics weren't offensive.

More than just a used record shop, Young at Heart was a gathering place for music lovers from all over the map. Vinyl enthusiasts from the Twin Cities to Thunder Bay, from West Duluth to North Dakota came to Wosniak's shop to dig through the endless stacks of wax. Twin Cities weekly newspaper *City Pages* called it "the Babel of vinyl" and encouraged its readers to visit when in Duluth.

Wozniak so loved his store that he practically lived in it during the last few years it was open. He kept several shelves stocked with canned goods and boxed dinners, which he would prepare and eat at the store to avoid leaving for meals.

When Wozniak retired in 1997, relatives put the contents of his store up for sale in order to help finance his retirement. While its doors have closed, the memory of the store will be preserved. The Minnesota Historical Society purchased Young at Heart memorabilia, including its cash register and several hand-decorated 45-rpm record boxes. The Society included these items in an exhibit entitled "Sounds Good to Me: Music in Minnesota" at St. Paul's History Center as an example of mom-and-pop music stores.

Random Radio: Airwave Pirates

In the late 1990s, the airwaves over Duluth's East Hillside were filled with an incredibly eclectic mix of music emanating from Scott Lunt's basement and beamed at 100 watts of power over the radio frequency 93.5 FM.

Random Radio was a "pirate" radio station—that is, a station that operated without an FCC license. The station earned its name three ways. First, the programming (everything from rock to jazz to spoken-word) touched so many different corners, listeners never quite knew what they were in store for. Second, the station operated only when Lunt (a.k.a. "DJ Starfire") or one of his crew had the spare time to be on the air. And third, because of the station's low wattage and its placement on Duluth's Hillside, listeners had only a random chance of picking it up on their radios. It came in best through car stereos, and while Duluthians over the hill couldn't pick it up, listeners along the South Shore in Wisconsin claimed clear reception.

Random Radio's programming included a great deal of local music, such as that of Lunt's own country-inspired group, Father Hennepin. The station also featured live performances by guest musicians, including Duluth's own internationally recognized Low. Lunt had the foresight to record those appearances, and assembled many of them on a CD entitled *Random Acts of Radio* (the CD is available locally at the Electric Fetus).

But crime doesn't pay (neither does operating a low-watt, commercial-free radio station), and the Feds eventually caught up with Lunt. He received a letter from the FCC listing the laws he was violating and was forced to shut the station down shortly afterward or face stiff fines.

If you want a taste of what Random Radio was like, visit Fitger's Brewhouse in the Fitger's complex on Thursday nights for the Starfire Lounge, where Lunt and his team of DJs spin an eclectic mix of songs old and new, with lots of local music in the mix. And although it's officially off the air, some claim that, just like Lake Superior's ghost ship the *Bannockburn*, on foggy nights when the big lake's waters run rough, you can still hear the efforts of local music lovers drifting over the air at 93.5 FM....

The Aerial Bridge Didn't Always Lift

Duluth's Aerial Lift Bridge—the largest in the world—has become an icon for the city, used in the logos of everything from newspaper Web sites to food service companies. The original bridge, however, didn't lift. The bridge was built in 1905—a welcome structure to those who lived on Minnesota Point and who had relied upon ferries to cross the canal since it was dug in 1871. (During winter months, a temporary suspension bridge was used.) The 1905 bridge, patterned after a suspended car bridge in Rouen, France, used a gondola to ferry passengers and goods (and, later, streetcars) across the canal. It was called the Aerial Transfer Bridge.

Redesigned in 1930 as a lift bridge, the bridge first lifted for a ship on March 29, 1930, when the *Essayons*, a Corps of Engineers tug, passed through the canal as a test. It has since raised about 400,000 times.

Between 1966 and 1973, tourists were allowed to stay on the bridge as it raised and lowered. Today, police fine those who purposefully trespass on the bridge for rides. At least two tragedies are connected with the bridge.

In 1982, a 19-year-old man from Grand Rapids, Minnesota, grabbed onto the bottom of the bridge; when the bridge was 70 feet above the water, he fell to his death. And on June 10, 1990, a 50-year-old Duluth woman panicked when the bridge's warning bells sounded as she walked across the bridge. She either leaned out to grab a vertical beam or tried to jump, but became caught in the bridge's superstructure. The bridge cut her in half.

To learn more about the bridge, see *Duluth Shipping News* editor Thomas Holden's complete Aerial Bridge history at www.duluthshippingnews.com/aerialliftbridge.htm.

The original aerial bridge ferried passengers and goods using a gondola.

D. Clint Prescott House

54th Ave. W. & Central Pl. • c. 1888–1948
architect unknown

James Allen Scott, author of *Duluth's Legacy Volume 1: Architecture*, calls the Prescott House "The best costumed participant in [Duluth's] Mardi Gras of prosperity" and says that "nowhere on the house could the observer find a moment of visual rest." Iron executive D. Clint Prescott's Queen Anne-style home was indeed a treat for the eyes. Again, the eloquent Mr. Scott describes it beautifully: "[The] three-story house was a carnival of dormers and gables, porches, and verandas, carvings and spindles, chimneys and towers, bargeboards and lattices, and gaily dressed lightning rods."

Prescott worked for the Marinette Iron Works Company, which relocated to Duluth from Marinette, Wisconsin, in 1890. He moved his family to Chicago before the end of the century, and the house took on a series of owners and later became a hospital before it was eventually abandoned. Like many empty mansions, rumors of hauntings persisted until the house was destroyed in 1948.

The Duluth Preservation Alliance uses a drawing of the D. Clint Prescott House as its logo.

Hartley House

1305 E. Superior St. • 1889–1954 • Oliver G. Traphagen, architect

You'd be hard pressed to spend any amount of time in Duluth without bearing witness to the mark left by Guilford and Caroline E. Hartley. That Tudor Revival building rising above the Lakewalk east of the Portland Malt Shop? That's their office building. The Kitchi Gammi Club? Mr. Hartley played a principal role in its construction (note the similarity between the Kitch and the Hartley's office building). Hartley Park? Well, you get the picture. A busi-

nessman with eclectic interests, Guilford Hartley focused on industry, politics, cattle, agriculture, transportation, and the press (he owned one of Duluth's early newspapers). He also helped found the Northland Country Club.

In 1889 he and his wife, Caroline, had Oliver Traphagen design a house one block from what is now the Rose Garden and Leif Erickson Park. The Romanesque mansion stood nearly four stories tall and included a carriage house. The house became the first in Duluth to be wired for electricity and the first to have a telephone. Chester Creek ran along its eastern edge.

The lots upon which the house once stood are now home to a Walgreens Drug Store and its parking lot.

First Methodist Episcopal Church

215 N. 3rd Ave. W. • 1892–1966 • architect unknown

Built for $120,000 in 1892, the Gothic red sandstone First Methodist Episcopal Church seated 2,200 parishioners when all its galleries were open. All of its windows were stained glass, and paintings adorned the interior walls. Its chimes were the first to be installed in Duluth. The ten bells, the largest of which weighed 1,200 pounds, played in two keys and were the gift of Thomas and George Martin, who paid $10,000 for them in 1921. The chimes rang each day at noon, before Sunday services, and on national holidays and other special occasions.

Because most of its parishioners (which once included the Charles and Clara Congdon family) had moved away from the downtown area, the church closed its doors after its last service on November 6, 1966. It was replaced by the Pietro Belluschi-designed First United Methodist Church at Skyline Parkway and Central Entrance (also known as the "Coppertop Church," see page 59).

The church also held a historic pipe organ made by the Austin firm of Hartford, Connecticut. The organ, a gift from a parishioner, had 1,500 pipes and was originally water driven. The instrument was dismantled before the church was torn down. Its cathedral chimes and stops were transplanted into the new church's organ.

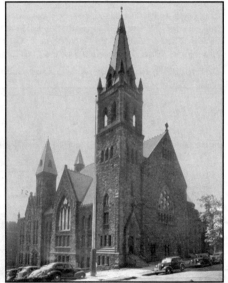

Duluth Curling Club

1330 London Rd. · 1912–1984 · Frederick G. German, architect

Curling is a shuffleboard-like sport played on a sheet of ice with brooms and rocks with handles—Scottish bocce ball, if you will. Local residents have participated in organized curling since Christmas Day of 1891, when the Duluth Curling Club was born on a $400 rink at 3rd Avenue East and Superior Street. (By the way, Superior's Raymond "Bud" Somerville led the U.S. Olympic curling team to a bronze medal in 1992; he was 55 years old.)

Built in 1912, the Duluth Curling Club eclipsed all other curling facilities in sheer number of rinks, with 12. Ice

skaters and hockey players used rinks on the second floor and in the summer the space was used for roller skating.

In 1984 the curling club caught fire and was demolished just before work on the I-35 extension began. The lot on which it stood is now a parking lot next to the Rose Garden. Today, the Curling Club plays its matches at its facility inside the Duluth Entertainment and Convention Center.

The Duluth Boat Club

You can't live next to the largest body of fresh water in the world without finding plenty of ways to have fun with it, and from early on Duluthians found recreation on the great lake. In 1886 eleven local men got together to form the Duluth Boat Club and soon after built a clubhouse along the lake at 7th Avenue West along the St. Louis Bay (pictured below; adjacent to where Bayfront Festival Park stands today). Eventually a second club house had to be built at 10th Street on the bay side of Minnesota Point.

According to the current Duluth Boat Club, the old club "offered rowing, sailing, canoeing, swimming, tennis, and other sports [and] also hosted lavish banquets, festivals and dances." At its peak the exclusive club had 1,400 members and became the hub of social activities for Duluth's elite.

The Boat Club produced twenty national rowing championship teams led by coach James Ten Eyck, Jr., and in 1916 played host to the national championships. But by 1926 Ten Eyck had left and automobiles were all the rage. Starving for funds, the club closed its doors.

Duluth was without a boating organization until 1956, when the Duluth Rowing Club was formed. The current club credits its growing youth program to its members' volunteer mentoring and dedication.

The Duluth Rowing Club changed its name to the Duluth Boat Club in the fall of 1999. Members have proposed building a $2 million to $2.5 million facility at 14th Street and St. Louis Avenue. The new facility would be youth-oriented, handicapped-accessible, and affordable, setting it apart from the exclusive Boat Club of years gone by.

Duluth Incline Railway & Pavilion

7th Ave. W. • Railway: 1891–1939 | Pavilion: 1891–1901 • Traphagen & Fitzpatrick, pavilion architects

The Incline Railway was a system of steam engines and cables that pulled tram cars up and down two sets of elevated tracks on what is now 7th Avenue West to get commuters from their homes at the top of the hill down to Superior Street and their jobs downtown. On weekends and evenings, residents hopped on the Incline for a ride up to its expansive pavilion. There, Duluthians enjoyed dances, vaudeville performances, or dined in one of its restaurants. Others picnicked outdoors or took a ride in a hot-air balloon.

Unfortunately, in 1901 a fire began in the pavilion and destroyed it. The fire spread to the power station, and the heat melted the railway's cables, releasing a flaming trolley car that raced toward Superior Street, crashed through the railway's depot gates, crossed Superior Street, and came to a halt in the

railyards near the Union Depot. No one was injured.

The Incline Railway served Duluth until Labor Day, 1939. After that, it was dismantled and sold as scrap.

Old Cascade Park

4th St. below Mesaba Ave. • 1895–1975

The City of Duluth didn't always run roughshod over its natural beauty in order to make a few developers rich. As far back as 1890, the city was purchasing land to reserve as parks. Cascade Park, a 3.19-acre space complete with a creek and waterfalls, was part of the first wave of park development. In 1895 the city added a sandstone pavilion and bell tower at the heart of the park, giving it a whimsical, castle-like atmosphere.

Clark House Creek ran through the park and right through the pavilion, its waterfall cascading through an opening on the building's lakeview facade. Unfortunately, the bell tower was destroyed during a storm in 1897. Portions of the creek were altered to flow underground as the area surrounding the park developed.

Only two-and-a-half acres of Cascade Park survive. When Mesaba Avenue was widened in 1975 to accommodate traffic heading toward the Duluth Heights neighborhood and the mall, part of the park was sacrificed. Its sandstone structures were destroyed and the remainder of the creek was forced underground. The city then rebuilt the bell tower, though in a different design than the original.

Top of the Temple Opera Building

201 E. Superior St. • 1889–c. 1940
Charles McMillen & E.S. Stebbins, architects

When the Masonic Temple Opera Block opened its doors in 1889, it housed the first Duluth Public Library, a Masonic lodge, an opera house, and business offices. The six-story building was designed in the Moorish Romanesque style complete with an onion-shaped dome at its top. But when Guilford Hartley bought the building, things changed.

In 1910 Hartley financed the construction of the Orpheum Theatre, a vaudeville house designed by J.E.O. Pridemore and built at the back of the opera house, replacing the ornate 2nd Avenue East entrance and facade with an awning and Classic Revival pillars. Hartley later had the top three floors and the dome of the Temple Opera Building removed.

The Orpheum closed in the 1930s. In 1941 the building was dramatically converted into the NorShor Theatre, an art deco movie house featuring the world's first milk bar (see page 110). Portions of the Orpheum are actually still inside the structure of the NorShor, whose entrance is on Superior Street. When first built, the NorShor featured a tower of lights that reached 65 feet in the air. (Some say Hartley had the Temple Opera Building altered to make the tower more visible, but he died in 1922). The Temple Opera Building currently houses office space and Browser's N'eTc., an Internet coffee shop run by a Hartley descendant (see page156).

Lyceum Theatre

Superior St. at 5th Ave. W. • 1891–1966 • Traphagen & Fitzpatrick, architects

When the Lyceum Theatre opened for business in July of 1891, it was proudly hailed as the "handsomest and costliest building in the Northwest." The building stood six stories high in a style the *Duluth Daily Tribune* called "reposeful and majestic Romanesque" and contained an auditorium surrounded by business offices. Its facade was a treat for the eyes.

The Lyceum featured a triple-arched, two-story entryway on Superior Street complete with stone lions to guard the entry and the ornate carvings of Duluth's master stone artisan, Norwegian immigrant O. George Thrana (Thrana's work still graces many of Duluth's old buildings). The Lyceum seated 1,500 and its stage was the second largest in the "Northwest."

Opera divas, actors, and vaudevillians trod its stage's boards for 30 years before it was converted to a movie theater. It operated until November 1960, and in January 1966 was destroyed to make room for KDLH-TV's studios. You can still see some remains of the Lyceum: its stairway's stone lions, appropriately enough, have found a home at the Lake Superior Zoo, and the drama and comedy masks that flanked its entrance now grace the Duluth Playhouse Theater.

The Lyceum Theatre's ornate, two-story Superior Street entrance.

U.S. Government Building

431 W. 1st St. • 1894–1934
Traphagen & Fitzpatrick, architects

A fine example of the many stone Romanesque Revival buildings that once flourished throughout Duluth, the U.S. Government Building's square stone tower reached five stories into the sky. The building stood at 5th Avenue West and 1st Street, across the street from what is now the home of the *Duluth News-Tribune*. The heavy stone structure was often called the Post Office building, because it also held Duluth's central post office.

When it was dismantled in 1934, its arched doorway was supposed to go to Leif Erickson Park to act as a gateway to the park (if it did indeed move to the park, it is no longer there). A single nine-ton piece of stone featuring a carved eagle was also removed and was to be given to the Naval Reserve Station on Minnesota Point, but it was too heavy. Workers dismantling the building found a bottle; in the bottle was a cloth with the message "goodby, Friends." It was dated November 11, 1892, and signed by "James Peterson, 14th Ave. E. and Charles Bowman, 465 23rd W."

Appendix
(credits, bibliography, & index)

Photo & Illustration Credits

All illustrations, maps, and photos by Tony Dierckins, except:

The illustration of the Spirit Little Cedar Tree (page 252) was drawn by Kent Aldrich of The Nomadic Press.

The image of the Aerial Transfer Bridge (page 256) is from a postcard c. 1905; publisher unknown.

The images used for the collage of Duluth's grand old hotels (page 197) are from the private postcard collection of Jerry Paulson.

The image of Old Cascade Park (page 263) is from the private postcard collection of Bob Swanfeld.

The image of the Duluth Union Depot (page 79) is from a postcard originally published by A. Gallagher.

The photo of the Squaw Bay caves (page 55) is courtesy of Joe Taatjes.

The following photos appear courtesy of the Northeast Minnesota Historical Center (NEMHC):
Morgan Park Goodfellowship Club (page 85), Hartley House (page 258), First Methodist Episcopal Church (page 259), Duluth Incline Railway Pavilion (page 262), Temple Opera Building (page 264), Lyceum Theatre (page 265), U.S. Government Building (page 266).

The NEMHC photos of the D. Clint Prescott home (page 257) and the Duluth Boat Club (page 261) were originally published in the 1890 edition of *Duluth Illustrated* (J.P. Craig, publisher).

The NEMHC photos of the Duluth Incline Railway (page 262) and the Duluth Curling Club (page 260) are Hugh McKenzie photographs.

Further Reading

Books, pamphlets, and Web sites

Aubut, Sheldon T. and Maryanne C. Norton. *Images of America: Duluth, Minnesota*. Arcadia Publishing, Chicago, IL: 2001.

Buchanon, James. *The Twin Ports: A Guide to Duluth and Superior*. Nodin Press, Minneapolis, MN: 1992.

Eichten, Gary, et al. *Minnesota Public Radio Online*. http://www.mpr.org/index_main.shtml

El-Hai, Jack. *Lost Minnesota: Stories of Vanished Places*. University of Minnesota Press, Minneapolis, MN: 2000.

Fedo, Michael. *The Lynchings in Duluth*. Minnesota Historical Society Press, St. Paul, MN: 2000.

Harnish, Sue, et. al. *Mission Creek Nature Trail* (pamphlet). Junior League of Duluth, Duluth, MN: 1975.

Hertzel, Laurie, ed. *Boomtown Landmarks*. Pfeifer-Hamilton Publishers, Duluth, MN: 1992.

Lundgren, Paul and Brad Nelson and Heidi Bakk-Hansen, eds. *Ripsaw Online*. http://www.ripsawnews.com

MacDonald, Dora Mary. *This is Duluth*. Paradigm Press, Ashland, WI: 1999.

Morgan Park/Smithville Community Club 1994 Calendar. Morgan Park/Smithville Community Club, Duluth, MN: 1994.

Nash, Anedith and Robert Silberman. *Morgan Park: Continuity and Change in a Company Town*. 1992 (Publisher unknown).

Perich, Shawn. *The North Shore: a four-season guide to Minnesota's favorite destination*. Pfeifer-Hamilton Publishers, Duluth, MN: 1992.

Powell, Mrs. Thomas. *Congdon Creek Park* (pamphlet). Junior League of Duluth. Duluth, MN: publication date unknown.

Ryan, Mark. *The History of Seven Bridges Road*. http://www.geocities.com/SoHo/Lofts/4839/SevenBridges/

Scott, James Allen. *Duluth's Legacy: Volume 1, Architecture*. City of Duluth, Duluth, MN: 1974.

Simonowicz, Nina. *Nina's North Shore Guide*. University of Minnesota Press, Minneapolis, MN: 1999.

Stonehouse, Frederick. *Haunted Lakes*. Lake Superior Port Cities, Inc., Duluth, MN: 1997.

Thomas, Thomas R. "Duluth's Aerial Lift Bridge." *Duluth Shipping News*. http://www.duluthshippingnews.com/aerialliftbridge.htm

Tierney, Carol. *Chester Creek Nature Trail* (pamphlet). Junior League of Duluth. Duluth, MN: 1974.

Newspapers

The Duluth News-Tribune (Duluth, MN)

The Duluth Herald (Duluth, MN; no longer in publication)

The Truth (Duluth, MN; no longer in publication)

Index

Index, continued

Index, continued

Index, continued

Index, continued

Index, continued

Index, continued

Look for these other books by

About the Authors

St. Paul native **Tony Dierckins** first moved to Duluth in 1984 to attend the University of Minnesota Duluth. He has moved away twice but was drawn back each time, making the city his permanent home in 1996. Dierckins has taught writing and graphic design at UMD and has coauthored over a dozen books, including *Greetings from Duluth*, *The Mosquito Book, The WD-40 Book,* and the *Duct Tape* books and calendars. He also created the CoasterBook series published by Running Press.

Kerry Elliott was born in Kaukauna, Wisconsin, and grew up in Duluth. She too moved away but was drawn back to make her home in Duluth. Elliott works for for Maurices, Inc., at its corporate headquarters in downtown Duluth and is a former feature writer and film reviewer for the *Ripsaw*, a regional weekly arts & entertainment paper. This is her first book.